AF765167

Patient-Focused and Feedback Research in Psychotherapy

In the last 15 years feedback interventions have had a significant impact on the field of psychotherapy research and have demonstrated their potential to enhance treatment outcomes, especially for patients with an increased risk of treatment failure. Current investigations on feedback research are concerned with potential moderators and mediators of these effects, as well as the design and the implementation of feedback into routine care. After summarizing the current state of feedback research, this book provides empirical investigations of contemporary feedback research. These efforts aim at answering three overarching questions: 1) How should we implement feedback systems into routine practice and how do therapist and patient attitudes influence its effects?, 2) How can we design feedback reports and decision support tools?, and 3) Why do patients become at risk of treatment failure and how should therapists intervene with these patients? The studies included in this book reflect the current state of feedback research and provide promising pathways for future endeavours that will enhance our understanding of feedback effects.

This book was originally published as a special issue of *Psychotherapy Research.*

Wolfgang Lutz (Ph.D., Full Professor) is head of the Department of Clinical Psychology and Psychotherapy and the director of the Outpatient Clinic and Postgraduate Clinic Training at the University of Trier, Germany.

Kim de Jong (Ph.D.) is Assistant Professor at the Institute of Psychology, Unit Clinical Psychology, at Leiden University, the Netherlands.

Julian Rubel (Ph.D.) is research fellow at the Department for Clinical Psychology and Psychotherapy at the University of Trier, Germany.

Patient-Focused and Feedback Research in Psychotherapy

Edited by
Wolfgang Lutz, Kim de Jong and Julian Rubel

Routledge
Taylor & Francis Group
LONDON AND NEW YORK

First published 2017 by Routledge

2 Park Square, Milton Park, Abingdon, Oxfordshire OX14 4RN
711 Third Avenue, New York, NY 10017

Routledge is an imprint of the Taylor & Francis Group, an informa business

First issued in paperback 2018

Copyright © 2017 Society for Psychotherapy Research

All rights reserved. No part of this book may be reprinted or reproduced or utilised in any form or by any electronic, mechanical, or other means, now known or hereafter invented, including photocopying and recording, or in any information storage or retrieval system, without permission in writing from the publishers.

Notice:
Product or corporate names may be trademarks or registered trademarks, and are used only for identification and explanation without intent to infringe.

British Library Cataloguing in Publication Data
A catalogue record for this book is available from the British Library

ISBN 13: 978-1-138-69996-0 (hbk)
ISBN 13: 978-0-367-02901-2 (pbk)

Typeset in Plantin
by RefineCatch Limited, Bungay, Suffolk

Publisher's Note
The publisher accepts responsibility for any inconsistencies that may have arisen during the conversion of this book from journal articles to book chapters, namely the possible inclusion of journal terminology.

Disclaimer
Every effort has been made to contact copyright holders for their permission to reprint material in this book. The publishers would be grateful to hear from any copyright holder who is not here acknowledged and will undertake to rectify any errors or omissions in future editions of this book.

Contents

Citation Information

The chapters in this book were originally published in *Psychotherapy Research*, volume 25, issue 6 (November 2015). When citing this material, please use the original page numbering for each article, as follows:

Introduction
Patient-focused and feedback research in psychotherapy: Where are we and where do we want to go?
Wolfgang Lutz, Kim de Jong, & Julian Rubel
Psychotherapy Research, volume 25, issue 6 (November 2015), pp. 625–632

Chapter 1
A mixed-method investigation of patient monitoring and enhanced feedback in routine practice: Barriers and facilitators
Mike Lucock, Jeremy Halstead, Chris Leach, Michael Barkham, Samantha Tucker, Chloe Randal, Joanne Middleton, Wajid Khan, Hannah Catlow, Emma Waters, & David Saxon
Psychotherapy Research, volume 25, issue 6 (November 2015), pp. 633–646

Chapter 2
Feedback and therapist effects in the context of treatment outcome and treatment length
Wolfgang Lutz, Julian Rubel, Anne-Katharina Schiefele, Dirk Zimmermann, Jan Rasmus Böhnke, & Werner W. Wittmann
Psychotherapy Research, volume 25, issue 6 (November 2015), pp. 647–660

Chapter 3
Why do some therapists not deal with outcome monitoring feedback? A feasibility study on the effect of regulatory focus and person–organization fit on attitude and outcome
Kim de Jong & Marije de Goede
Psychotherapy Research, volume 25, issue 6 (November 2015), pp. 661–668

Chapter 4
The effect of implementing the Outcome Questionnaire-45.2 feedback system in Norway: A multisite randomized clinical trial in a naturalistic setting
Ingunn Amble, Tore Gude, Sven Stubdal, Bror Just Andersen, & Bruce E. Wampold
Psychotherapy Research, volume 25, issue 6 (November 2015), pp. 669–677

Chapter 5
Feedback mechanisms of change: How problem alerts reported by youth clients and their caregivers impact clinician-reported session content
Susan R. Douglas, Bae Jonghyuk, Ana Regina Vides de Andrade, M. Michele Tomlinson, Ryan Pamela Hargraves, & Leonard Bickman
Psychotherapy Research, volume 25, issue 6 (November 2015), pp. 678–693

Chapter 6

Predicting outcome of substance abuse treatment in a feedback study: Can recovery curves be improved upon?
Paul Crits-Christoph, Hannah M. Markell, Robert Gallop, Mary Beth Connolly Gibbons, Bridget McClure, & John Rotrosen
Psychotherapy Research, volume 25, issue 6 (November 2015), pp. 694–704

Chapter 7

Daily monitoring of temporal trajectories of suicidal ideation predict self-injury: A novel application of patient progress monitoring
Emma Restifo, Shraddha Kashyap, Geoff R. Hooke, & Andrew C. Page
Psychotherapy Research, volume 25, issue 6 (November 2015), pp. 705–713

Chapter 8

Extreme deviations from expected recovery curves and their associations with therapeutic alliance, social support, motivation, and life events in psychosomatic in-patient therapy
Thomas Probst, Michael J. Lambert, Thomas H. Loew, Reiner W. Dahlbender, & Karin Tritt
Psychotherapy Research, volume 25, issue 6 (November 2015), pp. 714–723

Chapter 9

Using the Assessment for Signal Clients as a feedback tool for reducing treatment failure
Melissa M. White, Michael J. Lambert, Benjamin M. Ogles, Stevie B. McLaughlin, Russell J. Bailey, & K. Morgan Tingey
Psychotherapy Research, volume 25, issue 6 (November 2015), pp. 724–734

For any permission-related enquiries please visit:
http://www.tandfonline.com/page/help/permissions

Notes on Contributors

Ingunn Amble, Outpatient Clinic, Modum Bad Psychiatric Center, Vikersund, Norway.

Ana Regina Vides de Andrade, Department of Economics, Vanderbilt University, Nashville, TN, USA.

Russell J. Bailey, Department of Counseling and Psychological Services, Brigham Young University, Provo, UT, USA.

Michael Barkham, Department of Psychology, Centre for Psychological Services Research, University of Sheffield, Sheffield, UK.

Leonard Bickman, Department of Psychology and Human Development, Vanderbilt University, Nashville, TN, USA.

Hannah Catlow, South West Yorkshire Partnership NHS Foundation Trust, UK.

Paul Crits-Christoph, Department of Psychiatry, University of Pennsylvania, Philadelphia, PA, USA.

Reiner W. Dahlbender, Clinic for Psychosomatic Medicine and Psychotherapy, University Clinic of Ulm, Ulm, Germany.

Marije de Goede, Department of Social and Organizational Psychology, Utrecht University, Utrecht, The Netherlands.

Kim de Jong, Institute of Psychology, Unit Clinical Psychology, Leiden University, Leiden, The Netherlands.

Susan R. Douglas, Department of Psychology and Human Development, Vanderbilt University, Nashville, TN, USA.

Robert Gallop, Department of Mathematics, West Chester University, West Chester, PA, USA.

Mary Beth Connolly Gibbons, Department of Psychiatry, University of Pennsylvania, Philadelphia, PA, USA.

Tore Gude, Research Institute, Modum Bad Psychiatric Center, Vikersund, Norway.

Jeremy Halstead, Clinical Psychology, University of Leeds, Leeds, UK.

Ryan Pamela Hargraves, Emma, Nashville, TN, USA.

Geoff R. Hooke, Department of Psychology, University of Western Australia, Perth, WA, Australia.

Bror Just Andersen, Baerum District Psychiatric Center, Vestre Viken HF, Drammen, Norway.

Bae Jonghyuk, Department of Economics, Vanderbilt University, Nashville, TN, USA.

Shraddha Kashyap, Department of Psychology, University of Western Australia, Perth, WA, Australia.

Wajid Khan, South West Yorkshire Partnership NHS Foundation Trust, UK.

Michael J. Lambert, Department of Psychology, Brigham Young University, Provo, UT, USA.

Chris Leach, Centre for Applied Psychological and Health Research, University of Huddersfield, Huddersfield, UK.

Thomas H. Loew, Department of Psychosomatics, University Clinic of Regensburg, Regensburg, Germany.

Mike Lucock, Centre for Applied Psychological and Health Research, University of Huddersfield, Huddersfield, UK.

Wolfgang Lutz, Department of Psychology, University of Trier, Trier, Germany.

Bridget McClure, Joint Clinical Trials Office, Weill Cornell Medical College, New York, NY, USA.

Stevie B. McLaughlin, Department of Psychology, Brigham Young University, Provo, UT, USA.

Hannah M. Markell, Department of Psychiatry, University of Pennsylvania, Philadelphia, PA, USA.

Joanne Middleton, School of Psychological Sciences, University of Manchester, Manchester, UK.

Benjamin M. Ogles, Department of Psychology, Brigham Young University, Provo, UT, USA.

Andrew C. Page, Department of Psychology, University of Western Australia, Perth, WA, Australia.

Thomas Probst, Department of Psychology, University of Regensburg, Regensburg, Germany.

Chloe Randal, South West Yorkshire Partnership NHS Foundation Trust, UK.

Jan Rasmus Böhnke, Hull York Medical School & Department of Health Sciences, University of York, York, UK.

Emma Restifo, Department of Psychology, University of Western Australia, Perth, WA, Australia.

John Rotrosen, Department of Psychiatry, New York University School of Medicine, New York, NY, USA.

Julian Rubel, Department of Clinical Psychology and Psychotherapy, University of Trier, Trier, Germany.

David Saxon, Department of Psychology, Centre for Psychological Services Research, University of Sheffield, Sheffield, UK.

Anne-Katharina Schiefele, Department of Clinical Psychology and Psychotherapy, University of Trier, Trier, Germany.

Sven Stubdal, Outpatient Clinic, Modum Bad Psychiatric Center, Vikersund, Norway.

K. Morgan Tingey, Department of Psychology, Brigham Young University, Provo, UT, USA.

M. Michele Tomlinson, Hope Network, Grand Rapids, Michigan, USA.

Karin Tritt, Department of Psychosomatics, University Clinic of Regensburg, Regensburg, Germany.

Samantha Tucker, School of Psychological Sciences, University of Manchester, Manchester, UK.

Bruce E. Wampold, Department of Counseling Psychology, University of Wisconsin-Madison, Madison, WI, USA.

Emma Waters, Clinical Psychology, University of Leeds, Leeds, UK.

Melissa M. White, Department of Psychology, Brigham Young University, Provo, UT, USA.

Werner W. Wittmann, Otto-Selz-Institute for Applied Psychology, University of Mannheim, Mannheim, Germany.

Dirk Zimmermann, Department of Clinical Psychology and Psychotherapy, University of Trier, Trier, Germany.

INTRODUCTION

Patient-focused and feedback research in psychotherapy: Where are we and where do we want to go?

WOLFGANG LUTZ[1], KIM DE JONG[2], & JULIAN RUBEL[1]

[1]*Department of Psychology, University of Trier, Trier, Germany &* [2]*Department of Clinical Psychology, Leiden University, Leiden, The Netherlands*

Abstract

In the last 15 years feedback interventions have had a significant impact on the field of psychotherapy research and have demonstrated their potential to enhance treatment outcomes, especially for patients with an increased risk of treatment failure. This article serves as an introduction to the special issue on "Patient-focused and feedback research in psychotherapy: Where are we and where do we want to go?" Current investigations on feedback research are concerned with potential moderators and mediators of these effects, as well as the design and the implementation of feedback into routine care. This introduction summarizes the current state of feedback research and provides an overview of the three main research topics in this issue: (1) How to implement feedback systems into routine practice and how do therapist and patient attitudes influence its effects?, (2) How to design feedback reports and decision support tools?, and (3) What are the reasons for patients to become at risk of treatment failure and how should therapists intervene with these patients? We believe that the studies included in this special issue reflect the current state of feedback research and provide promising pathways for future endeavors that will enhance our understanding of feedback effects.

About two decades ago, *patient-focused* research (PFR) was introduced as a new research concept to outcome research in psychotherapy. Besides efficacy and effectiveness research, which are traditionally concerned with the average treatment effect of a given or new treatment approach, PFR is concerned with monitoring actual progress over the course of treatment and providing "real-time" feedback of this information to clinicians (Howard, Moras, Brill, Martinovich, & Lutz, 1996; Lambert, 2007; Lambert, Hansen, & Finch, 2001; Lutz, 2002).

Even though PFR is a relatively recent research area, it has become an international endeavor and one of the most prolific and cited areas within *Psychotherapy Research* over the last decades (Muran & Lutz, 2015). Starting with several large randomized controlled trials (RCTs), this research agenda, as well as its practical applications in routine care and the promising results of several studies, has been adopted in many countries and by several service systems. Examples include the following: the USA (Bickman, Kelley, Breda, de Andrade, & Riemer, 2011; Lambert, Whipple et al., 2001; 2003); the UK (Barkham et al., 2001); Norway (Amble, Gude, Stubdal, Andersen, & Wampold, 2014); Germany (Lutz, Böhnke, & Köck, 2011); Sweden (Holmqvist, Philips, & Barkham, 2015); the Netherlands (De Jong, Van Sluis, Nugter, Heiser, & Spinhoven, 2012); and Australia (Newnham & Page, 2010).

This line of research has had a substantial impact on national and international policy decisions and research collaborations. Amongst others in the USA, the "APA Presidential Task Force on Evidence-Based Practice" stated that: "The application of research evidence to a given patient always involves probabilistic inferences. Therefore, ongoing monitoring of patient progress and adjustment of treatment as needed are essential" (American Psychological Association 2006, p. 280). In England, routine outcome monitoring (ROM) and feedback was a component in a government initiative to improve access to psychological treatments ("Improving Access to psychological Therapy," IAPT; Clark et al., 2009). Most recently, the European research initiative stated in their roadmap for mental health research in Europe (ROAMER; Emmelkamp et al., 2014): "There is a clear need of research into routine outcome monitoring as a means of investigating the accountability of treatments, therapists and treatment centers" (p. 70). This broad international orientation is also reflected in the contributions of this special issue originating from six countries and three continents.

The development of PFR has been influenced by other movements within psychotherapy research and is related to ROM or practice-oriented research (POR). For example, in the most recent edition of the *Handbook for psychotherapy and behavior change*, Castonguay, Barkham, Lutz, and McAleavey (2013) differentiate practice-oriented research within psychotherapy into the three main approaches: patient-focused research, practice-based evidence, and practice research networks. PFR is based, as are scientist-practitioner networks and practice-based evidence, on the idea of an ongoing collaboration between practitioners and scientists (e.g., Boswell, Kraus, Miller, & Lambert, 2015; Castonguay & Muran, 2015; Holmqvist et al., 2015; Strauss et al., 2015). Practitioners deliver the actual treatment and collect data by assessing patients' progress during therapy. This provides researchers with continuously growing databases of patients' change information that can be utilized by researchers in pursuit of gaining a more thorough understanding of change patterns. In return, researchers have used this information to develop tools to support clinical decision making for clinical practice in real-time. The empirical progress or change information is directly fed back to therapists and patients as soon as it is available.

Feedback tools can be based on empirical data or rational decision strategies (e.g., Lutz, Stulz, Martinovich, Leon, & Saunders, 2014). They allow practitioners to track individual progress and adapt ongoing treatment, especially for patients with an early negative development (Lambert, 2007; Shimokawa, Lambert, & Smart, 2010). In that way, PFR establishes a permanent exchange between research and practice. Furthermore, data generated in projects following a patient-focused research paradigm can be used for supervision or can be used on a systems level as part of an evaluation or quality management system (e.g., Grossl, Reese, Norsworthy, & Hopkins, 2014; Swift et al., 2015). PFR methods and quality assurance (QA) or ROM in psychotherapy have formed a close relationship, although PFR, QA, and ROM do not have identical goals, and do, sometimes, have divergent goals, especially when QA or ROM are established by legal institutions or regulations defining strategies of external quality control (as for example, in the Netherlands; Stuurgroep ROM ggz, 2010).

The pivotal goal of PFR is the use and implementation of research into the actual treatment and thereby making psychotherapy in clinical practice a research-supported intervention. In this view it is not enough that a treatment has been shown, on average, to be effective based on efficacy and effectiveness trials. Instead the research support should be an integral part of each individual treatment, to the extent that the current state of research as well as the service system and treatment environment allows it. As such, PFR follows an alternative concept of treatment development and research. Traditionally, the development of a new treatment concept starts with a new clinical idea proposed by a clinical researcher or practicing clinician. Based on this idea, a new treatment paradigm consisting of a number of interventions is developed and eventually tested in a RCT. If these efforts result in evidence suggesting that the new intervention is effective, often a new movement promoting the proposed clinical mechanisms of change starts to be disseminated. This is a natural development of how new theoretical concepts of change are introduced into the field, but often with limited empirical knowledge related to the actual moderators and mediators of change (Kazdin, 2014). In contrast, PFR supports a research-practice perspective that is more focused on the improvement of actual outcomes and less based on a debate about therapeutic schools or theories. Accordingly, the core of this approach requires research to be conducted on the course of individual patients in order to learn about differences in individual change as well as subgroups of patients with specific patterns of change (e.g., Lutz, et al., 2014; Rubel et al., 2014; Stulz, Lutz, Leach, Lucock, & Barkham, 2007).

The first three studies testing the effects of feedback were conducted by Michael Lambert and his research group (Lambert, Whipple et al., 2001; Lambert, Whipple, Vermeersch et al., 2002; Whipple et al., 2003). In these studies, feedback to therapists on patients' progress was effective in improving patient outcomes, particularly for those patients who showed an increased risk for treatment failure (not on track patients; NOT). The percentage of NOT patients receiving feedback and reaching a reliable or clinical significant improvement was about 14% higher than the rate for the NOT patients without feedback. Furthermore, those NOT patients also had an 8% lower deterioration rate when their therapists received feedback. Additionally, feedback to therapists of NOT patients led to, on average, longer treatments but shorter treatments, on average, for on-track (OT) patients. Further studies yielded more dramatic effects as a result of implementing feedback systems. Lambert and his group devoted considerable energy to predicting treatment failure (e.g., Lambert, Whipple, Bishop et al., 2002) and came to believe that the essential value of feedback systems was to help clinicians become aware of pending treatment failure, something that they could not achieve through clinical intuition (Hannan et al., 2005). From their perspective progress feedback is an intervention aimed at NOT cases, not all cases, and thus should be judged by its impact on such cases rather than the entire caseload. Thus, they developed and tested clinical support tools (CST) with decision rules for when and in which clinical areas therapists should intervene for patients at risk for treatment failure (e.g., Whipple et al., 2003).

To date, key findings of these original studies have been replicated under different conditions in many investigations and have been reported in four systematic reviews (Carlier et al., 2012; Davidson, Perry, & Bell, 2015; Krägeloh, Czuba, Billington, Kersten, & Siegert, 2015; Newnham & Page, 2010) and four meta-analyses (Knaup, Koesters, Schoefer, Becker, & Puschner, 2009; Lambert & Shimokawa, 2011; Poston & Hanson, 2010; Shimokawa et al., 2010). For example, in a recent review on the effects of feedback Krägeloh and colleagues (2015) reported that of the 25 identified studies, 17 showed a significantly positive feedback effect on average or for NOT patients. However, evidence for the effects of feedback on treatment length was less convincing. Of the 17 studies that reported on these associations, only six found a significant association between treatment length and feedback.

More detailed information about the size of the effects was derived from several meta-analyses (Lambert & Shimokawa, 2011; Shimokawa et al., 2010). In these studies the significant effect sizes regarding improvement for NOT patients with feedback vs. treatment as usual (TAU) offered by the same therapists ranged between $g = .28$ (intent-to-treat sample, ITT) and $g = .53$ (at least four sessions in treatment, efficacy analysis). For OT patients the effects were smaller, ranging from $g = .18$ (ITT) to $g = .32$ (efficacy analysis) if patients and therapists were provided with feedback and from $g = .12$ (ITT) to $g = .30$ (efficacy analysis) if only therapists received the feedback. When CST's were employed the effect size reached between $g = .44$ (ITT) and $g = .70$ (efficacy analysis; Shimokawa et al., 2010). The effect of psychometric feedback on treatment length showed a heterogeneous picture, and the treatment length findings of the early studies could not be replicated, but the feedback effect on outcome was stable for different monitoring systems (OQ and PCOMS, see Lambert & Shimokawa, 2011).

Overall, over the last 10 years, feedback research has investigated a large variety of feedback modalities with regard to the feedback and monitoring systems used, the settings in which those were applied (e.g., child, group, couple, family, inpatient, outpatient, and counseling), the frequency with which feedback was provided during the course of treatment, the amount of information provided to clinicians (e.g., raw scores, expected treatment response curves, decision rules, and clinical support tools), the investigated diagnostic groups (e.g., eating disorders, addiction, and personality disorder), and the formalization of the usage of feedback. From this cumulative body of research we can conclude that feedback is effective, especially for not on track patients. Alerting therapists to patients at risk for treatment failure is essential for what needs to be fed back to therapists. Thus, evaluating the effects of feedback should focus on NOT cases. Furthermore, the accurate prediction of treatment failure is a condition of an effective feedback system and the feedback effects can be enhanced by using decision support tools, which include clinical suggestions to adapt or improve treatments with the risk of failure.

It can also be concluded, that the implementation of feedback systems leads to changes and adaptations in clinical interventions and is well received by patients. For example, in a German feedback study (Lutz et al., 2011; Lutz et al., 2015) on approximately 70% of the occasions, when therapists got feedback, therapists made some use of feedback either by taking some action or by drawing some consequence concerning their treatment formulation, for example, discussing the results with patients, trying to adjust their therapeutic interventions or trying to enhance the therapeutic alliance. Furthermore, the positive evaluations about feedback studies are very high. For example, when patients are asked, if they find it important to monitor the results of psychotherapeutic treatments, 66.8% answer with completely right and 26.1% of participants answer with partially right (further details see, e.g., Castonguay, et al., 2013; Lutz, et al., 2015; Strauss, et al., 2015). However, recent research has also shown that feedback is not equally effective for all therapists and patients. Simon, Lambert, Harris, Busath & Vazquez (2012) report that only for about 50% of the therapists feedback enhanced outcomes with NOT cases and had no impact for the other half of the therapists. Similarly, Lutz et al., (2015) analyzed therapist differences, which is an under investigated factor in feedback studies so far. Results suggest that therapists satisfaction with the feedback system and their use of the feedback information are important differential predictors. Likewise, De Jong et al. (2012) analyzed differences between therapists in using feedback. Female therapists and those with a higher commitment to feedback seemed to have a higher probability to use the information provided by the feedback system. Those therapists, who used the feedback system, were also more effective for NOT patients.

Furthermore, the debate about giving feedback directly to patients compared to providing feedback just to therapists resulted in mixed results and it is still unclear whether giving formal written feedback to patients results in a further enhancement of outcome (De Jong et al., 2014; Shimokawa et al., 2010). Accordingly, nowadays the leading questions are more fine-grained than in the beginnings of feedback research: What are patient and therapist variables that moderate the effects of feedback? How should feedback be designed to maximize its effects? Which elements of feedback reports are more important and which are less important? How can therapists use feedback most efficiently? How can therapists be motivated and trained to integrate psychometric feedback in their work? How can we facilitate the implementation of ROM and feedback systems? These questions underpin the aims of this special issue.

Accordingly, the goal of this special issue in *Psychotherapy Research* is to present new studies related to those more specific and detailed research questions and to stimulate future work in this area. Authors were briefed that the issue was about the knowledge base around patient-focused research and feedback in psychotherapy. The studies could focus on the empirical basis of patient-focused research/feedback (when is it useful, does it improve clinical practice, what are the circumstances/predictors of its functionality, how does it work, what are the limitations) and/or could focus on data, which covers some aspects of a feedback systems (e.g., acceptability to clinicians, patients, and administrators), and/or could focus on the theoretical background and future research aspects of the field (e.g., fundamental part of clinical work, and required part of clinical training). They were also briefed that the focus was not on the presentation of a specific version of outcome monitoring systems and promotional material for specific instruments. By contrast, the focus of the current special issue was on cutting-edge original articles that showed the current status as well as the pros and cons of the research field. Another important feature was that articles in the special issue should reflect the international perspective in this research field. Therefore, experts from six countries and three continents, working with different feedback systems were invited.

In addition to this introduction, the special issue comprises nine empirical papers investigating the most up to date research questions within the following areas of PFR:

- How to implement feedback systems into routine care and how do therapist and patient attitudes influence its effects? Implementation, acceptance, and feasibility of routine outcome monitoring.
- How to design feedback reports and decision support tools? The important elements of feedback reports.
- What are the reasons that patients are not on track or at risk for treatment failure? In which clinical areas should therapists get feedback, and how to intervene? Typical problems of patients who do not profit from treatment or are at risk for failure, dimensions of feedback and clinical support tools.

How to Implement Feedback Systems into Routine Care and How Do Therapist and Patient Attitudes Influence its Effects?

The first four papers address questions related to the implementation of feedback in routine care as well as feasibility and acceptance issues (Amble, Gude, Stubdal et al., 2014; De Jong & Goede, 2015; Lucock et al., 2015; Lutz et al., 2015). In the first study, Lucock et al. (2015) present an empirical investigation of these questions. Using an actual study example within the UK National Health Service, the authors identified barriers and facilitators of an effective implementation of outcome monitoring and feedback systems with a mixed methods approach. In this study, therapists were asked to complete quantitative questionnaires and their written and verbal feedback was subjected to qualitative thematic analyses. While their findings generally support the feasibility and acceptability of the implementation of ROM, the authors emphasize apparent therapist differences. These findings underline the importance of the participating therapists in feedback studies. In the second paper, taking the importance of therapist differences into account, Lutz et al. (2015) examine therapist effects on treatment outcome and treatment length in a German feedback study. In an outpatient sample treated in private practices, the authors consider several predictors of treatment outcome and length. Therapists' attitudes (a composite index of feedback usage and satisfaction with the feedback system) as well as patients' attitudes toward psychometric feedback influence the impact of feedback on outcome. In the third article, De Jong and De Goede (2015) report a feasibility study to explore two potential factors influencing therapists' attitude formation as well as treatment outcome in three outpatient mental healthcare centers in the Netherlands. The first factor investigated whether a therapists' regulatory focus—that is whether she/he is rather motivated to prevent failure or to achieve success. The second factor is the perceived match between the therapist's own values and the philosophy of the organization she/he is working in.

The last of these studies investigates the impact and consequences of a multisite implementation of the OQ feedback system in southern Norway (Amble, Gude, Stubdal et al., 2014). In six psychiatric clinics, the authors evaluate the implementation within a multisite randomized clinical trial design. Besides the overall effects of feedback, the authors investigate whether these effects differ between the sites and with regard to the treatment course of the patient (OT vs. NOT). Based on that study, Amble, Grude, Ulvenes, Stubdal, and Wampold (2015) investigated whether receiving a signal for NOT cases causes the effect of feedback.

How to Design Feedback Reports and Decision Support Tools?

The second topic in this issue, as well as a major theme within PFR, is the actual design of feedback reports. Decision support tools play a crucial role in efforts to enhance the effects of feedback. Therefore, the next three papers of this special issue investigate specific elements of feedback reports and try to identify the essential clinically useful information that helps to improve patient outcomes (Crits-Christoph et al., 2015; Douglas et al., 2015; Restifo, Kashyap, Hooke, & Page, 2015).

The first of these papers searched for the mechanisms through which feedback leads to more pronounced treatment effects. Douglas et al. (2015) hypothesize that therapists who receive feedback on the problems of their patients address specific contents more immediate and more frequently than without feedback. The authors use data from clients treated within a home-based community mental health treatment. Therapists were provided with computerized feedback on the problem areas of their patients. Such problem-specific feedback is consistent with the results of a recent study providing evidence for an enhanced feedback effect if feedback is based on multiple domains in comparison to a single domain (Dyer, Hooke, & Page, 2014).

In order to evaluate the progress of patients over the course of treatment and to give feedback, decision tools that compare the actual progress to a benchmark are necessary. Since the early days of feedback studies, decision tools or expected treatment response (ETR) curves based on data of already treated patients are investigated. Early studies using mostly initial impairment as the basis for ETR resulted in about 17–18% of explained variance in the rate of change (e.g., Lambert, Whipple, Bishop et al., 2002; Lutz, Martinovich, & Howard, 1999), whereas additional predictors such as previous therapy, chronicity and treatment expectation added only a small additional amount of explained variance to the ETR curves (e.g., 22% in Lutz et al., 1999). This topic is addressed in the next article by Crits-Christoph et al. (2015) that focuses on predictors of ETR curves for patients treated in four US community-based outpatient substance abuse treatment clinics. General intake variables, such as the initial score in the OQ-45, as well as substance abuse specific variables (e.g., craving) were investigated with regard to their associations with patients' change curves. Specifically, the results were used to deduce implications for the design of ETR curves in disorder specific settings (e.g., substance abuse treatments; also see Schuman, Slone, Reese, & Duncan, 2014).

In the next article, Restifo et al. (2015) present an innovative application of ROM and feedback for the prediction of self-harming behaviors following suicidal ideation. Using latent class growth analysis, the authors identify change patterns of suicidal ideation in psychiatric inpatients. The authors investigate whether and how information on typical change patterns could be used in routine inpatient care to estimate the probability that suicidal ideation results in self-harming behaviors and how this tool could be used to avoid self-harm.

What are the Reasons that Patients are Not on Track or at Risk for Treatment Failure?

The final two papers deal with the reasons why patients get off track and in which areas therapists should intervene to prevent treatment failure (Probst et al., 2014; White et al., 2015). As described above, clinical support tools (CSTs) for patients that are NOT allow therapists to tailor their interventions and therefore appear to enhance the effect of feedback. Both papers in this section take a closer look at patients' typical response patterns on therapy process measures typically used in CSTs. Probst et al. (2014) compare the scores in the Assessment for Signal Clients (ASC; Lambert, 2007) scales of patients with extreme positive deviations from the above-discussed ETR curves with those of patients with extreme negative deviations. Using this approach with patients from a psychosomatic inpatient clinic in Germany, the authors investigate whether prioritizing the ASC domains (therapeutic alliance, social support, motivation, and life events) could further enhance the effects of clinical support tools. In the same vein, White et al. (2015) investigate ASC data of cases that were identified as NOT in a feedback study carried out in a hospital-based outpatient clinic in the USA. The ASC was completed immediately after the identification of a patient as being at risk for treatment failure. These ASC data were subjected to a cluster analysis to characterize typical patterns of problem areas within these signal clients. Knowing typical problem areas and/or conjoint problem areas of patients who do not profit from therapy in the first place, again allows the development of more effective support tools for important domains. This area of investigation, which focusses on the further refinement of the clinical support tools, seems to be another promising area of future investigations.

In sum, this special issue provides an overview of new developments in the field of patient-focused and feedback research that we hope will inspire new, innovative studies and research collaborations. We believe that the studies included in this special issue reflect the current state of feedback research and flag promising pathways for future endeavors that will increase our understanding of feedback effects. Feedback tools can and will likely be more easily implemented in the future by using tools from eMental health research (e.g., Emmelkamp et al., 2014). The more technology develops, the easier it is to implement these tools into daily routine. Given that 20 years ago psychotherapy research was limited to a few patients treated in a university setting and assessed in a pre-post design, this new line of research allows us to study psychotherapy in practice, based on large databases and to integrate this information directly into the field, while promoting further integration of science and practice. Thus, the implementation of feedback in the training and supervision of future therapists would help them to build a clinical identity, which includes research as an integral part of the treatment.

Acknowledgement

We would like to thank Michael J. Lambert and Michael Barkham for commentaries on previous versions of this manuscript.

References

American Psychological Association. (2006). Report of the 2005 presidential task force on evidence-based practice. *American Psychologist*, *61*, 271–285.

Amble, I., Gude, T., Stubdal, S., Andersen, B. J., & Wampold, B. E. (2014). The effect of implementing the outcome questionnaire-45.2 feedback system in Norway: A multisite randomized clinical trial in a naturalistic setting. *Psychotherapy Research*, Advance online publication. doi:10.1080/10503307.2014.928756

Amble, I., Gude, T., Ulvenes, P., Stubdal, S., & Wampold, B. E. (2015). How and when feedback works in psychotherapy: Is it the signal? *Psychotherapy Research*. Advance online publication. doi:10.1080/10503307.2015.1053552

Barkham, M., Margison, F., Leach, C., Lucock, M., Mellor-Clark, J., Evans, C., … & McGrath, G. (2001). Service profiling and outcomes benchmarking using the CORE-OM: Toward practice-based evidence in the psychological therapies. *Journal of Consulting and Clinical Psychology*, *69*(2), 184–196.

Bickman, L., Kelley, S. D., Breda, C., de Andrade, A. R., & Riemer, M. (2011). Effects of routine feedback to clinicians on mental health outcomes of youths: Results of a randomized trial. *Psychiatric Services*, *62*(12), 1423–1429.

Boswell, J. F., Kraus, D. R., Miller, S. D., & Lambert, M. J. (2015). Implementing routine outcome monitoring in clinical practice: Benefits, challenges, and solutions. *Psychotherapy Research*, *25*(1), 6–19.

Carlier, I. V., Meuldijk, D., Van Vliet, I. M., Van Fenema, E., Van der Wee, N. J., & Zitman, F. G. (2012). Routine outcome monitoring and feedback on physical or mental health status: evidence and theory. *Journal of Evaluation in Clinical Practice*, *18*(1), 104–110.

Castonguay, L., Barkham, M., Lutz, W., & McAleavy, A. (2013). Practice-oriented research: Approaches and applications. In M. J. Lambert (Ed.), *Bergin and Garfield's handbook of psychotherapy and behavior change*, (6th ed., pp. 85–133). New York, NY: Wiley & Sons.

Castonguay, L. G., & Muran, J. C. (2015). Fostering collaboration between researchers and clinicians through building practice-oriented research: An introduction. *Psychotherapy Research*, *25* (1), 1–5.

Clark, D. M., Layard, R., Smithies, R., Richards, D. A., Suckling, R., & Wright, B. (2009). Improving access to psychological therapy: Initial evaluation of two UK demonstration sites. *Behaviour Research and Therapy*, *47*(11), 910–920.

Crits-Christoph, P., Markell, H. M., Gallop, R., Gibbons, M. B. C., McClure, B., & Rotrosen, J. (2015). Predicting outcome of substance abuse treatment in a feedback study: Can recovery curves be improved upon? *Psychotherapy Research*. Advance online publication. doi:10.1080/10503307.2014.994146

Davidson, K., Perry, A., & Bell, L. (2015). Would continuous feedback of patient's clinical outcomes to practitioners improve NHS psychological therapy services? Critical analysis and assessment of quality of existing studies. *Psychology and Psychotherapy: Theory, Research and Practice*, *88*(1), 21–37.

De Jong, K., & De Goede, M. (2015). Why do some therapists not deal with outcome monitoring feedback? A feasibility study on the effect of regulatory focus and person-organization fit on attitude and outcome. *Psychotherapy Research*. Advance online publication. doi:10.1080/10503307.2015.1076198

De Jong, K., Timman, R., Hakkaart-Van Roijen, L., Vermeulen, P., Kooiman, K., Passchier, J., & Busschbach, J. V. (2014). The effect of outcome monitoring feedback to clinicians and patients in short and long-term psychotherapy: A randomized controlled trial. *Psychotherapy Research*, *24*(6), 629–639.

De Jong, K., Van Sluis, P., Nugter, M. A., Heiser, W. J., & Spinhoven, P. (2012). Understanding the differential impact of outcome monitoring: Therapist variables that moderate feedback effects in a randomized clinical trial. *Psychotherapy Research*, *22*(4), 464–474.

Douglas, S., Jonghyuk, B., Vides de Andrade, A., Tomlinson, M., Hargraves, R., & Bickman, L. (2015). Feedback mechanisms of change: How problem alerts reported by youth clients and their caregivers impact clinician-reported session content. *Psychotherapy Research*, Advance online publication. doi:10.1080/10503307.2015.1059966

Dyer, K., Hooke, G. R., & Page, A. C. (2014). Effects of providing domain specific progress monitoring and feedback to therapists and patients on outcome. *Psychotherapy Research.* Advance online publication. doi:10.1080/10503307.2014.983207

Emmelkamp, P. M. G., David, D., Beckers, T., Muris, P., Cuijpers, P., Lutz, W., & Vervliet, B. (2014). Advancing psychotherapy and evidence-based psychological interventions. *International Journal of Methods in Psychiatric Research*, *23*(S1), 58–91.

Grossl, A. B., Reese, R. J., Norsworthy, L. A., & Hopkins, N. B. (2014). Client feedback data in supervision: Effects on supervision and outcome. *Training and Education in Professional Psychology*, *8*(3), 182–188.

Hannan, C., Lambert, M. J., Harmon, C., Nielsen, S. L., Smart, D. W., Shimokawa, K., & Sutton, S. W. (2005). A lab test and algorithms for identifying clients at risk for treatment failure. *Journal of Clinical Psychology*, *61*(2), 155–163.

Holmqvist, R., Philips, B., & Barkham, M. (2015). Developing practice-based evidence: Benefits, challenges, and tensions. *Psychotherapy Research*, *25*(1), 20–31.

Howard, K. I., Moras, K., Brill, P. L., Martinovich, Z., & Lutz, W. (1996). Evaluation of psychotherapy: Efficacy, effectiveness, and patient progress. *American Psychologist*, *51*(10), 1059–1064.

Kazdin, A. E. (2014). Moderators, mediators, and mechanisms of change in psychotherapy. In W. Lutz & S. Knox (Eds.), *Quantitative and qualitative methods in psychotherapy* (pp. 87–101). New York, NY: Routledge.

Knaup, C., Koesters, M., Schoefer, D., Becker, T., & Puschner, B. (2009). Effect of feedback of treatment outcome in specialist mental healthcare: meta-analysis. *The British Journal of Psychiatry*, *195*(1), 15–22.

Krägeloh, C. U., Czuba, K. J., Billington, D. R., Kersten, P., & Siegert, R. J. (2015). Using feedback from patient-reported outcome measures in mental health services: a scoping study and typology. *Psychiatric Services*, *66*(3), 224–241.

Lambert, M. (2007). Presidential address: What we have learned from a decade of research aimed at improving psychotherapy outcome in routine care. *Psychotherapy Research*, *17*(1), 1–14.

Lambert, M. J., Hansen, N. B., & Finch, A. E. (2001). Patient-focused research: Using patient outcome data to enhance treatment effects. *Journal of Consulting and Clinical Psychology*, *69*(2), 159–172.

Lambert, M. J., & Shimokawa, K. (2011). Collecting client feedback. *Psychotherapy*, *48*(1), 72–79.

Lambert, M. J., Whipple, J. L., Bishop, M. J., Vermeersch, D. A., Gray, G. V., & Finch, A. E. (2002). Comparison of empirically-derived and rationally-derived methods for identifying patients at risk for treatment failure. *Clinical Psychology & Psychotherapy*, *9*(3), 149–164.

Lambert, M. J., Whipple, J. L., Hawkins, E. J., Vermeersch, D. A., Nielsen, S. L., & Smart, D. W. (2003). Is it time for clinicians to routinely track patient outcome? A meta-Analysis. *Clinical Psychology: Science and Practice*, *10*(3), 288–301.

Lambert, M. J., Whipple, J. L., Smart, D. W., Vermeersch, D. A., Nielsen, S. L., & Hawkins, E. J. (2001). The effects of providing therapists with feedback on patient progress during psychotherapy: Are outcomes enhanced? *Psychotherapy Research*, *11*(1), 49–68.

Lambert, M. J., Whipple, J. L., Vermeersch, D. A., Smart, D. W., Hawkins, E. J., Nielsen, S. L., & Goates, M. (2002). Enhancing psychotherapy outcomes via providing feedback on client progress: A replication. *Clinical Psychology & Psychotherapy*, *9*(2), 91–103.

Lucock, M., Halstead, J., Leach, C., Barkham, M., Tucker, S., Randal, C., ... Saxon, D. (2015). A mixed method investigation of patient monitoring and enhanced feedback in routine practice: Barriers and facilitators. *Psychotherapy Research.* Advance online publication. doi:10.1080/10503307.2015.1051163

Lutz, W. (2002). Patient-focused psychotherapy research and individual treatment progress as scientific groundwork for an empirically based clinical practice. *Psychotherapy Research*, *12* (3), 251–272.

Lutz, W., Böhnke, J. R., & Köck, K. (2011). Lending an ear to feedback systems: evaluation of recovery and non-response in psychotherapy in a German outpatient setting. *Community Mental Health Journal*, *47*(3), 311–317.

Lutz, W., Hofmann, S. G., Rubel, J., Boswell, J. F., Shear, M. K., Gorman, J. M., ... & Barlow, D. H. (2014). Patterns of early change and their relationship to outcome and early treatment termination in patients with panic disorder. *Journal of Consulting and Clinical Psychology*, *82*(2), 287–297.

Lutz, W., Martinovich, Z., & Howard, K. I. (1999). Patient profiling: An application of random coefficient regression models to depicting the response of a patient to outpatient psychotherapy. *Journal of Consulting and Clinical Psychology*, *67*(4), 571–577.

Lutz, W., Rubel, J., Schiefele, A. K., Zimmermann, D. Böhnke, J., & Wittman, W. W. (2015). Feedback and therapist effects in the context of treatment outcome and treatment length. *Psychotherapy Research.* Advance online publication. doi:10.1080/10503307.2015.1053553

Lutz, W., Stulz, N., Martinovich, Z., Leon, S., & Saunders, S. M. (2014). Patient-focused research in psychotherapy: methodological background, decision rules and feedback tools. In W. Lutz & S. Knox (Eds.), *Quantitative and qualitative methods in psychotherapy* (pp. 204–217). New York, NY: Routledge.

Muran, J. C., & Lutz, W. (2015). A train of thought: 25 years of psychotherapy research. *Psychotherapy Research*, *25*(3), 277–281.

Newnham, E. A., & Page, A. C. (2010). Bridging the gap between best evidence and best practice in mental health. *Clinical Psychology Review*, *30*(1), 127–142.

Poston, J. M., & Hanson, W. E. (2010). Meta-Analysis of psychological assessment as a therapeutic intervention. *Psychological Assessement*, *22*(2), 203–212.

Probst, T., Lambert, M. J., Loew, T. H., Dahlbender, R. W., & Tritt, K. (2014). Extreme deviations from expected recovery curves and their associations with therapeutic alliance, social support, motivation, and life events in psychosomatic in-patient therapy. *Psychotherapy Research.* Advance online publication. doi:10.1080/10503307.2014.981682

Restifo, E., Kashyap, S., Hooke, G. R., & Page, A. C. (2015). Daily monitoring of temporal trajectories of suicidal ideation predict self-injury: A novel application of patient progress monitoring. *Psychotherapy Research.* Advance online publication. doi:10.1080/10503307.2015.1006707

Rubel, J., Lutz, W., Kopta, S. M., Köck, K., Minami, T., Zimmermann, D., & Saunders, S. M. (2014). Defining early positive response to psychotherapy: An empirical comparison between clinically significant change criteria and growth mixture modeling. *Psychological Assessment*, *27*(2), 478–488.

Schuman, D. L., Slone, N. C., Reese, R. J., & Duncan, B. (2014). Efficacy of client feedback in group psychotherapy with soldiers referred for substance abuse treatment. *Psychotherapy Research.* Advance online publication. doi:10.1080/10503307.2014.900875

Shimokawa, K., Lambert, M. J., & Smart, D. W. (2010). Enhancing treatment outcome of patients at risk of treatment failure: Meta-analytic and mega-analytic review of a psychotherapy quality assurance system. *Journal of Consulting and Clinical Psychology*, *78*(3), 298–311.

Simon, W., Lambert, W. J., Harris, M. W., Busath, G., & Vazquez, A. (2012). Providing patient progress information and clinical support tools to therapists: Effects on patients at risk of treatment failure. *Clinical Psychology & Psychotherapy*, *22*(6), 638–647.

Strauss, B. M., Lutz, W., Steffanowski, A., Wittmann, W. W., Boehnke, J. R., Rubel, J., ... & Kirchmann, H. (2015). Benefits and challenges in practice-oriented psychotherapy research in Germany: The TK and the QS-PSY-BAY projects of quality assurance in outpatient psychotherapy. *Psychotherapy Research*, *25*(1), 32–51.

Stulz, N., Lutz, W., Leach, C., Lucock, M., & Barkham, M. (2007). Shapes of early change in psychotherapy under routine outpatient conditions. *Journal of Consulting and Clinical Psychology*, *75*(6), 864–874.

Stuurgroep ROM ggz (2010). *Visie op ROM in de GGZ*. Amersfoort, the Netherlands: GGZ Nederland.

Swift, J. K., Callahan, J. L., Rousmaniere, T. G., Whipple, J. L., Dexter, K., & Wrape, E. R. (2015). Using client outcome monitoring as a tool for supervision. *Psychotherapy*, *52*(2), 180–184.

Whipple, J. L., Lambert, M. J., Vermeersch, D. A., Smart, D. W., Nielsen, S. L., & Hawkins, E. J. (2003). Improving the effects of psychotherapy: The use of early identification of treatment and problem-solving strategies in routine practice. *Journal of Counseling Psychology*, *50*(1), 59–68.

White, M. M., Lambert, M. J., Ogles, B. M., Mclaughlin, S. B., Bailey, R. J., & Tingey, K. M. (2015). Using the assessment for signal clients as a feedback tool for reducing treatment failure. *Psychotherapy Research*. Advance online publication. doi:10.1080/10503307.2015.1009862

A mixed-method investigation of patient monitoring and enhanced feedback in routine practice: Barriers and facilitators

MIKE LUCOCK[1,2], JEREMY HALSTEAD[3], CHRIS LEACH[1,2], MICHAEL BARKHAM[4], SAMANTHA TUCKER[5], CHLOE RANDAL[1], JOANNE MIDDLETON[5], WAJID KHAN[1], HANNAH CATLOW[1], EMMA WATERS[3], & DAVID SAXON[4]

[1]*South West Yorkshire Partnership NHS Foundation Trust, UK;* [2]*Centre for Applied Psychological and Health Research, University of Huddersfield, Huddersfield, UK;* [3]*Clinical Psychology, University of Leeds, Leeds, UK;* [4]*Department of Psychology, Centre for Psychological Services Research, University of Sheffield, Sheffield, UK;* [5]*School of Psychological Sciences, University of Manchester, Manchester, UK*

Abstract

Objective: To investigate the barriers and facilitators of an effective implementation of an outcome monitoring and feedback system in a UK National Health Service psychological therapy service. **Method**: An outcome monitoring system was introduced in two services. Enhanced feedback was given to therapists after session 4. Qualitative and quantitative methods were used, including questionnaires for therapists and patients. Thematic analysis was carried out on written and verbal feedback from therapists. Analysis of patient outcomes for 202 episodes of therapy was compared with benchmark data of 136 episodes of therapy for which feedback was not given to therapists. **Results**: Themes influencing the feasibility and acceptability of the feedback system were the extent to which therapists integrated the measures and feedback into the therapy, availability of administrative support, information technology, and complexity of the service. There were low levels of therapist actions resulting from the feedback, including discussing the feedback in supervision and with patients. **Conclusions:** The findings support the feasibility and acceptability of setting up a routine system in a complex service, but a number of challenges and barriers have to be overcome and therapist differences are apparent. More research on implementation and effectiveness is needed in diverse clinical settings.

Introduction

There is substantial evidence for the efficacy and effectiveness of psychological therapies (Lambert, 2013). Despite this body of literature, a significant number of patients do not benefit. Hansen, Lambert, and Forman (2002) report that about a third of patients receiving psychotherapy in RCTs either show no benefit or deteriorate. The rates of poor response are reported to be higher in routine services, with Hansen et al. (2002) reporting 56% of patients making no reliable change across studies in routine practice involving over 6000 patients with an additional average reliable deterioration rate of 8%. The importance of deterioration in psychotherapy has been highlighted (e.g., Lilienfeld, 2007) and Mohr (1995), in a review of 46 studies, identified patient, therapist, and therapy variables associated with negative outcome. The patient characteristics identified included borderline personality, obsessive–compulsive problems with severe interpersonal difficulties, poor motivation, and those patients expecting psychotherapy to be painless. This evidence underlines the importance of identifying patients at risk of a poor treatment response.

There is now widespread acknowledgment that an important way of improving outcomes involves monitoring the progress of patients during therapy and providing timely feedback on the monitoring data to therapists. This activity has yielded a burgeoning literature comprising texts (e.g., Lambert, 2010), reviews (e.g., Carlier et al., 2012), special issues (e.g., Fitzpatrick, 2012), and opinion pieces (e.g., Macdonald & Mellor-Clark, 2015). Monitoring progress and providing feedback is consistent with the traditions of patient-focused research (Howard, Moras, Brill, Martinovich, & Lutz, 1996) and the scientist practitioner approach (Hayes, Barlow, & Nelson, 1999). However, only in recent years have patient monitoring and feedback systems become embedded in routine practice. Examples are Lambert's work using the Outcome Questionnaire (Lambert et al., 2004); the Clinical Outcomes in Routine Evaluation (CORE) OM and CORE system in the UK (Barkham et al., 2010); and Miller and Duncan's development and implementation of two 4-item measures of treatment progress and therapeutic alliance (Miller, Duncan, Sorrell, & Brown, 2005). Part of the rationale for using these systems rests on evidence that early response to therapy predicts outcome (Lutz et al., 2006; Lutz, Stulz, & Köck, 2009; Stulz, Lutz, Leach, Lucock, & Barkham, 2007). In particular, there is evidence that poor early response to therapy is a predictor of a poor outcome (Kuyken, 2004; Lambert et al., 2002). Another justification for patient monitoring and feedback systems is the evidence that therapists are poor judges of their patients' outcomes (Garb, 2005; Sapyta, Reimer, & Bickman, 2005). Moreover, they are poor at predicting which of their patients are likely to deteriorate (Hannan et al., 2005). This finding is consistent with long-standing evidence that clinical judgement can be relatively poor and inferior to statistical predictions (Dawes, Faust, & Meehl, 1989; Meehl, 1954). Tracey, Wampold, Lichtenberg, and Goodyear (2014) argue that a further justification for attending to feedback about patients' progress is that it is a necessary but not sufficient requirement for developing the expertise of therapists.

Lambert and colleagues introduced the notion of patients who are "not on track" (NOT) as a means of identifying patients who are not achieving the expected recovery trajectory and therefore at risk of treatment failure. They found that providing feedback to therapists on the progress of these patients improved outcomes (Lambert et al., 2001, 2002). The addition of a set of clinical support tools, which provided information to therapists about the quality of the therapeutic relationship, the patient's social support, motivation, and experience of life events, further improved outcomes for NOT patients (Whipple et al., 2003). There is further evidence of moderate effects of feedback on outcome from other settings and countries (e.g., Byrne, Hooke, Newnham, & Page, 2012; Hansson, Rundberg, Ö sterling, Ö jehagen, & Berglund, 2013; Probst et al., 2013).

Set against this promising body of evidence, a recent independent review of patient outcome feedback systems by Davidson, Perry, and Bell (2015) heeded caution in relation to the extent to which findings could be generalized to non-US, and specifically UK, settings. The authors note that only the later studies—post-2009—are likely to represent the diversity and severity of patients seen in the UK National Health Service (NHS) and the impact of feedback in these studies appears to be reduced. Accordingly, the present study investigated the feasibility of setting up an outcome feedback system within a routine UK NHS service setting that met the needs of a more diverse and broad spectrum of patient needs.

Despite this growing body of evidence, there have been few studies investigating mediators related to feedback systems, such as therapist behaviour (e.g., how they act on the feedback) or organizational factors. Boswell, Kraus, Miller, and Lambert (2015) discuss a number of these factors and identify some of the benefits, obstacles, and challenges associated with routine outcome monitoring based on their experience with different systems over many years. They identify issues such as time burden, multiple stakeholders with different needs, and turnover of staff, particularly local "champions," as well as fear and mistrust by therapists. Further research is required to understand the contribution of such factors to feedback, which might then inform improved methods for presenting feedback, engaging therapists, and understanding how clinicians make use of the feedback provided to them (Sapyta et al., 2005). Boswell et al. (2015) point out that despite research on feedback in psychotherapy, more needs to be learned about the implementation and sustained use of outcome monitoring and feedback systems in order to improve adoption and compliance. This should involve identifying organizational issues that may act as barriers to and facilitators of implementing patient monitoring and feedback systems in routine services. Services will vary in a number of key aspects, all of which may impact on the feasibility of running an effective feedback system. This situation is likely to be more important in complex services, for example, with multiple clinical bases, where a range of therapies is provided (including group work) and where patients receive more than one episode of therapy. Hence, the present study aimed to identify the barriers and facilitators to effective implementation and clinician engagement within a complex routine UK service setting.

The current study therefore had three specific aims: (1) to assess the acceptability and feasibility, including organizational factors, of running an outcomes monitoring and feedback system in a routine UK NHS psychological therapy service; (2) to investigate if and how clinicians make use of feedback; and (3) to track the relationship between early change and clinical outcome, comparing outcomes for patients in this study with benchmark data from a study that did not involve feedback about progress.

Method

Design

The design comprised an organizational intervention and implementation of a patient monitoring and feedback system framed within a practice-oriented research paradigm (Castonguay, Barkham, Lutz, & McAleavy, 2013). The outcome monitoring and feedback system comprised not only feedback on patient outcomes but also feedback on the alliance, social support, motivation, and stressful life events. In light of these additional components, we referred to this package as *enhanced* feedback. These components provided a focus for an evaluation of how therapists made use of this information. Therapists had access to outcome data throughout therapy but an enhanced feedback report was provided to therapists between the fourth and fifth sessions for each of their patients. A key design component of the study was the inclusion of two neighbouring but contrasting NHS services, one a smaller service and the other a larger and more complex service, in order to inform the extent to which complexity affected feasibility and acceptability.

Mixed methods were employed to investigate the feasibility, acceptability, and effectiveness of the patient monitoring and enhanced feedback system. There were seven main sources of data: (1) outcome measures completed by patients each session; (2) a therapist questionnaire measuring how they used the feedback; (3) a questionnaire measuring therapists' experiences of the overall system; (4) therapists' experiences of the system, expressed at review meetings; (5) a post-discharge questionnaire collecting patient experiences of the system; (6) feedback from patient focus groups; and (7) comparisons with benchmark data from a neighbouring service without a feedback system.

Setting

Both services were based within the psychological therapies services of a large UK NHS Trust and provided therapy for patients with more severe, complex, and enduring mental health problems, including personality difficulties and interpersonal problems. The services were based in neighbouring metropolitan districts in West Yorkshire with both the smaller and larger services serving populations of about 200,000 people. Psychotherapeutic services are free to patients but require referral. The smaller service operated from a single base, with a single administrative support system, while the larger service operated from three substantial clinical bases: a health centre, a district general hospital, and a community centre. They will be referred to in this paper as the "small" and "large" services, respectively.

The new patient monitoring and enhanced feedback system was set up so that all therapists would participate, including trainees and temporary staff employed to deal with the waiting list in the larger service. A total of 31 therapists from the large service and 11 from the small service provided therapy for patients who consented to be included in the study. The total sample of 42 therapists comprised 26 permanent and qualified therapists, 8 trainee clinical psychologists, and 8 therapists either employed on a temporary basis to address the waiting list or who were based in another part of the service and provided short-term, sessional input. Of the 26 permanent and qualified therapists, 7 were cognitive behavioural therapists, 3 psychodynamic psychotherapists, and 16 clinical psychologists, whose main therapeutic orientations were psychodynamic, cognitive behaviour therapy (CBT), integrative psychotherapy, or cognitive analytic therapy. Some therapists worked part-time, so whole-time equivalents ranged from 0.2 to 1.0.

Similar types of therapy were provided in each service and mainly comprised psychodynamic psychotherapies and CBT. Group therapies were also provided within both services and focused on mood management and self-management skills, incorporating mindfulness and CBT approaches. In some cases, patients received more than one type of therapy (for example, individual followed by group therapy or vice versa). These are referred to as episodes of therapy. The large service underwent a major service re-organization during the course of the study, which introduced a triage system comprising a brief assessment/intervention of up to three sessions for a large number of patients who had been waiting a long time for treatment.

The benchmark data was collected as part of a previous and separate research study that included sessional outcome measurement, but without a feedback system (see Stulz et al., 2007). This service was in the same UK NHS Trust, in a neighbouring metropolitan district with a population of about 320,000.

Measures

The study utilized a package of measures that tapped five areas: patient outcomes, process, clinical support tools, therapist feedback, and patients' experiences. A hallmark of measure selection was that they should be brief and thereby enable the package of measures to have good bandwidth in terms of the breadth of data capture within routine service delivery.

Patient outcome (feedback sample). CORE-10 (Barkham et al., 2013). The CORE-10 is a brief, pantheoretical questionnaire for routine use in practice settings and is a shortened version of the 34-item CORE-OM (Barkham et al., 2001; Evans et al., 2002). The CORE-10 taps 3 domains: (1) *Problems*: Depression (2 items), Anxiety (2 items), Physical (1 item), and Trauma (1 item); *Functioning*: General functioning (1 item), Social functioning (1 item), and Close relationships (1 item); and (3) *Risk*: To self (1 item). The CORE-10 does not tap the domain of subjective well-being that is included in the CORE-OM. As with the CORE-OM, the CORE-10 items are rated on a 5-point scale (0 = *not at all* to 4 = *most or all of the time*). The clinical score is computed as a mean of all the completed items, multiplied by 10 to give a possible range between 0 and 40. This is equivalent to a simple sum of the responses when all 10 items are completed. The CORE-10 has been shown to have good internal reliability (alpha) of 0.90 and a correlation with the CORE-OM of 0.94 in a clinical sample and 0.92 in a non-clinical sample and a 90% reliable change index of 6 (Barkham et al., 2013).

Patient outcome (benchmark comparison). Two parallel 18-item short forms of the CORE-OM (CORE-SF-A & B, Barkham et al., 2001; Evans et al., 2002) representing the same three domains plus subjective well-being had been used for monitoring patient progress in the benchmark study, which preceded the development of the CORE-10. Each of these short forms comprises four items on subjective well-being, six on problems, six on functioning, and two detecting risk to self and others. The alpha coefficients for the two short forms are reported as .94 (Form A) and .94 (Form B) (Barkham et al., 2001). Items are rated on the same 5-point scale as the CORE-OM and CORE-10. The CORE-SF clinical score is computed as a mean of all the completed items, multiplied by 10 to give a possible range between 0 and 40, making it comparable to the CORE-10 scores.

Process measures. (1) The Assessment for Signal Cases (ASC; Lambert et al., 2007). The ASC comprises 40 items and taps patients' functioning using a 5-point Likert scale with anchors of 1 (strongly disagree) to 5 (strongly agree). It was developed and used by Lambert and colleagues in feedback studies to help therapists identify problems and was linked to clinical support tools (Lambert et al., 2007). There are four subscales: therapeutic alliance (11 items), social support (11 items), motivation for therapy (9 items), and life events (9 items). A modified version of the ASC was used in the present study. The wording of eight items was modified, without changing the meaning, to take account of the UK context.[1] For example, "I felt connected to a higher power" was replaced with "I have felt supported by religion/faith." Responses to this questionnaire are not reported on here but it was an important component of the enhanced feedback after session 4. (2) Helpfulness Alliance and Stage Measure (HASQ). This is a 12-item brief measure with 1 item asking about the helpfulness of the session, 5 items assessing therapeutic alliance the short form Agnew Relationship Measure (ARM-5, Cahill et al., 2012), and a 6-item checklist assessing stage of change and based on Stiles' assimilation model (Stiles, 2002). The HASQ also included a space for comments about the patient's current experience of therapy.

Feedback questionnaires. Three questionnaires relating to the feedback were used, two completed by the therapist and one by the patient.

The therapist questionnaires were as follows:

(1) Feedback Response Questionnaire (FRQ) recorded how therapists responded to the enhanced feedback. This focused on how helpful the enhanced feedback report was, whether it reflected their view of the patient's progress, and how therapists viewed and responded to the report. They were asked to tick one or more of seven responses shown in Figure 2, for example, taking it to supervision or exploring feedback with the patient.

(2) Feedback System Questionnaire (FSQ) included items on therapists' experiences of the system and its impact on their practice. It included questions on interference with routine practice, helpfulness of various aspects of the feedback to therapy (e.g., the traffic light system, graphs, feedback reports), extent of access to graphs, helpfulness to risk assessment, assessment and formulation, developing a therapeutic alliance, and impact on aspects of the therapy

provided (e.g., treatment goals, type of therapy, outcome, number of sessions). Items were rated on a 10-point scale. Each item offered the opportunity for therapists to make comments, which formed part of the data for thematic analysis. The questionnaire was completed by therapists prior to the review meetings and provided the structure for the meetings.

(3) Patient Experience Questionnaire (PEQ) comprised seven statements tapping patients' views and experiences of the patient monitoring and enhanced feedback system, including completing the process and outcome measures every session and their views regarding the impact on therapy. Items were rated on a 7-point scale from *strongly disagree* to *strongly agree*. The items are presented in Table IV.

Procedure

The research proposal and related procedures were approved by the Bradford Research Ethics Committee (reference 10/H1302/80) as part of the National Research Ethics Service. All patients entering the larger and smaller services over an 18-month period were invited to take part in the study. Those who provided consent were asked to complete the CORE-10 (Barkham et al., 2013) before each session and the HASQ after each session. To support the enhanced assessment and feedback, the adapted form of the ASC (Lambert et al., 2007) was administered at session 4. All measures were completed in paper form and collected by the administrative and research team. The research team entered the ratings into a database.

Feedback procedure. Feedback on patient progress as recorded by the CORE-10 was provided in both services before session 5 in the form of a simple traffic light system indicating likely change: green indicating an improvement of 5 or more points by session 4, red indicating a deterioration of 5 or more points, and amber for those patients who had neither improved or deteriorated by 5 points or more. This 5-point change was informed by the reliable change index of 6 for the CORE-10 (Barkham et al., 2013) and was a pragmatic decision by the service to provide a simple, easily understood and over-inclusive criterion for judging whether a red feedback alert should be given. Where problems were highlighted on the ASC and HASQ, therapists were directed to sections of a therapist support manual, which included signposting to local support services. Figure 1(a) and 1(b) show an example of two sections from an enhanced feedback report for a patient whose CORE-10 scores had increased by 5 points at the fourth session. This patient had strong negative ratings on ASC items reflecting life events and social support. Figure 1(a) shows these ASC factors highlighted and the other factors on the ASC and HASQ not highlighted. Figure 1(b) shows the negatively rated items from the two ASC factors. In addition to the enhanced feedback after session 4, therapists had access to graphs on their patients' progress (CORE-10 scores) throughout therapy via a shared network drive accessible from their desktop PCs.

Feedback System

Therapists' views. Therapists' views about the system were collected at review meetings and from questionnaires. The review meetings were held at the mid-point of the 2-year study and towards the end of the study. Notes were taken at these meetings by the research team and key issues affecting the feasibility and acceptability of the system were discussed and agreed between all participants. Therapists also completed the FRQ after each enhanced feedback report had been received. Towards the end of the study, therapists completed the FSQ that provided information on their experience of the use and acceptability of the system.

Patients' views. Patients who had received more than four sessions and whose therapist had received a feedback report were sent the PEQ by post after discharge and asked to return it by post. They were also asked to indicate their willingness to be involved in a focus group to provide more in-depth feedback on their experience of the system. Two focus groups were subsequently held, with seven patients attending one and five attending the other.

Selection of Sample

Figure 2 presents a flow diagram charting the selection of the sample for which clinical outcomes were calculated. The total sample comprised 409 episodes of therapy, 333 delivered in the large service and 76 in the small service. An initial inclusion criterion for the study was that episodes of therapy included at least five therapy sessions, yielding 222 (larger service) and 58 (smaller service) episodes of therapy. A further criterion required episodes of therapy to include a CORE-10 completed at sessions 1 and 4, together with at least one more CORE-10 completed after session 4. These criteria ensured all clients could have received a feedback report indicating progress at session 4 with further outcome monitoring after session 4. This criterion reduced

(a)

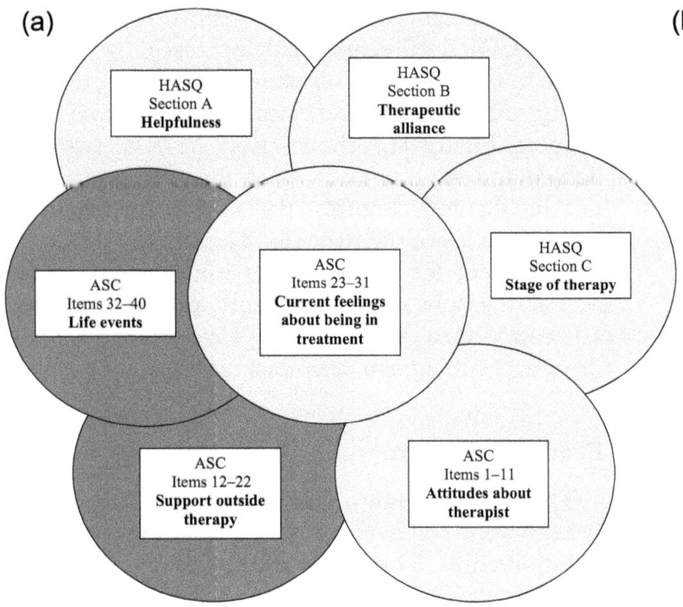

(b)

Factor	Example standout items at session 4	
Support outside therapy (in the last week)	Item:	Client said:
	I could count on my friendships when things went wrong	Strongly disagree
	I could talk about problems with my friends	Strongly disagree
	I could talk about problems with my family	Slightly disagree
	I got the emotional help and support I needed from someone in my family	Slightly disagree
	There was a special person who was there for me when I was in need	Strongly disagree
	There was a special person with whom I could share my ups and downs	Strongly disagree
	I had support from social groups (like: church, Mosque, Temple, college, AA, clubs, etc)	Strongly disagree
	I have felt supported by religion/faith	Strongly disagree
	Some subjects were so sensitive I couldn't talk with anyone about them	Strongly agree
Life events (during the past week)	Item:	Client said:
	Something happened with another person that I found upsetting	Strongly agree
	I felt rejected or betrayed by someone	Strongly agree
	I made a mistake that I can't undo	Slightly agree
	There was trouble at home work or college	Strongly agree
	I had health problems (such as physical pain)	Strongly agree
	I avoided facing a crisis or difficulty	Slightly agree
	I had difficulty adjusting to an event or occurrence in my life	Slightly agree

Figure 1. (a) Feedback report: Section reporting ASC and HASQ results. The red portions indicate the areas where your client may benefit from extra support. (b) Feedback report: Section reporting negatively rated ASC items (Red areas in Figure 1a) (Colour in online version).

the sample to 202 episodes, 147 and 55 episodes for the large and small services, respectively. For this sample, 64% of patients were female, with a mean (SD) age of 39 years (12.0). In the benchmark sample, 69% of patients were female, with a mean (SD) age of 36 years (10.6).

Analysis

Quantitative analysis. Patients were categorized as NOT (red traffic light) if CORE-10 scores had increased by 5 points or more between sessions 1 and 4; amber cases had neither improved nor deteriorated by more than 5 points; and green cases (categorized as "early responders") had improved by 5 or more points. This is different from the definition of NOT used in the studies by Lambert et al. in which the term refers to patients who do not progress along expected recovery trajectories. Clinical outcomes and the relationship between progress at session 4 and final outcome were calculated for those patients whose therapists had received enhanced feedback and who attended at least five therapy sessions, representing a significant dose of therapy. The benchmark comparison group had also all attended at least five therapy sessions. Effect sizes were calculated by using study-specific means and SDs to yield separate effect sizes (ES) for the Feedback and Benchmark study. Comparisons between samples are reported using *t*-tests. When the Levene test for equality of variances indicated significant differences in variance, adjusted *t*-values and degrees of freedom are reported.

Qualitative analysis. The research team, comprising principal investigators and research assistants, identified initial themes (codes) from the notes taken at the first set of feedback meetings using thematic analysis (Braun & Clarke, 2006). These were then discussed with the therapists at the second round of meetings. Further thematic analysis incorporated written comments in the FSQ to ensure that all the overarching themes and subthemes were captured.

Results

The rates of successfully providing feedback reports between sessions 4 and 5 are proxy measures of the success of the system in providing prompt feedback in each service. Reports were provided in 55 (95%) cases for the smaller service and 147 (66%) cases for the larger service (see lower portion of Figure 2).

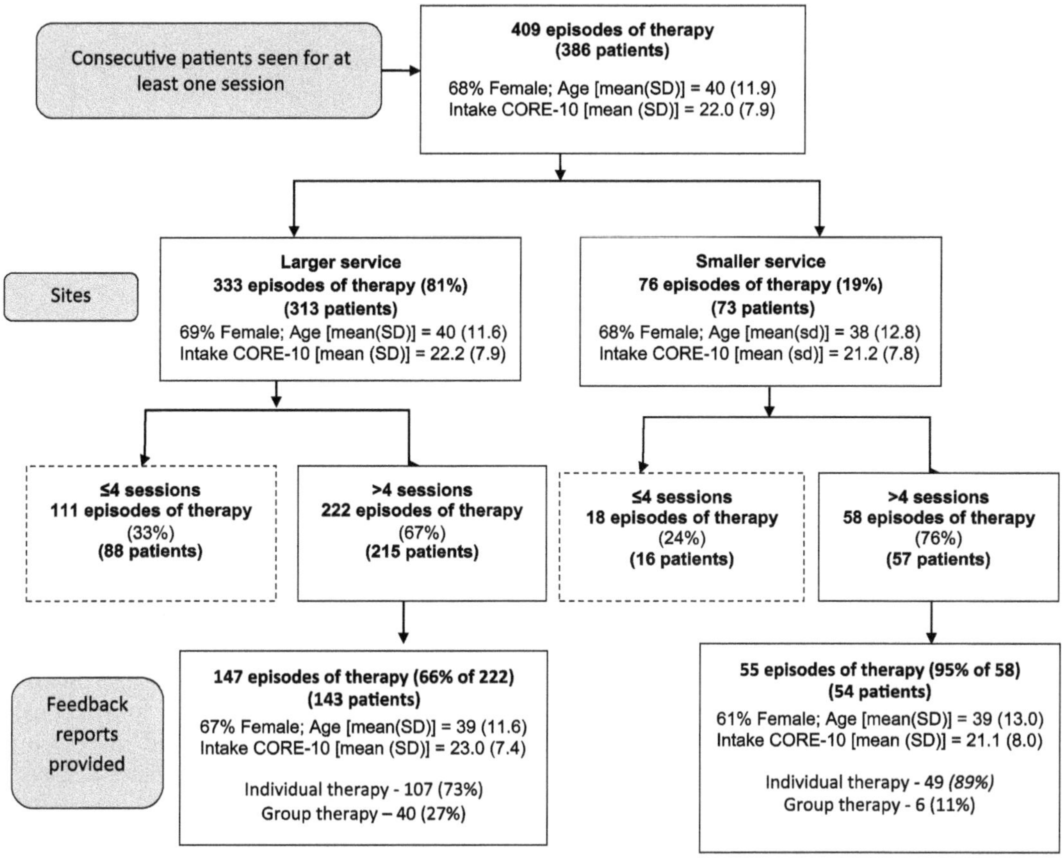

Figure 2. Flow diagram of patients within the two services.

Intake Scores

Figure 2 also shows intake scores on the CORE-10 for the two services, with similar mean (SD) scores of 21.1 (8.0) for the smaller service and 23.0 (7.4) for the larger service. The overall mean intake CORE for the full sample of 202 (M = 22.5, SD = 7.6) is significantly larger than the mean intake CORE-SF for the benchmark sample (N = 136, M = 18.6, SD = 8.5; $t(336) = 4.4$, $p < 0.001$), but both the feedback and the benchmark sample means are well above the clinical cut-off for the CORE.

Early Change Compared to Final Change

Table I shows the numbers and percentages of episodes of therapy that were categorized within the

Table I. Relationship between early and overall changes on the CORE-10 for study sample (with feedback) and benchmark (no feedback).

		Number (%) of patients meeting reliable change categories on the CORE-10 across therapy episodes		
		Deteriorated ≥ 6 (Session 1 to last)	No change	Improved ≥ 6 (Session 1 to last)
Status at session 4	*N* (%)	*N* (%)	*N* (%)	*N* (%)
Current study (N = 202)				
Not on track (Red)	26 (13)	9 (35)	12 (46)	5 (19)
No change (Amber)	116 (57)	8 (7)	73 (63)	35 (30)
Early responders (Green)	60 (30)	0 (0)	16 (27)	44 (73)
Totals		17 (8)	101 (50)	84 (42)
Benchmark comparator (N = 136)				
Not on track (Red)	12 (9)	3 (25)	7 (58)	2 (17)
No change (Amber)	86 (63)	9 (11)	55 (64)	22 (26)
Early responders (Green)	38 (28)	1 (3)	11 (29)	26 (68)
Totals		13 (10)	73 (54)	50 (37)

three traffic light categories at session 4 and whether they improved or deteriorated at the end of therapy. For patients in the Feedback sample, 60 (30%) showed early improvement of 5 or more points at session 4 (Green feedback), 116 (57%) showed no change at session 4 (Amber feedback), and 26 (13%) showed a deterioration of 5 or more points at session 4 (Red feedback). By the final session, 84 (42%) had improved at or beyond the reliable change index of 6 points for the CORE-10, 101 (50%) had shown no reliable improvement, and 17 (8%) had shown reliable deterioration.

Of the 26 patients who had significantly deteriorated at session 4, 9 (35%) reliably deteriorated at final outcome while 5 (19%) reliably improved. The equivalent figures for the benchmark data were 3 (25%) and 2 (17%), respectively. Of the 60 early responders at session 4, none had significantly deteriorated at final outcome while 44 (73%) reliably improved. Of the 38 early responders in the benchmark data, 1 (3%) had significantly deteriorated at final outcome and 26 (68%) reliably improved. Overall, the proportions of patients in the different change categories at final outcome did not differ for the feedback study compared with the benchmark data ($\chi^2(2, N = 338) = 0.81$).

Effect Sizes for the Feedback and Benchmark Samples

Pre–post effect sizes for the current study and the benchmark data are presented in Table II. Effect sizes (both positive and negative) are slightly, but non-significantly, larger for the current study ($M = 0.56$, SD = 1.00 for the feedback sample and $M = 0.43$, SD = 0.89 for the benchmark sample; $t(336) = 1.25$, $p = 0.21$). Table II also shows that both data sets show a negative effect size for the group who had deteriorated at session 4. In addition, the mean number of sessions was significantly higher for the Benchmark study ($M = 20.1$, SD = 17.2) than the Feedback study ($M = 12.8$, SD = 7.3; $t(167.9) = 4.79$, $p < 0.001$).

Table II. Effect sizes at end of therapy for each study by session 4 status.

Session 4 status	Feedback study (n = 202)	Benchmark study (n = 136)	ES(diff)
Green	1.28	1.03	0.25
Amber	0.36	0.24	0.12
Red	− 0.18	− 0.10	0.08
Overall	0.56	0.43	0.13

Therapists' Views on the Feedback System

Table III presents the results of the FSQ. This focused on therapists' overall views of the service and was completed by 15 permanent, qualified therapists (4 from small service, 11 from large service) out of 24 who were working in the services at the time (7 from small service, 17 from larger service, 62.5% response rate). The main therapeutic orientations of these 15 therapists were CBT ($N = 5$), psychodynamic ($N = 4$), integrative ($N = 5$), and cognitive analytic therapy ($N = 1$). Seven (47%) therapists indicated they regularly accessed graphs and 8 (53%) indicated they did not access the graphs. A total of 13 (87%) therapists indicated that the feedback had not affected the number of sessions provided and 2 (13%) indicated that it led to fewer sessions being provided. Only 3 (20%) therapists agreed that feedback identified something they were not already aware of while 8 (53%) stated they specifically discussed the measures in supervision, and 5 (33%) therapists said they shared and discussed the feedback reports in supervision. In all, 9 (60%) therapists indicated they would like to continue with aspects of the feedback system as part of their routine therapy.

In all, 142 FRQs were completed by therapists in relation to the enhanced feedback reports. A total of 115 (81%) reflected patients' progress and 91 (64%) said the feedback report had been helpful to them and to their patient. Figure 3 shows the percentage of various actions resulting from receipt of an enhanced feedback report and indicates low levels of discussion of the feedback in supervision as well as in exploring it with patients. In addition, Figure 3 shows a very low incidence of changes to treatment and consulting the therapist support manual. For NOT patients, therapists tended to be less likely to explore the feedback with patients and less likely to find the feedback report helpful to the therapy they were offering.

The thematic analysis identified four themes from verbal and written feedback from the review meetings and the open questions of the FSQ. These themes were identified as affecting the feasibility, effectiveness, and acceptability of the system.

(1) *The extent to which therapists integrated the measures and feedback into the therapy.* There was a range of experiences regarding the extent to which the outcomes monitoring and feedback system were found to be helpful to the therapeutic process. This view is supported by data presented in Table III, which shows the variability in ratings on the

Table III. Therapists' ratings on the FSQ (n = 15).

Items	Range	Mode (*N*)	Mean (SD)
Helpfulness (0 = *very unhelpful*; 10 = *very helpful*)			
How helpful have you found the feedback reports?	3–10	5 (5)	5.5 (2.0)
How helpful have you found the traffic light system?	2–10	7 (5)	6.1 (2.2)
How helpful were the feedback reports in relation to accessing risk?	0–8	5 (4)	4.7 (2.2)
How helpful was the feedback in relation to assessment and formulation?	2–8	7 (5)	5.4 (1.5)
Impact (0 = *not at all*; 10 = *very much*)			
How much did recruiting patients to the research interfere with normal therapeutic practice?	0–7	7 (4)	4.2 (2.5)
To what extent do you think the feedback reports reflect your patient's progress?	4–10	5 (4)	5.6 (1.6)
To what extent has the feedback affected treatment goals	0–8	0 (5)	2.1 (2.4)
To what extent has the feedback affected the type of therapy provided?	0–7	0 (9)	1.5 (2.4)
To what extent has the feedback affected the outcome of therapy?	0–5	0 (5)	1.5 (1.8)

FSQ. Some therapists fully integrated the system into therapy and discussed the measures at each session. At least one therapist discussed each questionnaire item with patients at every session and found the measures and their use in therapy to be "invaluable." Other therapists had concerns that the repeated measures were not helpful to the client or to the therapeutic relationship. There were also differences in the extent to which therapists were willing to use therapy time to complete the questionnaires with some strongly believing they should not be completed in the therapy room. At the review meetings, there was a broad agreement that therapists found that initial concerns about adverse effects on the therapy were reduced the more they became familiar with the system. However, a few therapists remained concerned about fundamental elements of the system such as whether the outcome measures could reflect the progress and the benefits patients gained from therapy.

(2) *Availability of administrative support.* Therapists considered that the lack of administrative support adversely affected questionnaire completion, particularly in satellite clinic bases. This was also clear to the research team. Some therapists felt the resulting additional responsibility of ensuring complete data-sets detracted or impinged on their therapeutic time with the client. Lack of administrative support also adversely affected the timely administration of measures and ensuring therapist codes were attached to the questionnaires, which reduced the proportion of feedback reports successfully provided at the larger service.

(3) *Information technology (IT).* IT problems adversely affected access to the graphs of the patients' progress throughout therapy. The application containing the database and related graphs crashed on a number of occasions, which some therapists reported was a disincentive to routinely accessing the graphs.

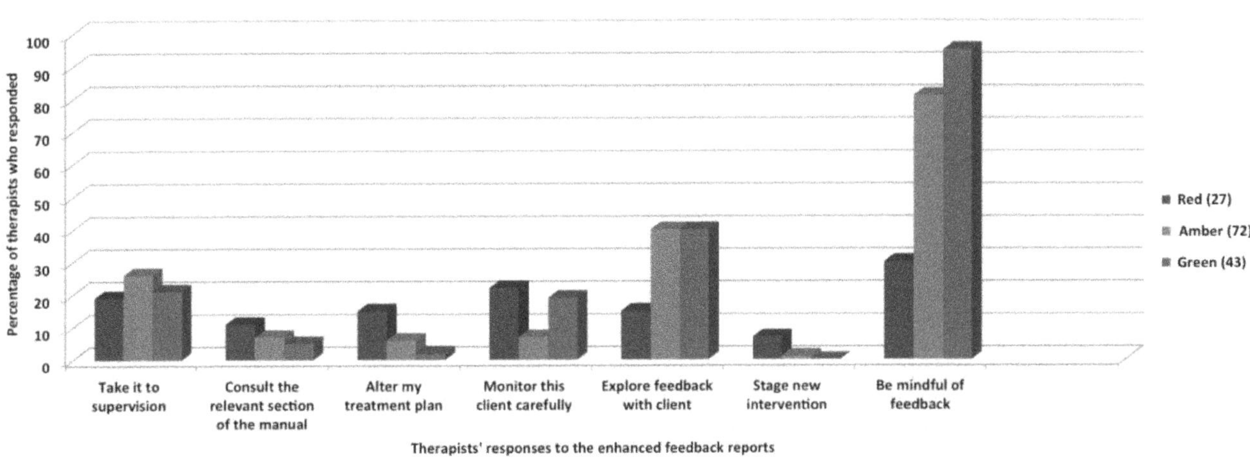

Figure 3. Therapists' responses to feedback reports after session 4 for the three groups (n = 142) (Colour in online version).

(4) *Complexity of the service and service changes.* These challenges were greater at the larger site and included the number of clinic bases, internal transfers of clients between episodes of therapy and therapists (e.g., when patients received both individual and group work), and service reorganizations. Immediately prior to the start of data collection, the large service also moved its main base with little warning. Attempts were made to track the changes in episodes of therapy but this was not always successful. Group work also presented challenges to the successful completion of measures at each session.

In addition to these themes, some therapists reported finding the system more helpful to therapy over time and there was a general view that the traffic light system was helpful and easily understood. Some therapists who were concerned that looking at the feedback reports would interfere with the therapeutic process came to see it as another useful channel of communication. Therapists expressed concerns about the concept of patients being NOT, when patients are going through a difficult stage in therapy such as exposure or trauma work. Therapists also reported that information on the alliance and on stresses in a person's life were particularly helpful, the latter helping set realistic treatment goals for people with very adverse life situations. A few therapists reported that some patients had found completion of the forms burdensome and were given "time off" from completing them. Therapists noted that some patients found it difficult to complete the post-session questionnaires after an intense session.

Patients' Views of the Feedback System

Table IV presents the mean ratings on the PEQ for 56 patients who had been discharged and their therapist had received an enhanced feedback report after session 4. The questionnaire was introduced a few months after the study began. It was sent to 179 patients, yielding a response rate of 31%. Table IV shows positive views of the system in terms of understanding why the forms were completed, ease of completion, and the time taken. Ratings were still positive, but less so on the questions relating to the impact on therapy.

Patients' views expressed at the two reference groups highlighted problems with the questionnaires, such as formatting and wording, and difficulties reflecting on the benefits of the therapy session immediately after an emotionally difficult session. However, there was general support for the idea of tracking progress using standardized questionnaires. Patients attending the reference groups all thought therapists should look at the responses to the questionnaire items but some questioned whether the therapists always did so.

Discussion

The aims of this study were to investigate the feasibility and acceptability of an outcome monitoring and enhanced feedback system, what therapists did with the feedback, and the relationship between early change and outcome. We discuss each of these aims in turn.

In terms of our first aim concerning feasibility and acceptability, we highlight barriers and facilitators that can be categorized as operating at any one of three levels: patient level, therapist level, and service/organizational level. At the patient level, feedback from patients was, on the whole, positive. They saw the value of regular outcome monitoring, felt the measures were relevant, and did not find it too much of a burden, except for some concerns about completing questionnaires at the end of distressing therapy sessions. Feedback about improvements that could have been made to the layout of the forms supports the practice of involving service users in the research process (Brett, Staniszewska, & Mockford, 2010). It was also acknowledged that their involvement should have happened earlier in the research process.

Table IV. Patients' ratings on the PEQ (n = 56).

Items	Range	Mode (*N*)	Mean (SD)
Experiences (1 = *strongly disagree*; 7 = *strongly agree*)			
I understand why I am being asked to fill in the forms	1–7	7 (36)	6.3 (1.3)
I find the forms easy to fill in	1–7	7 (23)	5.8 (1.4)
I am comfortable with the place in which I fill in the forms	1–7	7 (23)	5.9 (1.3)
The time it takes me to fill in the forms is acceptable	3–7	7 (29)	6.2 (1.0)
Filling in the forms has helped my therapy	1–7	6 (16)	5.2 (1.6)
The forms capture everything my therapist needs to know about my problems, progress, and therapy	1–7	7 (14)	5.1 (1.8)
My therapist uses information from my forms in the session	1–7	4 (14)	4.7 (2.0)

At the therapist level, the main facilitator to engagement and a positive view of the system was the extent to which therapists integrated the measures and feedback into the therapy. This was, in turn, related to how compatible the therapists felt the system was to their own therapeutic approach. Youn, Kraus, and Castonguay (2012) argue that therapists may resist using outcomes monitoring and feedback systems because they believe it may interfere with the therapeutic alliance. A few therapists in our study did express this concern, although the study did not directly measure the impact on the alliance between the patient and therapist. We found no clear relationship between therapeutic orientation and integration with practice in that those therapists reporting integration practised CBT, psychodynamic therapy, and integrative therapy. Concerns about measures being collected too often and encroaching on the therapy time and space may be reduced with data inputting systems using hand-held computer devices and/or online, but for a few therapists, the objections to the system were more fundamental and attributable to a perceived incompatibility with their therapeutic approach. There is clearly evidence from this study of variability in the extent to which therapists took account of the feedback on their patients' progress. Another possible factor influencing this variability is the extent to which they feel supported. A supportive culture is likely to facilitate reflective practice.

At the organizational level, the lack of availability of administrative support in some service bases, IT problems, and service complexity and reorganizations all adversely affected the acceptability, feasibility, and effectiveness of the system. The administrative support and IT problems could be mitigated with a more reliable system and such systems have been developed and reviewed (e.g., Barkham et al., 2010; Lutz, Bönke, & Köck, 2011). Systems involving inputting by patients on hand-held devices or online and linked to therapists' computers provide efficient and prompt feedback to therapists and this is clearly the way forward. Ideally, these systems should also have the capability to capture the different episodes of therapy that may follow one another so that outcomes, and benchmarks of expected outcomes, relate to particular interventions. This is particularly important where both individual and group therapy are provided for patients and where stepped care service models are used. For example, in the UK, Improving Access to Psychological Therapies Services provide low-intensity interventions that may then be stepped up to a high-intensity therapy such as CBT, Counselling for Depression, or Interpersonal Therapy (Clark, 2011). Feedback systems should also be flexible enough to be used in group therapy. It is possible that patients in group therapy may be at particular risk of experiencing a deterioration that goes unnoticed by therapists.

The second aim was to look at what therapists do with feedback and this is one of the few studies to do that. Lutz et al. (2011) investigated responses of therapists to feedback in a German study and reported some action or reformulation as a result of feedback on about 70% of occasions. However, the percentages for most responses were relatively low with the highest—approximately 50%—relating to a discussion of the questionnaire answers with the patient. Our study also found low levels of the various responses to feedback. Of particular note was the finding that, for NOT patients, therapists tended to be less likely to explore the feedback with patients and to find the feedback report less helpful to therapy. The reasons for this finding are not clear. It may reflect a discomfort with negative feedback or a bias in therapists wishing to see their patients doing well and themselves as effective therapists (Walfish, McAlister, O'Donnell, & Lambert, 2012). In a similar vein, it is proposed that feedback works on the basis of a discrepancy between the feedback and the (ultimate) goal of patient improvement (e.g., De Jong, 2014). Accordingly, if that real or perceived discrepancy is not present, the utility and/or impact of feedback will be reduced. But this is only speculation. The clear implication of this finding is the need to understanding *how* therapists make sense of and respond to NOT feedback in particular and also to develop systems, methods, and a culture that encourages therapists to take account of feedback.

Lambert's studies suggest it is only the NOT patients whose outcomes improve with feedback. Hence, it is important to understand how therapists understand and respond to such feedback. The third aim was to understand how early change related to outcome and it is important to acknowledge that although progress at session 4 did predict outcome, this was not the case for all patients. Indeed, approximately 20% of patients who had reliably deteriorated at session 4 went on to record outcome scores meeting the criterion of reliable improvement. This is a small percentage and the numbers in this study were low, so this should not deflect from the clear message that early response is a predictor of outcome. However, it is important to acknowledge that a minority of patients may indeed feel worse before they improve. This phenomenon may be more prevalent with severe mental health problems as the early stages of therapy may involve elements such as becoming aware of and exploring distressing issues and exposure to traumatic memories. Acknowledgement of this phenomenon may help keep therapists engaged in the process and underlines the importance of acknowledging that any measure of change should be considered by therapists (and patients) in a broader context. On a similar theme, therapists found the information from the ASC scale helpful in that it provided some context with which to consider the patients' progress, for example, for those with complex and adverse life situations.

The third aim also involves comparison of outcomes for this study with the benchmark study. Recovery and deterioration rates tended to be similar when based on the reliable change index. In both studies, deterioration rates were in the region of 8%–10% (Table I). These elevated rates are consistent with the Mohr (1995) review, which suggested higher deterioration rates with more severe and complex problems. It is important to point out that this deterioration rate was for patients receiving at least five therapy sessions. The deterioration rate was less for those receiving fewer sessions. There was a significant difference in the mean number of sessions provided in the two studies, with the patients in the current study receiving fewer sessions than in the benchmark study. Discussion within the service suggested the shorter length of therapy was due to changes towards a more managed service with more time-limited individual and group therapies being provided rather than the consequence of feedback.

It is important, however, to consider the impact of feedback on treatment length and the efficiency of the service. The service provided in the current study would seem to be more efficient in that similar outcomes were achieved with significantly fewer sessions. The method used to measure early deterioration was based on statistically reliable change, mirroring the criteria used for reliable improvement (Jacobson & Truax, 1991). However, we used a less stringent criterion than reliable change in order to identify patients at risk of a poor outcome. Indeed, it is probably too simplistic to view reliable deterioration as a mirror opposite of reliable improvement. There is a case for the criterion for deterioration to be less stringent—that is, more sensitive to indications of clinical deterioration rather than being viewed as no reliable change. In this context, we would support the approach taken by Lambert for monitoring system to flag up those patients who do not follow the expected course of improvement, particularly as these are the patients who appear to benefit most from feedback.

Several caveats need to be stated. First it is unclear the extent to which findings can be generalized to other service delivery systems. Although the services used were based in routine UK NHS settings, the diversity of services within the UK and internationally makes it unlikely that any single study could be representative of the wide range of services providing psychological therapy. Second, the study investigated a newly introduced feedback system and it is possible therapists would have been more positive and more responsive to the feedback with a more established system. However the study does highlight barriers and facilitators that will apply across other services and it is especially important to consider these issues in complex services providing therapy to patients with severe and complex problems.

In this context, Davidson et al. (2015) reviewed 10 feedback studies and two meta-analyses and questioned the generalizability of findings of existing feedback studies to other settings. They point out that the early studies by Lambert and colleagues were all carried out in a university counselling centre, predominantly with female students. Although further studies have found beneficial effects of feedback, the review reports *reduced* effect sizes in feedback studies with more severe mental health problems. Interestingly, such a tendency may dovetail with findings that therapist effects *increase* with greater patient severity (Saxon & Barkham, 2012). Indeed, there is the possibility that inherent variability across therapists—that is, therapist effects—moderates the activity of feedback per se. We certainly found evidence of considerable variability in therapists' responses to utilizing feedback.

Reflecting on the combined weight of evidence, our study provides clear implications for the implementation of acceptable and effective monitoring and feedback systems. These include providing reliable information systems that can accommodate complexities such as working in different settings, individual and group therapy, and multiple episodes of therapy. They should also enable completion of patient-completed questionnaires outside the therapy space but with rapid or real-time access for therapists. Consideration should also be given to enabling patients to have direct access to progress graphs. These systems will be flexible enough to allow individual therapists to use the system in a way that suits their own therapeutic approach.

Overall, the findings add support to the body of evidence suggesting the positive impact of feedback systems and the acceptability of such systems to most patients and therapists. However, they also support the observations of Davidson et al. (2015) that more research on the implementation and effectiveness of feedback systems in more diverse patient settings and services is required. Similarly, we are mindful of the natural variability across therapists and would advocate that future research in the field of feedback takes account of this key phenomenon.

Acknowledgements

We would like to thank all the therapists, administrative staff, and managers who supported this research as well as service users who gave us such valuable feedback. We would also like to thank Bronwen Ashton, Sheila Downward, Alison Moreton, Faten Sabouni, and Lorraine Scargill for their valuable contribution. We also thank Michael Lambert and Wolfgang Lutz for their expert advice and support.

Funding

This study was funded by the National Institute for Health Research (NIHR) under its Research for Patient Benefit Programme [grant reference number PB-PG-0909-20319]. The views expressed are those of the authors and not necessarily those of the NHS, the NIHR, or the Department of Health.

Note

[1] Permission was given to authors by Michael Lambert.

References

Barkham, M., Margison, F., Leach, C., Lucock, M., Mellor-Clark, J., Evans, C., … McGrath, G. (2001). Service profiling and outcomes benchmarking using the CORE-OM: Toward practice-based evidence in the psychological therapies. *Journal of Consulting and Clinical Psychology, 69*(2), 184–196. doi:10.1037//0022-006X.69.2.184

Barkham, M., Bewick, B., Mullin, T., Gilbody, S., Connell, J., Cahill, J. … & Evans, C. (2013). The CORE-10: A short measure of psychological distress for routine use in the psychological therapies. *Counselling and Psychotherapy Research, 13*(1), 3–13. doi:10.1080/14733145.2012.729069

Barkham, M., Mellor-Clark, J., Connell, J., Evans, R., Evans, C., & Margison, F. (2010). The CORE measures & CORE system: Measuring, monitoring, and managing quality evaluation in the psychological therapies. In M. Barkham, G. E. Hardy, & J. Mellor-Clark (Eds.), *Developing and delivering practice-based evidence: A guide for the psychological therapies* (pp. 175–219). Chichester: Wiley.

Boswell, J. F., Kraus, D. R., Miller, S. D., & Lambert, M. J. (2015). Implementing routine outcome monitoring in clinical practice: Benefits, challenges, and solutions. *Psychotherapy Research, 25*(1), 6–19. doi:10.1080/10503307.2013.817696

Braun, V., & Clarke, V. (2006). Using thematic analysis in psychology. *Qualitative Research in Psychology, 3*(2), 77–101. doi:10.1191/1478088706qp063oa

Brett, J., Staniszewska, S., & Mockford C. (2010). *The PIRICOM Study. A systematic review of the conceptualisation, measurement, impact and outcomes of patient and public involvement in health and social care research.* London: United Kingdom Clinical Research Collaboration. Retrieved from: http://www.ukcrc.org/wp-content/uploads/2014/03/Piricom+Review+Final+2010.pdf

Byrne, S. L., Hooke, G. R., Newnham, E. A., & Page, A. C. (2012). The effects of progress monitoring on subsequent readmission to psychiatric care: A six-month follow-up. *Journal of Affective Disorders, 137*(1–3), 113–116. doi:10.1016/j.jad.2011.12.005

Cahill, J., Stiles, W. B., Barkham, M., Hardy, G. E., Stone, G., Agnew-Davies, R., & Unsworth, G. (2012). Two short forms of the Agnew Relationship Measure: The ARM-5 and ARM-12. *Psychotherapy Research, 22*(3), 241–255. doi:10.1080/10503307.2011.643253

Carlier, I. V. E., Meuldijk, D., Van Vliet, I. M., Van Fenema, E., Van der Wee, N. J. A., & Zitman, F. G. (2012). Routine outcome monitoring and feedback on physical or mental health status: Evidence and theory Feedback on physical or mental health status. *Journal of Evaluation in Clinical Practice, 18*(1), 104–110. doi:10.1111/j.1365-2753.2010.01543.x

Castonguay, L. G., Barkham, M., Lutz, W., & McAleavy, A. (2013). Practice oriented research: Approaches and applications. In M. J. Lambert (Ed.), *Bergin & Garfield's handbook of psychotherapy and behaviour change* (6th ed., pp. 85–133). Hoboken, NJ: Wiley.

Clark, D. M. (2011). Implementing NICE guidelines for the psychological treatment of depression and anxiety disorders: The IAPT experience. *International Review of Psychiatry, 23*(4), 318–327. doi:10.3109/09540261.2011.606803

Davidson, K., Perry, A., & Bell, L. (2015). Would continuous feedback of patient's clinical outcomes to practitioners improve NHS psychological therapy services? Critical analysis and assessment of quality of existing studies. *Psychology and Psychotherapy: Theory, Research and Practice, 88*(1), 21–37. doi:10.1111/papt.12032

Dawes, R., Faust, D., & Meehl, P. (1989). Clinical versus actuarial judgment. *Science, 243*, 1668–1674. doi:10.1126/science.2648573

De Jong, K. (2014). Deriving implementation strategies for outcome monitoring feedback from theory, research and practice. *Administration Policy and Mental Health.* doi:10.1007/s10488-014-0589-6

Evans, C., Connell, J., Barkham, M., Margison, F., Mellor-Clark, J., McGrath, G., & Audin, K. (2002). Towards a standardised brief outcome measure: Psychometric properties and utility of the CORE-OM. *The British Journal of Psychiatry, 180*(1), 51–60. doi:10.1192/bjp.180.1.51

Fitzpatrick, M. (2012). Blurring practice-research boundaries using progress monitoring: A personal introduction to this issue of *Canadian Psychology. Canadian Psychology/Psychologie canadienne, 53*(2), 75–81. doi:10.1037/a0028051

Garb, H. N. (2005). Clinical judgment and decision making. *Annual Review of Clinical Psychology, 1*(1), 67–89. doi:10.1146/annurev.clinpsy.1.102803.143810

Hannan, C., Lambert, M. J., Harmon, C., Nielsen, S. L., Smart, D. W., Shimokawa, K., & Sutton, S. W. (2005). A lab test and algorithms for identifying clients at risk for treatment failure. *Journal of Clinical Psychology, 61*(2), 155–163. doi:10.1002/jclp.20108

Hansen, N. B., Lambert, M. J., & Forman, E. M. (2002). The psychotherapy dose-response effect and its implications for treatment delivery services. *Clinical Psychology: Science and Practice, 9*(3), 329–343. doi:10.1093/clipsy.9.3.329

Hansson, H., Rundberg, J., Österling, A., Öjehagen, A., & Berglund, M. (2013). Intervention with feedback using Outcome Questionnaire 45 (OQ-45) in a Swedish psychiatric outpatient population. A randomized controlled trial. *Nordic Journal of Psychiatry, 67*(4), 274–281. doi:10.3109/08039488.2012.736534

Hayes, S. C., Barlow, D. H., & Nelson, R. O. (1999). *The scientist–practitioner – Research and accountability in clinical and educational settings* (2nd ed.). New York: Pergamon.

Howard, K. I., Moras, K., Brill, P. L., Martinovich, Z., & Lutz, W. (1996). Evaluation of psychotherapy: Efficacy, effectiveness, and patient progress. *American Psychologist, 51*, 1059–1064. doi:10.1037//0003-066X.51.10.1059

Jacobson, N. S., & Truax, P. (1991). Clinical significance: A statistical approach to defining meaningful change in psychotherapy research. *Journal of Consulting and Clinical Psychology, 59*(1), 12–19. doi:10.1037/0022-006X.59.1.12

Kuyken, W. (2004). Cognitive therapy outcome: The effects of hopelessness in a naturalistic outcome study. *Behaviour Research and Therapy, 42*, 631–646. doi:10.1016/S0005-7967(03)00189-X

Lambert, M. J. (2010). *Prevention of treatment failure: The use of measuring, monitoring, and feedback in clinical practice.* Washington, DC: American Psychological Association.

Lambert, M. J. (2013). The efficacy and effectiveness of psychotherapy. In M. J. Lambert (Ed.), *Bergin & Garfield's handbook of psychotherapy and behavior change* (6th ed., pp. 169–218). Hoboken, NJ: Wiley.

Lambert, M. J., Bailey, R. J., Kimball, K., Shimokawa, K., Harmon, S. C., & Slade, K. (2007). *Clinical support tools manual—Brief version-40.* Salt Lake City, UT: OQ Measures.

Lambert, M. J., Morton, J. J., Hatfield, D., Harmon, C., Hamilton, S., Reid, R. C., ... Burlingame, G. M. (2004). *Administration and scoring manual for the Outcome Questionnaire-45.* Orem, UT: American Professional Credentialing Services. Retrieved from: www.oqfamily.com.

Lambert, M. J., Whipple, J. L., Bishop, M. J., Vermeersch, D. A., Gray, G. V., & Finch, A. E. (2002). Comparison of empirically-derived and rationally-derived methods for identifying patients at risk for treatment failure. *Clinical Psychology and Psychotherapy, 9*(3), 149–164. doi:10.1002/cpp.333

Lambert, M. J., Whipple, J. L., Smart, D. W., Vermeersch, D. A., Nielsen, S. L., & Hawkins, E. J. (2001). The effects of providing therapists with feedback on patient progress during psychotherapy: Are outcomes enhanced? *Psychotherapy Research, 11*(1), 49–68. doi:10.1093/ptr/11.1.49

Lilienfeld, S. O. (2007). Psychological treatments that cause harm. *Perspectives on Psychological Science, 2*(1), 53–70. doi:10.1111/j.1745-6916.2007.00029.x

Lutz, W, Bönke J. R., & Köck, K. (2011). Lending an ear to feedback systems: Evaluation of recovery and non-response in psychotherapy in a German outpatient setting. *Community Mental Health Journal, 47*(3), 311–317. doi:10.1007/s10597-010-9307-3

Lutz, W., Lambert, M. J., Harmon, S. C., Stultz, N., Tschitsaz, A., & Schurch, E. (2006). The probability of treatment success, failure and duration – What can be learned from empirical data to support decision making in clinical practice? *Clinical Psychology and Psychotherapy, 13*(4), 223–232. doi:10.1002/cpp.496

Lutz, W., Stulz, N., & Köck, K. (2009). Patterns of early change and their relationship to outcome and follow-up among patients with major depressive disorders. *Journal of Affective Disorders, 118*(1–3), 60–68. doi:10.1016/j.jad.2009.01.019

Macdonald, J., & Mellor-Clark, J. (2015). Correcting psychotherapists' blindsidedness: Formal feedback as a means of overcoming the natural limitations of therapists. *Clinical Psychology & Psychotherapy, 22*, 249–257.

Meehl, P. E. (1954). *Clinical versus statistical prediction: A theoretical analysis and review of the literature.* Minneapolis: University of Minnesota Press

Miller, S. D., Duncan, B. L., Sorrell, R., & Brown, G. S. (2005). The Partners for Change outcome management system. *Journal of Clinical Psychology, 61*(2), 199–208. doi:10.1002/jclp.20111

Mohr, D. C. (1995). Negative outcome in psychotherapy: A critical review. *Clinical Psychology: Science and Practice, 2*(1), 1–27. doi:10.1111/j.1468-2850.1995.tb00022.x

Probst, T., Lambert, M. J., Loew, T. H., Dahlbender, R. W., Göllner, R., & Tritt, K. (2013). Feedback on patient progress and clinical support tools for therapists: Improved outcome for patients at risk of treatment failure in psychosomatic in-patient therapy under the conditions of routine practice. *Journal of Psychosomatic Research, 75*(3), 255–261. doi:10.1016/j.jpsychores.2013.07.003

Sapyta, J., Riemer, M., & Bickman, L. (2005). Feedback to clinicians: Theory, research, and practice. *Journal of Clinical Psychology, 61*(2), 145–153. doi:10.1002/jclp.20107

Saxon, D., & Barkham, M. (2012). Patterns of therapist variability: Therapist effects and the contribution of patient severity and risk. *Journal of Consulting and Clinical Psychology, 80*, 535–546. doi:10.1037/a0028898

Stiles, W. B. (2002). Assimilation of problematic experiences. In J. C. Norcross (Ed.), *Psychotherapy relationships that work: Therapist contributions and responsiveness to patients* (pp. 357–365). New York, NY: Oxford University Press.

Stulz, N., Lutz, W., Leach, C., Lucock, M., & Barkham, M. (2007). Shapes of early change in psychotherapy under routine outpatient conditions. *Journal of Consulting and Clinical Psychology, 75*, 864–874. doi:10.1037/0022-006X.75.6.864

Tracey, T. J. G., Wampold, B. E., Lichtenberg, J. W., & Goodyear, R. K. (2014). Expertise in psychotherapy. An elusive goal? *American Psychologist, 69* (3), 218–229. doi:10.1037/a0035099

Walfish, S., McAlister, B., O'Donnell, P., & Lambert, M. J. (2012). An investigation of self-assessment bias in mental health providers. *Psychological Reports, 110*, 639–644. doi:10.2466/02.07.17.PR0.110.2.639-644

Whipple, J. L., Lambert, M. J., Vermeersch, D. A., Smart, D.W., Nielsen, S. L., & Hawkins, E. J. (2003). Improving the effects of psychotherapy: The use of early identification of treatment failure and problem solving strategies in routine practice. *Journal of Counseling Psychology*, 50(1), 59–68. doi:10.1037/0022-0167.50.1.59

Youn, S. J., Kraus, D. R., & Castonguay, L. G. (2012). The treatment outcome package: Facilitating practice and clinically relevant research. *Psychotherapy, 49*(2), 115–122. doi:10.1037/a0027932

Feedback and therapist effects in the context of treatment outcome and treatment length

WOLFGANG LUTZ[1], JULIAN RUBEL[1], ANNE-KATHARINA SCHIEFELE[1], DIRK ZIMMERMANN[1], JAN RASMUS BÖHNKE[2], & WERNER W. WITTMANN[3]

[1]Department of Clinical Psychology and Psychotherapy, University of Trier, Trier, Germany; [2]Hull York Medical School & Department of Health Sciences, University of York, York, UK & [3]Otto-Selz-Institute for Applied Psychology, University of Mannheim, Mannheim, Germany

Abstract

Objective: This study estimates feedback and therapist effects and tests the predictive value of therapists' and patient attitudes toward psychometric feedback for treatment outcome and length. **Methods:** Data of 349 outpatients and 44 therapists in private practices were used. Separate multilevel analyses were conducted to estimate predictors and feedback and therapist effects. **Results:** Around 5.88% of the variability in treatment outcome and 8.89% in treatment length were attributed to therapists. There was no relationship between the average effectiveness of therapists and the average length of their treatments. Initial impairment, early alliance, number of diagnoses, feedback as well as therapists' and patients' attitudes toward feedback were significant predictors of treatment outcome. Treatments tended to be longer for patients with a higher number of approved sessions by the insurance company, with higher levels of interpersonal distress at intake, and for those who developed negatively (negative feedback) over the course of their treatment. **Conclusions:** Therapist effects on treatment outcome and treatment length in routine care seem to be relevant predictors in the context of feedback studies. Therapists' attitudes toward and use of feedback as well as patients' attitudes toward feedback should be further investigated in future research on psychometric feedback.

Introduction

Patient-focused research (PFR) represents one important research strategy to address the widely complained scientist–practitioner gap in providing feedback tools to implement research results "in real time" into clinical practice (e.g., Castonguay, Barkham, Lutz, & McAleavy, 2013; Howard, Moras, Brill, Martinovich, & Lutz, 1996; Lambert, 2007). Central to PFR is the continuous monitoring of patient outcomes over the course of treatment and a psychometric feedback of this information to therapists (and potentially patients). These assessment results are used to evaluate the current state and to predict the future course of an individual patient and can signal early, potentially negative developments and initiate a change in treatment strategy (e.g., Hannan et al., 2005; Meehl, 1954). Research suggests that this enhanced emphasis on outcome orientation and psychometric feedback is a promising path for a further improvement of the effectiveness of psychotherapy, especially for those patients showing negative developments early in treatment (Carlier et al., 2012; Shimokawa, Lambert, & Smart, 2010). In addition, some studies showed continuous feedback could support an optimized resource allocation since patients who show negative developments stay longer in treatment than patients who show positive developments, whereas patients with positive developments (on track) stay shorter in treatment (e.g., Lambert & Shimokawa, 2011; Lambert et al., 2003). A continuous outcome monitoring and feedback could be also a promising path to differentiate patients who need more sessions of treatment from those who already profit from smaller amounts (e.g., Lutz, Ehrlich, et al., 2013; Stulz, Lutz, Leach, Lucock, & Barkham, 2007).

However, early feedback studies were conducted within settings in which relatively short treatments were provided to only moderately impaired patients (e.g., college counseling centers; Newnham & Page, 2010; Lutz et al., 2014; Poston & Hanson, 2010; Shimokawa et al., 2010). Recent studies investigated feedback effects in more disturbed outpatients (De Jong, van Sluis, Nugter, Heiser, & Spinhoven, 2012; Simon, Lambert, Harris, Busath, & Vazquez, 2012), in psychosomatic in-patients (Byrne, Hooke, Newnham, & Page, 2012; Probst et al., 2013), in patients with eating disorders (Simon et al., 2013), and for patients receiving long-term treatments (≥35 weeks; De Jong et al., 2014). These more recent investigations generally showed less pronounced feedback effects. Different explanations have been discussed for this reduced effect (Riemer & Bickman, 2011; Simon et al., 2012). A closer look revealed that feedback is not uniformly effective for every patient and therapist. De Jong et al. (2012), for example, found substantial differences between therapists regarding their use of feedback. Having a higher commitment to use the feedback as well as being female showed to be significantly associated with a higher probability to make use of the feedback for the ongoing treatment. Therapists in turn who reported to use the feedback showed to be more effective for negatively developing patients. Additionally, patients of therapists who were more committed to use the feedback at the beginning of the study showed a faster treatment response. Likewise, Simon et al. (2012) reported that only 50% of the therapists in their study were able to use the feedback to substantially improve client' outcomes. For the other half of therapists it made no difference whether or not they got feedback about the progress of their patients. Until now, only these two studies investigated therapist differences and their effects on outcome in the context of feedback studies. But, these investigations have been limited to treatment outcome and did not examine the influence of these variables on treatment length.

Related to the differences between therapists reported in these feedback studies is the discussion about therapist differences in their ability to successfully provide psychological interventions (Baldwin & Imel, 2013; Saxon & Barkham, 2012). Theoretically, it is quite intuitive that therapists differ with regard to their average effectiveness, their ability to form a sustainable relationship with their clients, their reasoning regarding how much therapy is enough, and other process-relevant variables. Research suggests that about 5–8% of the variability in outcomes is due to therapist differences and depends in part on differences in the study designs and the severity of the patients' impairment (Baldwin & Imel, 2013; Crits-Christoph et al., 1991; Saxon & Barkham, 2012). It seems that the effect increases for more severely impaired patients and is higher in naturalistic compared to controlled samples (Lutz, Leon, Martinovich, Lyons, & Stiles, 2007; Saxon & Barkham, 2012).

Most research from naturalistic samples has focused on therapist effects on outcome and findings on treatment length are sparse. Randomized controlled trials (RCTs) are in this regard only of limited usefulness, since they usually have a treatment protocol with a fixed number of treatment sessions. Therapist effects on treatment length could unveil systematic differences in treatment lengths which are due to the therapists' individual concepts of how much treatment is enough or therapists' ability to maintain a treatment and not letting patients drop-out. The identification of therapists who generally provide longer treatments is also an important issue in the context of scarce financial resources in mental health-care settings. These therapists might profit from tools helping to differentiate patients who need more sessions from patients who need fewer sessions. Only one feedback study systematically investigated therapist effects on treatment length. Okiishi, Lambert, Nielsen, and Ogles (2003) found that patients seen by the best three therapists in their study not only experienced on average more change in OQ-45 scores from pre- to post-treatment but also stayed shorter in treatment than those patients seen by the three worst therapists. However, systematic differences between therapists' average treatment lengths have not been investigated independently from treatment outcome.

Therefore, in the current investigation first the question about how psychometric feedback, therapists' as well as patients' attitudes toward feedback and therapist differences influence treatment outcome and treatment length is addressed when controlling for several additional patient intake characteristics. The second question addresses whether there is an association between therapists' average treatment length and therapists' average treatment outcome.

Methods

The "Techniker Krankenkasse (TK) Project"

In collaboration with the TK, a German health insurance company, a quality monitoring study was conducted, which included decision rules and feedback tools. The *TK project* was the first study to evaluate the practical feasibility of a quality assurance and feedback system in private practices within the German health insurance system (Lutz, Wittmann, Böhnke, Rubel, & Steffanowski, 2013; Strauss et al., 2015; Wittmann et al., 2011). The main goal was to test whether a quality management strategy using feedback was feasible and associated with better outcomes compared to therapies, which were subject to the traditional peer review system of quality assurance (see also Lutz, Wittmann et al., 2013; Strauss et al., 2015; Wittmann et al., 2011). This study was designed as a cluster-RCT involving psychotherapists from three different therapeutic approaches: cognitive behavioral therapy (CBT), psychodynamic therapy and psychoanalysis.[1] The participating therapists were randomly allocated to (i) the traditional case report model of quality assurance including psychometric assessments at intake, termination and follow-up (control, CG) and (ii) an alternative approach to quality management including continuous psychometric testing and feedback (intervention, IG). Depending on how long patients were treated, self-reports were obtained after session 10, 20, 40, 55, and 75 in CBT and after session 10, 20, 45, 55, 75, and 95 for psychodynamic treatments. Each assessment was fed back to the therapists in the IG within a few days whereas no information was provided to the therapists of the CG. To increase the usefulness of the feedback, therapists from the IG were provided with rationally derived decision rules about their patients' progress based on an extension of clinically significant change criteria (for more details on the design of the feedback see Lutz, Böhnke, & Köck, 2011). Therapists who participated in the IG were provided with a simplified approval procedure. Instead of the usual 25 sessions more sessions were approved for treatments in the intervention group (CBT: 45; PD: 50). This modification to the usual application procedure resulted in a higher number of approved sessions in the IG compared to the CG (Table I).

Study Sample

In the current study, a subsample of the TK health insurance sample (N = 751, 177 therapists) was used, which included only therapists who treated at least 5 patients. This selection was necessary to reach a minimal precision for the estimates of within- and between-therapist variability for determining the therapist effects (see also Baldwin et al., 2011). Furthermore, only patients were included who provided a pre- and post-score in the Brief Symptom Inventory (BSI; Franke, 2000) as well as additional information on diagnoses, early alliance, and feedback (IG). Thus, the analysis sample included 44 therapists and 349 patients in which each therapist treated between 5 and 18 patients (M = 9.25, SD = 3.84, median = 8). A standardized assessment procedure including a structured diagnostic interview (related to ICD-10 criteria; Hiller, Zaudig, & Mombour, 2004) was conducted with the patients from the IG. In the CG diagnoses were based on clinical judgments. The primary axis one diagnoses in the study sample were distributed as follows: 39.0% of the patients had a major depressive disorder (n = 136), 9.2% (n = 32) had a dysthymic disorder, 20.1% (n = 70) had an adjustment disorder, 18.9% (n = 66) had an anxiety disorder, 2.0% (n = 7) had an eating disorder, 8.6% (n = 30) had other diagnoses, and 2.3% (n = 8) were not diagnosed with an axis one disorder. Additionally, about 10.3% (n = 36) of the patients were diagnosed with a personality disorder. The number of diagnoses in the analyzed sample ranges from one to four with an average value of M = 1.52. Further demographic characteristics for patients and therapists are provided in Tables I and II, respectively.

Instruments and Data Collection

Brief Symptom Inventory (BSI). Symptom severity was measured using the BSI (Franke, 2000; German translation of Derogatis, 1975), a 53-item self-report inventory, which asks about physical and psychological symptoms within the last week. It is the short form of the Symptom Check-List-90-Revised (SCL-90-R; Derogatis, 1975). Item responses are based on a 5-point Likert scale ranging from 0 ("not at all") to 4 ("extremely"). As the primary therapy outcome indicator, the Global Severity Index (GSI) was computed for pre- and post-treatment by averaging all BSI items. For this index an internal consistency of α = .92 and a retest-reliability of r_{tt} = .90 are reported (Franke, 2000).

Inventory of Interpersonal Problems (IIP-D). Initial interpersonal distress was assessed with the *IIP-D* (Horowitz, Strauß, & Kordy, 2000). For the present project the 64-item version of the IIP-D was used, which measures interpersonal problems regarding behavior, thoughts, and emotions. Item responses are based on a 5-point Likert scale ranging from 0 ("not") to 4 ("very"). For the overall mean score an internal consistency of α = .94 and a retest-reliability (10 weeks) of r_{tt} = .98 are reported (Horowitz et al., 2000).

Penn Helping Alliance Questionnaire (HAQ). Therapeutic alliance was assessed from a patient's

Table I. Descriptive patient characteristics (Mean [*SD*]) and 95% CI for the completer sample, the study sample, and the sample of excluded patients grouped by the treatment condition and on average.

	Completer sample		Study sample		Excluded sample	
	IG (*n* = 507)	CG (*n* = 244)	IG (*n* = 268)	CG (*n* = 81)	IG (*n* = 239)	CG (*n* = 163)
Age	44.4 (11.4)	45.6 (11.1)	44.3 (11.3)	46.0 (10.5)	44.3 (11.4)	45.3 (11.5)
	44.8 [43.97, 45.57]		44.8 [43.65, 46.00]		44.8 [43.59, 45.83]	
Female	67.3%	68.0%	64.2%	65.4%	70.7%	69.3%
	67.5% [64.1%, 70.8%]		64.5% [59.3%, 69.3%]		70.2% [65.5%, 74.4%]	
Number of diagnoses	1.61 (.75)	1.38 (.65)	1.56 (.73)	1.36 (.68)	1.69 (.78)	1.40 (.64)
	1.53 [1.48, 1.59]		1.52 [1.44, 1.59]		1.55 [1.47, 1.63]	
Approved sessions[a]	50.96 (16.4)	35.63 (18.4)	48.35 (9.4)	37.32 (22.7)	54.1 (21.5)	34.8 (15.7)
	46.08 [44.71, 47.44]		45.85 [44.32, 47.38]		46.29 [44.08, 48.50]	
Number of sessions	42.71 (21.4)	36.18 (19.0)	40.94 (19.0)	35.99 (19.8)	44.8 (23.8)	36.3 (18.6)
	40.63 [39.09, 42.18]		39.82 [37.76, 41.88]		41.38 [39.10, 43.66]	
GSI_{pre}	1.25 (.67)	1.14 (.63)	1.26 (.67)	1.09 (.62)	1.24 (.68)	1.16 (.63)
	1.21 [1.16, 1.26]		1.22 [1.15, 1.29]		1.20 [1.14, 1.27]	
GSI_{post}	0.62 (.56)	0.55 (.47)	.63 (.58)	.50 (.38)	.60 (.55)	.57 (.51)
	.59 [.56, .63]		.60 [.54, .66]		.59 [.54, .64]	
d_{GSI}	0.96 (.93)	0.90 (.97)	0.96 (.91)	0.90 (1.00)	.96 (.95)	.89 (.97)
	.94 [.87, 1.01]		.95 [.85, 1.04]		.93 [.84, 1.03]	
$d_{GSIadjusted}$	0.89 (.77)	0.98 (.77)	0.92 (.72)	1.02 (.72)	.96 (.73)	.96 (.73)
	.94 [.88, .99]		.97 [.88, 1.06]		.96 [.89, 1.03]	
HAQ_{pre}	53.8 (7.1)	56.2 (6.9)	53.4 (7.5)	55.8 (6.4)	54.3 (6.4)	56.4 (7.1)
	54.58 [54.06, 55.10]		53.97 [53.21, 54.74]		55.16 [54.46, 55.86]	
IIP_{pre}	1.55 (.55)	1.49 (.55)	1.53 (.54)	1.46 (.55)	1.58 (.56)	1.51 (.55)
	1.53 [1.49, 1.57]		1.53 [1.46, 1.57]		1.55 [1.50, 1.61]	

[a]Differences between control and intervention groups in terms of approved and number of sessions are due to the design of the original study (see also Strauss et al., 2015, and Methods section).

perspective with the HAQ after the first and after every 10th session (Alexander & Luborsky, 1986; German translation of Bassler, Potratz, & Krauthauser, 1995). The HAQ is an 11-item self-report questionnaire with a 6-point Likert scale ranging from 1 ("strongly agree") to 6 ("strongly disagree") so that lower mean scores imply a better alliance.

Feedback. Feedback in the TK project was based on three self-report questionnaires: the BSI (Franke, 2000) to cover general psychological distress, the IIP (Horowitz et al., 2000) to assess interpersonal impairment, and a disorder-specific instrument taking into account the main diagnosis of each patient (Beck Depression Inventory, Beck, Steer, & Carbin 1988; AKV – anxiety disorders, Ehlers & Margraf, 2001; Eating Disorder Inventory, Garner, 1991; HZI-K – compulsive disorders, Klepsch, Zaworka, Hand, Lünenschloss, & Jauering, 1993; SOMS – somatoform disorders, Rief, Hiller, & Heuser, 1997). Psychometric feedback after each assessment was generated based on clinical significant change calculations in relation to intake scores (Jacobson & Truax, 1991). The results of each instrument were integrated into an overall evaluation of patient progress, which described progress by one of three feedback reports: (i) "overall negative change", (ii) "no reliable change so far", and (iii) "good progress" indicating that the patient changed positively compared to the initial assessment. To be able to include patients from the control group in the analyses, feedback was dummy coded ("one negative feedback over the course of the treatment" and "no negative feedback over the course of the treatment") with the control group as reference category. For all patients from the IG group feedback after the 10th session was available. Due to varying treatment lengths, after the second assessment (session 20) feedback data were available for 93.3% of the patients in the IG, for 78.7% after the third, for 52.6% after the fourth, for 26.1% after the fifth, and for 9% after the sixth assessment.

Assessment of patients' attitudes toward routine outcome monitoring. Patients' attitudes toward routine outcome monitoring were assessed at the end of their therapy. An index of patients' attitudes toward feedback was composed of six items. In five of these items patients report their perception of the continuous outcome assessment procedure (e.g., "I find it important to monitor the results of psychotherapeutic treatments.") on a 5-point Likert scale ranging from 1 ("agree completely") to 5 ("disagree completely"). Additionally the index comprises one global item measuring patients' overall satisfactions with the project ("All together, how satisfied are you with the project?") on a 5-point

Likert scale ranging from 1 ("completely satisfied") to 5 ("dissatisfied"). The average of these six items was used as an indicator of patients' attitudes toward feedback. Thus, lower scores on that index imply more positive attitudes toward feedback. To be able to include patients from the CG and patients with missing values (to maintain statistical power for our analysis), this index was effect-coded: "very positive attitude" (n = 44; 12.6%; upper third), "average and negative attitude" (n = 90; 25.8%; lower two thirds), "missing" (n = 134; 38.4%), and "control group" (n = 81; 23.2%).

Assessment of therapists' attitudes toward routine outcome monitoring. Therapists' attitudes toward routine outcome monitoring were assessed at the end of each treatment. An index of therapists' attitudes toward feedback was composed of two indicators: The first indicator was the number of modifications made due to feedback. After the treatments, therapists were asked what they actually did with the provided feedback. A list of 10 different options was presented to the therapists.[2] For each of these options therapists could choose whether they used the feedback in the respective way or not. Since the distribution of the reported number of modifications made due to feedback was skewed to the right (many made just "one modification" for a patient), patients were grouped by whether their therapists applied only one modification or more than one modification due to feedback. The second indicator was an item asking therapists' about their overall satisfaction with the project. Therapists' answered on a 5-point Likert scale ranging from 1 ("completely satisfied") to 5 ("dissatisfied"). The first three categories and the last two categories were pooled in a "satisfied" and a "not satisfied" group, respectively.

Subsequently, we combined these two indicators into one composite index. This index constitutes therapists' attitudes toward the feedback system in terms of frequency of usage and overall satisfaction with the system. Similar to the approach described above for the patients' attitudes index, separate categories for patients of the CG and those with missing values were built. Using the categories of this index the complete sample was divided into six groups: "satisfied/one modification" (n = 57; 16.3%), "not satisfied/one modification" (n = 19; 5.4%), "satisfied/several modifications" (n = 107; 30.7%), "not satisfied/several modifications" (n = 26; 7.4%), "missing" (n = 59; 16.9%), and "control group" (n = 81; 23.2%).

Data Analysis Strategy

Since the data have a hierarchical structure with patients nested within therapists, multilevel models were used. Patients who are treated by the same therapist are likely to have more similar experiences than two randomly chosen patients treated by different therapists. Consequently, individual observations are not independent from each other, violating the assumption of independence. For these kinds of hierarchical data structure, multilevel modeling (MLM) has been established to be the method of choice because it addresses the fact that observations are not independent (e.g., Gallop & Tasca, 2014; Raudenbush & Bryk, 2002). For analyzing the present data, two-level models were used with patients on level 1 and therapists on level 2 (equations are reported in Appendix 1). The two-level model partitions the total variability into two components: variation within therapists (level 1) and variation between therapists (level 2). These components allow calculating the proportion of variance associated with each of the levels. The share of the total variance which is associated with level 2 is referred to in the literature as intraclass correlation or *therapist effect* (Baldwin & Imel, 2013). The larger the therapist effect the larger the differences between therapists concerning the dependent variable.

The analysis started in both cases with a *null model* that included no predictors. The other models were hierarchically built: Treatment outcome (GSI_{post}) was predicted by the following fixed effect predictors, each added in separate modeling steps on level one: initial symptom impairment (GSI_{pre}; *Model 1*), initial interpersonal problems (IIP_{pre}), early alliance (HAQ_{pre}), number of diagnoses (*Model 2*), early feedback (*Model 3*), therapists' attitudes toward feedback (*Model 4*), and patients' attitudes toward feedback (*Model 5*). Since the distribution of the GSI_{post} scores suggests non-normality, all analyses concerning this variable have been conducted with a transformed (root squared) version of this variable.

Variance explained in the different steps is calculated by subtracting the residual variation of the respective model from the residual variation of an identical model not including the newly added predictor variables and dividing this difference through the residual variance of the model with fewer predictor variables (Raudenbush & Bryk, 2002).

The same approach was used to predict treatment length (log-transformed to the base e). The same predictors were used and added on level one, only the number of approved sessions by the insurance company was added as an additional control variable in Model 1. Given that the study arms were confounded with differences in the number of approved sessions, this variable is an important contextual design factor, with the potential to influence differences in the length of the treatments. Therefore, in the analyses on treatment length, we controlled for the number of approved sessions when investigating the influence of other predictors. Data analyses were conducted with the free software environment R version 3.1.1 (R Development Core Team, 2014). The multilevel models have been estimated with the R package lme4 (Bates, Maechler, Bolker, & Walker, 2014).

Results

Comparison of the Full Sample and the Sample with at Least Five Patients per Therapist

To check for systematic selection effects the different subsamples were compared with regard to several variables. In a first step, the study patient sample (N = 349) was compared to the full patient sample (N = 751) and the sample of excluded patients (N = 402) regarding pre and post GSI scores, socio-demographic characteristics, as well as the predictor variables.

Figure 1 shows the pre- and post-distributions of GSI scores in density plots for those three samples. The three distributions are very similar at both time points. Additionally, Table I shows that the three samples do not differ significantly (overlapping 95% confidence intervals) with regard to socio-demographic variables (age and sex) as well as all the predictor and outcome variables included in the statistical analyses. The IG had significantly more approved and actually provided treatment sessions than the CG in each of the three samples. These differences resulted from the specific design of the study and were controlled in the following analyses.

Similarly, Table II shows that also the therapists from the three samples do not differ significantly (overlapping 95% confidence intervals) with regard to socio-demographic variables (age and sex), years of experience, proportion of cognitive behavioral therapists in the sample, working hours per week, average symptomatic intake impairment of their patients in the respective sample (BSI_{pre}), and the average interpersonal distress at intake of their patients in the respective sample (IIP_{pre}). Descriptively, the only difference between the samples is that more CBT therapists are in the study sample (71.8%) than in the excluded sample (59.8%).

Prediction of Treatment Outcome

The results of the MLM are reported in Table III. *Model 1* is the widely used model for the quantification of therapist differences taking only into account initial patient impairment (GSI_{pre}; Baldwin & Imel, 2013; Saxon & Barkham, 2012). The initial GSI score explained 22.40% of the variance in patient-rated outcomes (compared to the *null model*). A patient with an average GSI_{pre} score is on average 0.45 GSI_{post} scores less impaired than a patient who starts with a one point higher GSI_{pre} score. Dividing the residual level 2 variance (therapist variation) by the total variation results in a therapist effect of 5.88%. *Model 2 added* three additional intake characteristics: initial interpersonal distress (IIP_{pre}), early patient-rated alliance (HAQ_{pre}), and number of diagnoses[3] (*Model 2*). Only HAQ_{pre} and the number of diagnoses were significant predictors of treatment outcome and were kept as predictors in the subsequent models. These predictors explain incrementally 6.53% of the variance on the patient level. In *Model 3* feedback (dummy coded as "negative feedback" and "no negative feedback" with the control group patients as reference category) was included. Feedback explained 10.62% of the variance in patient reported outcome. Receiving a negative feedback sign at session 10 resulted for an averagely impaired patient in 0.35 points higher GSI_{post} scores compared to patients from the CG. Patients for whom their therapists receive no negative feedback over the course of treatment did not differ significantly from the CG with regard to their GSI_{post} scores. Thus, in

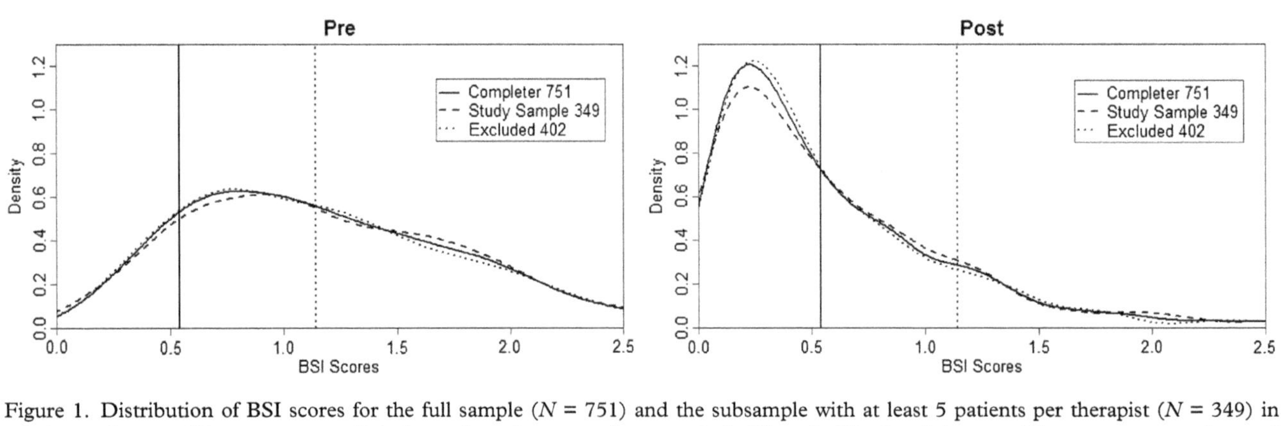

Figure 1. Distribution of BSI scores for the full sample (N = 751) and the subsample with at least 5 patients per therapist (N = 349) in relation to the cut-off between a non-clinical sample and an outpatient sample (solid vertical line) and the cut-off between an outpatient and an inpatient sample (dashed vertical line).

Table II. Descriptive therapist characteristics (Mean [*SD*]) and 95% CI for the completer sample, the study sample, and the sample of excluded patients for therapists grouped by treatment condition and on average.

	Completer sample		Study sample		Excluded sample	
	IG (n = 90)	CG (n = 87)	IG (n = 31)	CG (n = 13)	IG (n = 59)	CG (n = 74)
Age	48.5 (5.93)	48.5 (5.23)	49.8 (5.97)	49.0 (3.94)	47.9 (5.8)	48.4 (5.4)
	48.5 [47.64, 49.38]		49.6 [47.84, 51.36]		48.2 [47.15, 49.16]	
Female	45.6%	43.2%	51.6%	40.0%	42.4%	43.8%
	44.5% [37.1%, 52.2%]		48.8% [34.3%, 63.5%]		43.1% [34.7%, 51.9%]	
Years of experience	17.5 (6.20)	16.5 (5.09)	19.1 (6.37)	17.5 (4.95)	16.7 (6.0)	16.4 (5.1)
	17.1 [16.21, 17.98]		18.7 [16.80, 20.61]		16.6 [15.56, 17.54]	
Cognitive Behavior Therapy	58.6%	68.1%	77.4%	50.0%	48.2%	70.5%
	62.8% [55.0%, 70.0%]		71.8% [56.1%, 83.6%]		59.8% [50.8%, 68.3%]	
Working hours per week	37.9 (10.05)	37.1 (9.59)	40.9 (8.26)	39.1 (8.95)	36.4 (10.6)	36.8 (9.7)
	37.6 [36.05, 39.08]		40.4 [37.80, 43.08]		36.6 [34.80, 38.42]	
BSI_{pre}	1.24 (.44)	1.13 (.49)	1.26 (.31)	1.11 (.29)	1.23 (.49)	1.13 (.52)
	1.18 [1.11, 1.25]		1.22 [1.12, 1.31]		1.17 [1.09, 1.26]	
IIP_{pre}	1.56 (.39)	1.47 (.44)	1.54 (.23)	1.51 (.22)	1.58 (.46)	1.46 (.47)
	1.52 [1.45, 1.58]		1.53 [1.46, 1.60]		1.51 [1.43, 1.59]	

Note. All values were calculated for available cases; missings were deleted. Mean scores are shown for age, years of experience, working hours per week, as well as for aggregated BSI_{pre}, and IIP_{pre} scores; *SD*s in brackets. Female and CBT show percentages.

Models 4 and 5 a combination of the CG and the "no negative feedback" group serves as reference group.

In the next step, therapists' attitudes toward feedback were investigated (*Model 4*). This variable explained additionally 5.39% of the variation in patients' outcomes. Especially the group of patients for whom therapists were satisfied with the project and made only one modification due to the feedback showed significantly lower GSI_{post} scores (for an averagely impaired patient 0.17 points lower) than the control group.

In the last step, the influence of patients' attitudes toward feedback on treatment outcome was investigated (*Model 5*). This variable explained incrementally 5.72% of the variance in patients' outcomes. The group of patients that reported a positive attitude toward the feedback showed significantly lower GSI_{post} scores than the control

Table III. MLM results for models predicting treatment outcome ($\sqrt{GSI_{post}}$).

Models	Null model	Model 1	Model 2	Model 3	Model 4	Model 5
Fixed part						
Intercept	0.70***	0.70***	0.70***	0.66***	0.68***	0.68***
GSI_{pre}		0.25***	0.22***	0.23***	0.23***	0.23***
IIP_{pre}			0.02	–	–	–
HAQ_{pre}			−0.01*	−0.01*	−0.01**	−0.004+
Number of diagnoses			0.06**	0.04+	0.03	0.04+
Feedback						
Negative feedback				0.20***	0.22***	0.24***
No negative feedback				−0.03	–	–
Therapist attitude						
Not satisfied/several mod.					0.13+	–
Not satisfied/1 mod.					−0.03	–
Satisfied/several mod.					−0.05	–
Satisfied/1 mod.					−0.12*	–
Missing					−0.08	–
Patient attitude						
Positive						−0.25***
Average/negative						−0.08+
Missing						0.02
Random part						
Level 2	0.009	0.005	0.007	0.006	0.007	0.002
Level 1	0.103	0.080	0.075	0.067	0.063	0.063
Explained variance						
Level 1 (%)		22.4	27.5	35.1	38.8	39.0

Note. N = 349 patients, 44 therapists; Feedback neutral is not significantly different from the control group and serves together with the control group in further analysis as reference category.
***p = 0; **p < 0.001; *p < 0.05; +p < 0.1.

group (for an averagely impaired patient 0.32 points).

Relation of Treatment Outcome and Attitudes toward Feedback

To explore the relation between outcome and attitudes in more detail and facilitate interpretation, Figures 2 and 3 show the adjusted pre--post effect sizes (adjusted *d*) for the different therapist and patient attitude groups, respectively. Separate MLM with standardized (at the mean and SD of the GSI_{pre} scores) GSI_{post} scores as dependent variable were conducted to produce adjusted pre–post effect sizes and to compare the different levels of therapists' and patients' attitudes. Due to the standardization of the variables, the adjusted means can be interpreted as adjusted pre–post effect sizes (adjusted *d*). Figure 2 depicts the adjusted pre–post effects for the different therapist attitude groups, the control group, and the missing group. *MLM* revealed that the effects sizes of the group of patients for whom their therapists made several modifications due to feedback and are not satisfied with the monitoring system ("not satisfied/several modifications") are significantly lower than for all other attitude groups. Patients in this group had an effect sizes of $d_{adjusted}$ = .52. Patients for whom their therapists were satisfied with the project and made only one modification due to feedback ("one modification/satisfied") had the highest adjusted effect size ($d_{adjusted}$ = 1.13). Patients for whom their therapists were satisfied with the project and made several modifications due to feedback ("several modifications/satisfied") had the second to lowest adjusted effect size ($d_{adjusted}$ = 0.88) which was similar to the adjusted effect size of patients for whom their therapist were not satisfied and made only one modification due to feedback ($d_{adjusted}$ = 0.93). Patients from the CG ($d_{adjusted}$ = 0.99) had a similar adjusted effect size as patients with missing values on these variables ($d_{adjusted}$ = 1.00).

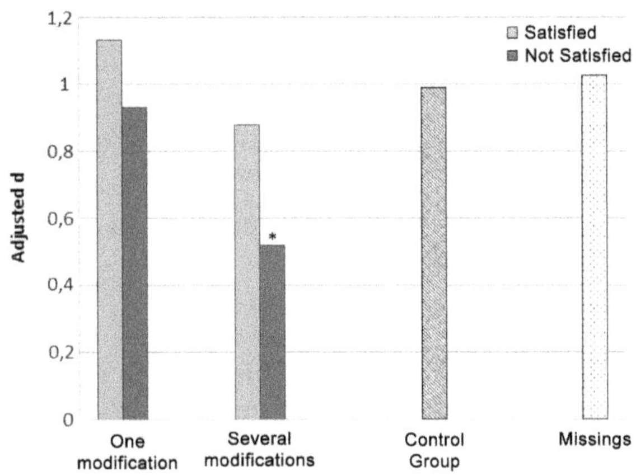

Figure 2. Effect sizes (*d*) for the different groups of therapists' attitudes toward feedback, the control group, and those patients for whom no information is reported (missings) adjusted for initial impairment (GSI_{pre}), early alliance (HAQ_{pre}), and number of diagnoses (*$p < 0.05$).

Figure 3 depicts the adjusted means of the pre–post effects sizes (adjusted *d*) for the different patient attitude groups, the control group, and the missing

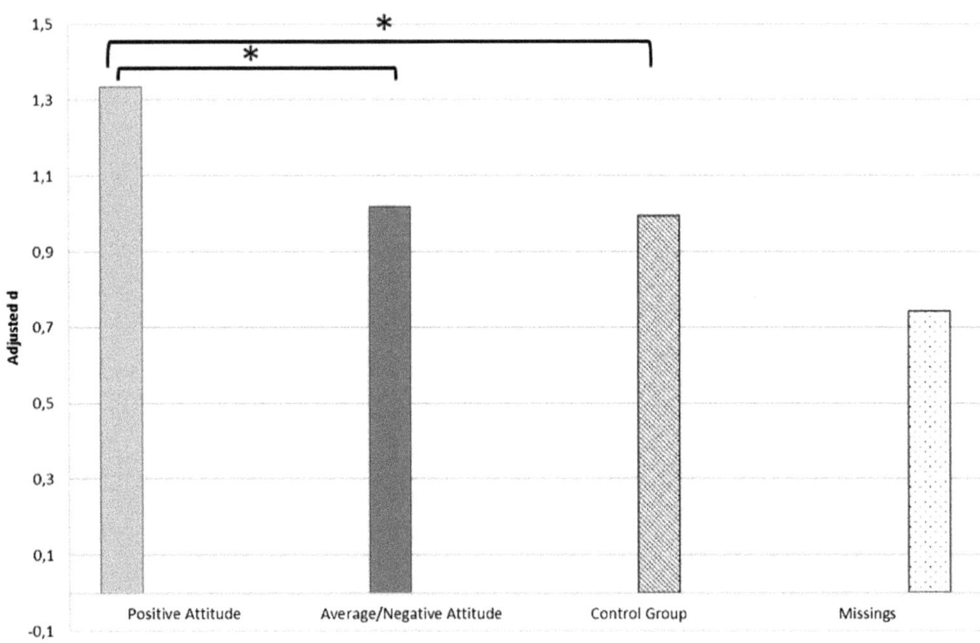

Figure 3. Effect sizes (*d*) for the different groups of patients' attitudes toward feedback, the control group, and those patients for whom no information is reported (missings) adjusted for initial impairment (GSI_{pre}), early alliance (HAQ_{pre}), and number of diagnoses (*$p < 0.05$).

group. Patients who reported positive attitudes toward feedback had descriptively the highest adjusted effect size ($d_{adjusted}$ = 1.33). *MLM* revealed that the positive attitude group was significantly different from the average/negative attitude group ($d_{adjusted}$ = 1.02) and the control group ($d_{adjusted}$ = 0.99). The missing group had significantly lower adjusted effect sizes than all other groups ($d_{adjusted}$ = 0.74).

Prediction of Treatment Length

The approach for the prediction of treatment length (number of sessions) was similar to the one above[4] and five models with an increasing number of predictors were used to test the incremental impact of these predictors (see Table IV). *Model 1* included the number of approved sessions by the insurance company as single predictor of treatment length. About 20.03% of the differences in treatment length could be explained by the number of approved sessions. After controlling for approved sessions, we found a therapist effect of about 8.89%. In *Model 2* additional intake characteristics were included in the analysis. Together, these variables explained 2.09% incremental variance compared to *Model 1*. Only patients' mean scores in the IIP at the beginning of the treatment and *number of diagnoses* were significant and marginally significant predictors, respectively. Thus, initial symptom impairment (GSI_{pre}) and early alliance (HAQ_{pre}) were excluded from subsequent analyses.

Model 3 tested the additional influence of the feedback on treatment length. Feedback explained additional 1.3% of the variation in treatment length. Patients with negative feedback had significantly longer treatments than all other patients.

Models 4 and *5* tested the additional influence of therapists' and patients' attitudes toward feedback on treatment length, respectively. Neither therapists' nor patients' attitudes toward feedback significantly explained additional variance in treatment length.

Associations between Therapist Effects on Outcome and Length

Finally, the association between therapist effects on outcome and treatment length was investigated. Figure 4 shows the association between therapist residuals from the outcome and the treatment length prediction model. On the *x* axis therapists' deviations from the average $\sqrt{GSI_{post}}$ score controlled for initial impairment (at the position of the average score, the residuals equal 0) are depicted. On the *y* axis the deviations from the average treatment length controlled for approved sessions

Table IV. MLM results for models predicting treatment length (ln(number of sessions)).

Models	Null model	Model 1	Model 2	Model 3	Model 4	Model 5
Fixed part						
Intercept	3.55***	3.55***	3.56***	3.52***	3.58***	3.58***
Approved session		0.02***	0.02***	0.02***	0.02***	0.02***
GSI_{pre}			−0.03	–	–	–
IIP_{pre}			0.15*	0.13**	0.13**	0.13**
HAQ_{pre}			−0.00	–	–	–
Number of diagnoses			0.07+	0.05	0.06	0.06
Feedback						
Negative feedback				0.14*	0.15*	0.15*
Therapist attitude						
Not satisfied/several mod.					0.04	–
Not satisfied/1 mod.					−0.04	–
Satisfied/several mod.					−0.10	–
Satisfied/1 mod.					−0.21*	–
Missing					−0.06	–
Patient attitude						
Positive						−0.07
Average/negative						−0.02
Missing						−0.15+
Random part						
Level 2	0.040	0.020	0.015	0.015	0.010	0.014
Level 1	0.256	0.205	0.200	0.197	0.199	0.194
Explained variance						
Level 1		20.03	21.7	23.0	22.7	24.3

Note. N = 336 patients, 44 therapists; Feedback neutral is not significantly different from the control group and serves together with the control group in further analysis as reference category.
***$p = 0$; **$p < 0.001$; *$p < 0.05$; +$p < 0.1$.

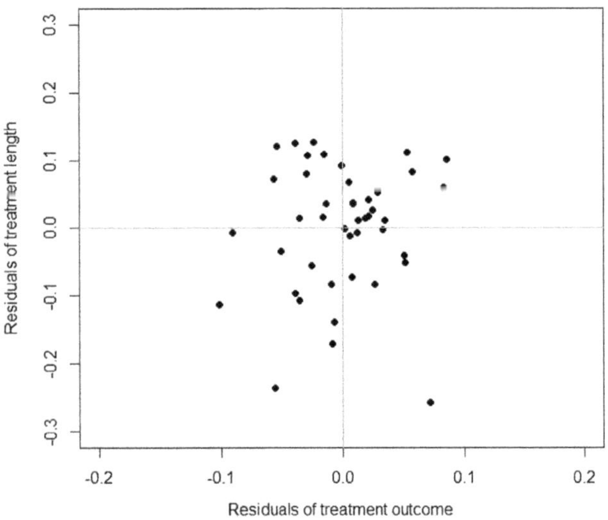

Figure 4. Scatterplot of therapist intercept residuals for GSI outcome scores and treatment length produced by *Model 1* for outcome and length, respectively. These represent how much each therapist's outcome and treatment length across their patients differ from the average treatment outcome and treatment length in this data-set, controlling for initial impairment as well as approved sessions. Negative residuals represent better outcomes as well as shorter treatments.

(at the position of the average score, the residuals equal 0) are depicted. Each point in the scatterplot represents the average $\sqrt{GSI_{post}}$ score of a therapist in reference to the average $\sqrt{GSI_{post}}$ score from all therapists as well as the average treatment length of a therapist in reference to the average treatment length from all therapists in our analysis sample. Thus, the intersection of the axes marks the concurrence of average effectivity (which relates to a score of $GSI_{post} = 0.49$) and average treatment length (which relates to an average treatment length of 35.0 sessions) per therapist. Therapists located in the upper left quadrant of the scatterplot are those who have on average relatively positive outcomes and rather long treatments. Therapists with good outcomes and short treatments are located in the bottom left quadrant, those with relatively bad outcomes and long treatments in the upper right quadrant, and those with bad outcomes and short treatments in the bottom right quadrant. There was no significant correlation between the average length of the treatments and the effectiveness of a therapist ($r = .09$; $p = 0.56$).

Discussion

Recent investigations which examined the effects of routine outcome monitoring and feedback suggest that feedback does not work uniformly for every patient and every therapist (De Jong et al., 2012; Simon et al., 2012). The present study investigated therapist effects on and predictors of treatment outcome and treatment length in a naturalistic setting. Therapist differences were found to account for 6.2% of the differences in patients' outcomes and for 9% of the differences in treatment lengths. There was no significant relation between therapists' average effectiveness and their average treatment length. Therapists' and patients' attitudes toward feedback both explained an additional share of 5.4% (therapist attitudes) and 5.7% (patient attitudes) of the variation in outcomes, respectively. For patients, a positive attitude was associated with better outcomes. For therapists it showed to be most promising when they were satisfied with the system and used the feedback for one specific modification per patient. Neither therapists' nor patients' attitudes toward feedback could incrementally explain significant variation in treatment length.

Furthermore, higher initial symptomatic impairment, lower early patient-rated alliance, and several diagnoses were consistently associated with worse outcome while initial interpersonal distress showed no significant relation. In accordance with previous studies negative feedback in the IG at session 10 was a significant predictor of worse treatment outcome. Although not on-track patients show improvements later on, they do not reach the same level at the end of therapy as on-track patients. A little less variation could be explained in treatment length compared to treatment outcomes (about 24% vs. 39%). Differences in treatment length were predicted by the number of approved sessions, by different intake levels of interpersonal distress (more interpersonal distress, longer treatments), and by feedback (negative feedback, longer treatments).

The finding that deteriorating patients (negative feedback at session 10) have worse treatment outcomes is well known. Previous studies showed that feedback is especially helpful for deteriorating patients even so not-on track patients do not reach the same outcome level as on-track patients (e.g., Lambert, 2007). Our study differs from previous efforts insofar as usually deteriorating patients from an IG (continuous assessments plus feedback to therapists) were compared with deteriorating patients from a control group (continuous assessments without feedback to therapists). In contrast to that, the current investigation compared deteriorating patients from the IG (continuous assessments plus feedback to therapists) with all patients from the CG for which only pre- and post-assessments were available. Without continuous assessments over the course of treatment in the CG, we could not match deteriorating patients from the CG to those from the IG (Strauss et al., 2015). Despite the different kinds of CGs, our findings are not in contrast to the findings of previous studies and our results emphasize the general importance to track treatment outcome continuously over the course of treatment and refer to the importance to provide feedback especially to those patients who show negative developments. Also in our study a more positive development after psychometric feedback was detected for the not-on track patients in the IG (discussed in more detail in Lutz et al., 2013).

Therapists' and patients' attitudes toward feedback showed to be potentially important variables to consider in future feedback studies. Regarding therapists' attitudes, especially those patients for whom their therapists were satisfied with the feedback system and who made only one modification due to the feedback showed the best outcomes. Patients showed worse outcomes when therapists were not satisfied with the feedback system and yet made several modifications due to the feedback. However, it should be noted that these associations are just correlational and not causal, since modifications and satisfaction were assessed at the end of each treatment. One specific modification (after feedback) seems to contribute to a positive outcome, if therapists are satisfied with the feedback. However, with regard to the post-hoc assessment of therapist satisfaction with the feedback system an alternative explanation might be that the outcome predicted the attitudes. Therapist and patients who had a good experience with therapy might look back on the feedback positively, especially those therapists who only had to make one modification, while those who had a worse experience view the feedback more negatively. Besides the impact of therapists' attitudes, results also suggest an influence of patients' attitudes toward feedback. It could be an important factor for the success of a treatment to provide patients with a sensible rationale for why these continuous assessments are an integral and important part of clinical practice (see also Boswell, Kraus, Miller, & Lambert, 2013; Castonguay et al., 2013; Flückiger et al., 2013).

The fact that therapists differ in both their attitudes as well as their use of feedback raises questions of treatment integrity within feedback studies (Wittmann & Lutz, 2014). Similarly to adhering to a treatment manual it should be checked whether therapists understand and actually integrate feedback information in their treatments when participating in the intervention group of such a study. Therefore, it is important to train therapists in the use of feedback instruments, document what they actually did with the feedback, and assess their attitude toward routine outcome monitoring.

Regarding treatment length it came as a surprise to us that higher initial symptom distress was not associated with more treatment sessions, when controlled for approved sessions. Therefore, we tested if this was a mere consequence of the fact that generally more sessions were approved for more distressed patients. If that would be the case the effect of initial symptom distress on treatment length would have been superimposed by the differential number of approved sessions. However, no significant relation could be found between GSI_{pre} scores and the number of approved sessions.

Another central aim of the present study was to quantify the therapist effects on treatment outcome and length. The variance on patient-rated outcome that could be attributed to differences between therapists (6.2%) was in the range of previous studies and meta-analysis in this field (Baldwin & Imel, 2013). About 9% of patients' differences in treatment length are due to differences between therapists. Since this is the first study investigating therapist effects on treatment lengths it is difficult to evaluate the absolute size of this effect. Nevertheless, it seems safe to say that more research in naturalistic samples on this currently neglected aspect could be worthwhile. Besides raising the question of why therapists differ in this regard (even after controlling for differences in their patients initial symptom distress), results from such studies could elucidate cognitive models and other determinants of therapists' choices. An incorporation of these models into more regulated treatment settings (e.g., clinical trials or structured intervention programs) could make these programs more amenable and possibly increase the acceptance on the side of the therapists.

It would be important for future research to replicate this finding in other samples, settings and potentially with other modeling strategies. Especially discrete-time event hazard models (e.g., Hox, 2010) might be an interesting alternative for the analysis of treatment length. We chose the presented modeling strategy in this study to build the treatment length models as similar to the established treatment outcome models as possible.

No relation between therapists' average effectiveness and their average treatment length was found. This suggests that the most effective therapists are not those who on average provide shorter or longer treatments. Although therapists' effectiveness and treatment lengths were unrelated, a joined investigation of therapist effects on outcome and length allows the identification of specific relations on a therapists' level (see Figure 4). The use of multilevel models also allows to control for the individual therapist's (or service's) case-mix, which can – as pointed out above – have an influence on patient outcome as well as treatment length.

A next step could be a closer look at the most effective therapists by means of video analyses, as well as patient and therapist interviews. There is a huge gap between our knowledge of how influential therapists are with regard to outcome and length of treatments and our knowledge of what makes therapists that influential. The aim might be to extract those elements that make therapists effective and transform them in parts of established clinical training programs (Castonguay, Eubanks, Goldfried, Muran, & Lutz, 2015). For health service research it is important to note that more effective therapists do not seem to provide generally shorter or longer treatments. Successful therapists seem to adapt their treatment length to the specific patient and the specific progress pattern. However, given that our findings are based on a limited number of therapists (N = 44), the results from these analyses should be treated with caution.

In addition to the limitations noted above, some further aspects limit the scope of this study and give suggestions for future research. Due to resistance among therapists and the study's steering committee, it was not possible to implement the standard control group of these studies in which patients filled out psychometric questionnaires over the course of the treatment but no feedback was given (Strauss et al., 2015). This CG would have allowed comparisons with the IG within patient subgroups showing similar change courses (e.g., deteriorating patients). Future research implementing such a design can look at differences in therapists' and patients' attitudes toward routine outcome monitoring among groups with similar change courses (on track/not on track).

Another issue is connected to the post-hoc assessment of the therapists' attitudes toward feedback. Since the feedback procedure was provided before the therapists' attitudes were assessed it is possible that the kind of feedback the therapists received over the course of the treatment influenced their attitudes. However, additional analyses for the IG revealed that the proportion of positive, neutral, or negative feedback (taking into account the total number of feedback reports given for this patient) had no statistically significant influence on either therapists' satisfaction or the number of modifications made due to feedback.

Furthermore, it should be noted that the diagnostic procedure was different between the CG and the IG. While in the CG diagnosis was based on clinical judgment, in the IG a standardized assessment procedure was conducted including a structured diagnostic interview (related to ICD-10 criteria; Hiller et al., 2004). This difference led to a slightly higher average number of diagnoses for the patients in the IG (see Table I), therefore we included the number of diagnoses as a potential covariate in all our prediction models.

Another shortcoming of the presented analyses is that the sample inclusion criteria were rather strict. It could be that those patients who met the inclusion criteria of this study (completion of intake and post-treatment assessment; at least 10 sessions) were rather satisfied with the treatment or are in other regards a specific, non-representative sample. However, we showed in this and previous reports that the study sample is similar to the completer sample and that the completer sample is similar to patients undergoing outpatient psychotherapy in Germany (Lutz, Wittmann, et al., 2013). Nevertheless, a replication could shed further light on the robustness of our findings.

Despite these limitations, the findings of this study add to the still growing body of literature on feedback and therapist effects. It seems that for the application of feedback tools in routine care it is necessary not only to train therapists in how to use the feedback, but also to convince them of the value these tools add by supporting (not replacing) their everyday clinical decision-making.

Disclosure statement

No potential conflict of interest was reported by the authors.

Notes

[1] Since not enough data were available for the psychoanalytic treatment modality, the present study includes only CBT and psychodynamic treatments.

[2] This list was composed of the statement "Due to the feedback, I ..." and the following 10 different options from which multiple choices were possible: "... discussed with the patient his/her answers in the questionnaire"; "... tried to assist the patient's resources"; "... tried to adjust my therapeutic interventions"; "... discussed with the patient his/her interpersonal problems"; "... prepared the end of the therapy"; "... tried to enhance the patient's motivation for therapy"; "... varied the intervals between sessions; "... tried to enhance the therapeutic alliance"; "... consulted additional sources of help (e.g., supervision, intervision, literature, further education); "... tried new homework with the patient."

[3] In a preliminary analysis, we checked if differences in diagnoses had an impact on outcome. In this analysis, seven dummy variables were created with depression as reference group: dysthymia, panic disorder, other anxiety disorders, adjustment disorder, eating disorder, personality disorders, and other disorders. Adding the dummy variables as predictors did not explain significant variation in $\sqrt{GSI_{post}}$ scores. Since the diagnostic category was not a significant predictor of treatment outcome and too many dummy variables in one model led to instable model estimations, we did not leave these non-significant predictors in next modeling step.

[4] For 13 patients from the analysis sample (N = 349) no information regarding treatment length was given and therefore had to be excluded (N = 336).

References

Alexander, L. B., & Luborsky, L. (1986). The Penn Helping Alliance Scales. In L. S. Greenberg & W. M. Pinsof (Eds.), *The psychotherapeutic process: A research handbook* (pp. 325–366). New York, NY: Guilford Press.

Baldwin, S. A., & Imel, Z. E. (2013). Therapist effects: Findings and methods. In M. J. Lambert (Ed.), *Bergin and Garfield's handbook of psychotherapy and behavior change* (6th ed., pp. 85–133). New York, NY: John Wiley & Sons.

Baldwin, S. A., Murray, D. M., Shadish, W. R., Pals, S. L., Holland, J. M., Abramowitz, J. S., ... Watson, J. (2011). Intraclass correlation associated with therapists: Estimates and applications in planning psychotherapy research. *Cognitive Behaviour Therapy, 40*(1), 15–33. doi:10.1080/16506073.2010.520731

Bassler, M., Potratz, B., & Krauthauser, H. (1995). Der "Helping Alliance Questionnaire" (HAQ) von Luborsky. Möglichkeiten zur Evaluation des therapeutischen Prozesses von stationärer Psychotherapie [The 'Helping Alliance Questionnaire' (HAQ) by Luborsky]. *Psychotherapeut, 40*, 23–32.

Bates, D., Maechler, M., Bolker, B., & Walker, S. (2014). lme4: Linear mixed-effects models using Eigen and S4 (R package version 1.1–7). Retrieved from http://CRAN.R-project.org/package=lme4

Beck, A. T., Steer, R. A., & Carbin, M. G. (1988). Psychometric properties of the Beck Depression Inventory: Twenty-five years of evaluation. *Clinical Psychology Review, 8*(1), 77–100. doi:10.1016/0272-7358(88)90050-5

Boswell, J. F., Kraus, D. R., Miller, S. D., & Lambert, M. J. (2013). Implementing routine outcome monitoring in clinical practice: Benefits, challenges, and solutions. *Psychotherapy Research, 25*, 6–19. doi:10.1080/10503307.2013.817696

Byrne, S. L., Hooke, G. R., Newnham, E. A., & Page, A. C. (2012). The effects of progress monitoring on subsequent readmission to psychiatric care: A six-month follow-up. *Journal of Affective Disorders, 137*(1–3), 113–116. doi:10.1016/j.jad.2011.12.005

Carlier, I. V. E., Meuldijk, D., Van Vliet, I. M., Van Fenema, E., Van der Wee, N. J. A., & Zitman, F. G. (2012). Routine outcome monitoring and feedback on physical or mental health status: Evidence and theory. *Journal of Evaluation in Clinical Practice, 18*(1), 104–110. doi:10.1111/j.1365-2753.2010.01543.x

Castonguay, L. C., Barkham, M., Lutz, W., & McAleavy, A. (2013). Practice-oriented research: Approaches and applications. In M. J. Lambert (Ed.), *Bergin and Garfield's handbook of psychotherapy and behavior change* (6th ed., pp. 85–133). New York, NY: John Wiley & Sons.

Castonguay, L. G., Eubanks, C. F., Goldfried, M. R., Muran, J. C., & Lutz, W. (2015). Research on psychotherapy integration: Building on the past, looking to the future. *Psychotherapy Research, 25*, 365–382.

Crits-Christoph, P., Baranackie, K., Kurcias, J., Beck, A., Carroll, K., Perry, K., ... Zitrin, C. (1991). Meta-analysis of therapist effects in psychotherapy outcome studies. *Psychotherapy Research, 1*(2), 81–91. doi:10.1080/10503309112331335511

De Jong, K., Timman, R., Hakkaart-Van Roijen, L., Vermeulen, P., Kooiman, K., Passchier, J., & Busschbach, J. V. (2014). The effect of outcome monitoring feedback to clinicians and patients in short and long-term psychotherapy: A randomized controlled trial. *Psychotherapy Research, 24*, 1–11.

De Jong, K., van Sluis, P., Nugter, M. A., Heiser, W. J., & Spinhoven, P. (2012). Understanding the differential impact of outcome monitoring: Therapist variables that moderate feedback effects in a randomized clinical trial. *Psychotherapy Research, 22*, 464–474. doi:10.1080/10503307.2012.673023

Derogatis, L. R. (1975). *Brief symptom inventory*. Baltimore, MD: Clinical Psychometric Research.

Ehlers, A., & Margraf, J. (2001). *Fragebogen zu körperbezogenen Ängsten, Kognitionen und Vermeidung (AKV)* [Questionnaire on body-directed anxieties, cognitions, and avoidance] (2., *überarbeitete und neunormierte Auflage). Weinheim: Beltz.*

Flückiger, C., Holforth, M. G., Znoj, H. J., Caspar, F., & Wampold, B. E. (2013). Is the relation between early post-session reports and treatment outcome an epiphenomenon of intake distress and early response? A multi-predictor analysis in outpatient psychotherapy. *Psychotherapy Research, 23*(1), 1–13.

Franke, G. (2000). *BSI. Brief Symptom Inventory: Deutsche Version (BSI. Brief Symptom Inventory: German Version). Manual.* Göttingen: Beltz.

Gallop, R., & Tasca, G. A. (2014). Multilevel modeling of longitudinal data for psychotherapy researchers: 2. The complexities. In W. Lutz & S. Knox (Eds.), *Quantitative and qualitative methods in psychotherapy research* (pp. 117–141). New York, NY: Routledge.

Garner, D. M. (1991). *Eating disorders inventory-2: Professional manual.* Lutz, FL: Psychological Assessment Resources.

Hannan, C., Lambert, M. J., Harmon, C., Nielsen, S. L., Smart, D. W., Shimokawa, K., & Sutton, S. W. (2005). A lab test and algorithms for identifying clients at risk for treatment failure. *Journal of Clinical Psychology, 61*, 155–163. doi:10.1002/jclp.20108

Hiller, W., Zaudig, M., & Mombour, W. (2004). *IDCL – International Diagnostic Checklists for ICD-10 and DSM-IV.* Bern: Huber.

Horowitz, L. M., Strauß, B., & Kordy, H. (2000). *Inventar Interpersonaler Probleme (IIP-D): Deutsche Version [Inventory of interpersonal problems (IIP-D): German Version].* Weinheim: Beltz Test GmbH.

Hox, J. (2010). *Multilevel analysis: Techniques and applications.* New York: Routledge.

Howard, K. I., Moras, K., Brill, P. L., Martinovich, Z., & Lutz, W. (1996). Evaluation of psychotherapy. Efficacy, effectiveness, and patient progress. *The American psychologist, 51*, 1059–1064. doi:10.1037/0003-066X.51.10.1059

Jacobson, N. S., & Truax, P. (1991). Clinical significance: A statistical approach to defining meaningful change in psychotherapy research. *Journal of Consulting and Clinical Psychology, 59*(1), 12–19. doi:10.1037/0022-006X.59.1.12

Klepsch, R., Zaworka, W., Hand, I., Lünenschloss, K., & Jauering, G. (1993). *Hamburger Zwangsinventar—Kurzform (HZI-K).* Manual [Hamburg Inventory for obsessive-compulsive disorders—short form]. *Göttingen: Beltz.*

Lambert, M. J. (2007). Presidential address: What we have learned from a decade of research aimed at improving psychotherapy outcome in routine care. *Psychotherapy Research, 17*(1), 1–14. doi:10.1080/10503300601032506

Lambert, M. J., & Shimokawa, K. (2011). Collecting client feedback. *Psychotherapy, 48*(1), 72–79. doi:10.1037/a0022238

Lambert, M. J., Whipple, J. L., Hawkins, E. J., Vermeersch, D. A., Nielsen, S. L., & Smart, D. W. (2003). Is it time for clinicians to routinely track patient outcome? A meta-analysis. *Clinical Psychology: Science and Practice, 10*, 288–301. doi:10.1093/clipsy.bpg025

Lutz, W., Böhnke, J. R., & Köck, K. (2011). Lending an ear to feedback systems: Evaluation of recovery and non-response in psychotherapy in a German outpatient setting. *Community Mental Health Journal, 47*, 311–317. doi:10.1007/s10597-010-9307-3

Lutz, W., Ehrlich, T., Rubel, J., Hallwachs, N., Röttger, M.-A., Jorasz, C., ... Tschitsaz-Stucki, A. (2013). The ups and downs of psychotherapy: Sudden gains and sudden losses identified with session reports. *Psychotherapy Research, 23*(1), 14–24. doi:10.1080/10503307.2012.693837

Lutz, W., Hofmann, S. G., Rubel, J., Boswell, J. F., Shear, M. K., Gorman, J. M., ... Barlow, D. H. (2014). Patterns of early change and their relationship to outcome and early treatment termination in patients with panic disorder. *Journal of Consulting and Clinical Psychology, 82*, 287–297. doi:10.1037/a0035535

Lutz, W., Leon, S. C., Martinovich, Z., Lyons, J. S., & Stiles, W. B. (2007). Therapist effects in outpatient psychotherapy: A three-level growth curve approach. *Journal of Counseling Psychology, 54*(1), 32–39. doi:10.1037/0022-0167.54.1.32

Lutz, W., Wittmann, W., Böhnke, J., Rubel, J., & Steffanowski, A. (2013). Zu den Ergebnissen des Modellprojektes der Techniker-Krankenkasse – Ein Plädoyer für mehr Psychotherapieforschung in Deutschland [The TK-project quality monitoring in outpatient psychotherapy from the perspective of the evaluation team – A plea for more psychotherapy research in Germany]. *PPmP-Psychotherapie Psychosomatik Medizinische Psychologie, 63*, 225–228.

Meehl, P. E. (1954). *Clinical versus statistical prediction: A theoretical analysis and a review of the evidence.* Minneapolis: University of Minnesota Press.

Newnham, E. A., & Page, A. C. (2010). Bridging the gap between best evidence and best practice in mental health. *Clinical Psychology Review, 30*(1), 127–142. doi:10.1016/j.cpr.2009.10.004

Okiishi, J., Lambert, M. J., Nielsen, S. L., & Ogles, B. M. (2003). Waiting for supershrink: An empirical analysis of therapist effects. *Clinical Psychology & Psychotherapy, 10*, 361–373. doi:10.1002/cpp.383

Poston, J. M., & Hanson, W. E. (2010). Meta-analysis of psychological assessment as a therapeutic intervention. *Psychological Assessment, 22*(2), 203.

Probst, T., Lambert, M. J., Loew, T. H., Dahlbender, R. W., Göllner, R., & Tritt, K. (2013). Feedback on patient progress and clinical support tools for therapists: Improved outcome for patients at risk of treatment failure in psychosomatic in-patient therapy under the conditions of routine practice. *Journal of Psychosomatic Research, 75*, 255–261. doi:10.1016/j.jpsychores.2013.07.003

R Development Core Team. (2014). *R: A language and environment for statistical computing.* Vienna: R Foundation for Statistical Computing. Retrieved from http://www.R-project.org/

Raudenbush, S., & Bryk, A. S. (2002). *Hierarchical linears models: Applications and data analysis methods* (2nd ed.). Newbury Park, CA: Sage.

Rief, W., Hiller, W., & Heuser, J. (1997). *SOMS—Das Screening für somatoforme Störungen (Manual zum Fragebogen)* [Screening for somatoform disorders]. *Bern: Huber.*

Riemer, M., & Bickman, L. (2011). Using program theory to link social psychology and program evaluation. In M. M. Mark, S. I. Donaldson, & B. Campbell (Eds.), *Social psychology and evaluation* (pp. 104–139). New York, NY: Guilford.

Saxon, D., & Barkham, M. (2012). Patterns of therapist variability: Therapist effects and the contribution of patient severity and risk. *Journal of Consulting and Clinical Psychology, 80*, 535–546. doi:10.1037/a0028898

Shimokawa, K., Lambert, M. J., & Smart, D. W. (2010). Enhancing treatment outcome of patients at risk of treatment failure: Meta-analytic and mega-analytic review of a psychotherapy quality assurance system. *Journal of Consulting and Clinical Psychology, 78*, 298–311. doi:10.1037/a0019247

Simon, W., Lambert, M. J., Busath, G., Vazquez, A., Berkeljon, A., Hyer, K., ... Berrett, M. (2013). Effects of providing patient progress feedback and clinical support tools to psychotherapists in an inpatient eating disorders treatment program: A randomized controlled study. *Psychotherapy Research, 23*, 287–300. doi:10.1080/10503307.2013.787497

Simon, W., Lambert, M. J., Harris, M. W., Busath, G., & Vazquez, A. (2012). Providing patient progress information and clinical support tools to therapists: Effects on patients at risk of treatment failure. *Psychotherapy Research, 22*, 638–647. doi:10.1080/10503307.2012.698918

Strauss, B. M., Lutz, W., Steffanowski, A., Wittmann, W. W., Boehnke, J. R., Rubel, J., ... Kirchmann, H. (2015). Benefits and challenges in practice-oriented psychotherapy research in Germany: The TK and the QS-PSY-BAY projects of quality assurance in outpatient psychotherapy. *Psychotherapy Research, 25*(1), 32–51. doi:10.1080/10503307.2013.856046

Stulz, N., Lutz, W., Leach, C., Lucock, M., & Barkham, M. (2007). Shapes of early change in psychotherapy under routine outpatient conditions. *Journal of Consulting and Clinical Psychology, 75*, 864–874. doi:10.1037/0022-006X.75.6.864

Wittmann, W. W., Lutz, W., Steffanowski, A., Kriz, D., Glahn, E. M., Völkle, M.C., ... Ruprecht, T. (2011). *Qualitätsmonitoring in der ambulanten Psychotherapie: Modellprojekt der Techniker Krankenkasse – Abschlussbericht.* Hamburg: Techniker Krankenkasse.

Wittmann, W. W., & Lutz, W. (2014, June). *The experience of a computer-based feedback system from the clients' perspective.* Paper presented at the 45th International Meeting of the Society for Psychotherapy Research (SPR), Copenhagen, DK.

Appendix 1

Model 1 for predicting treatment outcome

Level 1 (Patient level): $\sqrt{GSI_{post\,ij}} = \beta_{0j} + \beta_{1j} \times$ initial impairment_gm$_{ij}$ + e_{ij}

Level 2 (Therapist level): $\beta_{0j} = \gamma_{00} + r_{0j}$; $\beta_{1j} = \gamma_{10}$

Note. MLM *formulas* for Model 1 predicting treatment outcome (GSI) where patient *i* is nested within therapist *j*. Initial impairment was included as predictor on level 1. For Models 2–5 additional variables were tested as predictors at level 1: GSI_{pre}_gm, IIP_{pre_gm}, HAQ_{pre_gm}, number of diagnoses_gm, feedback, patient attitude, and therapist attitude. Variables with the suffix "_gm" are included as grand-mean centered.

Model 1 for predicting treatment length

Level 1 (Patient level): ln_treatment_length$_{ij}$ = $\beta_{0j} + \beta_{1j} \times$ approved sessions_gm$_{ij}$ + e_{ij}

Level 2 (Therapist level): $\beta_{0j} = \gamma_{00} + r_{0j}$; $\beta_{1j} = \gamma_{10}$

Note. MLM formulas for Model 1 predicting treatment length where patient *i* is nested within therapist *j*. Approved sessions were included as predictor at level 1. For Models 2–5 additional variables were tested as predictors at level 1: GSI_{pre}_gm, IIP_{pre_gm}, HAQ_{pre_gm}, number of diagnoses_gm, feedback, patient attitude, and therapist attitude.

Why do some therapists not deal with outcome monitoring feedback? A feasibility study on the effect of regulatory focus and person–organization fit on attitude and outcome

KIM DE JONG[1,2] & MARIJE DE GOEDE[3]

[1]*Institute of Psychology, Clinical Psychology Unit, Leiden University, Leiden, The Netherlands;* [2]*Research Department, GGZ Noord-Holland-Noord, Heerhugowaard, The Netherlands &* [3]*Department of Social and Organizational Psychology, Utrecht University, Utrecht, The Netherlands*

Abstract
Objective: Despite research on its effectiveness, many therapists still have negative attitudes toward using outcome monitoring feedback. The current study aims to investigate how the perceived match between values of an individual and those of the organization (Person–Organization fit; PO fit), and motivation to prevent failure or to achieve success (regulatory focus) are related to therapists' attitude, attitude changes over time, and outcomes. **Method:** Therapists (n = 20) filled out a feedback attitude questionnaire at two points in time: before the start of outcome monitoring, and after six months. In addition, they completed measures on PO fit and regulatory focus. **Results:** PO fit was predictive of outcomes, when feedback was provided, but did not predict therapists' attitude. Therapists with a strong prevention focus (prevent failures), had a more positive attitude toward feedback, but achieved slower symptom reduction in their at risk cases. A strong promotion focus (achieve success) was not predictive of attitude, but did result in faster symptom reduction in at risk patients when feedback was provided. **Conclusion:** Therapists motivational approach to work and the perceived match with the organization they work for, can influence both their attitude toward outcome monitoring and their outcomes.

Introduction

It has been more than a decade since the first study on outcome monitoring feedback came out, and many studies since then have demonstrated that using outcome monitoring and providing feedback to therapists about their patients' progress can improve outcomes in clinical practice, especially for patients who are not progressing well, so called not-on-track (NOT) patients (Lambert, 2007; Shimokawa, Lambert, & Smart, 2010). Despite its proven effectiveness, many therapists seem reluctant to use feedback, even when it is available to them. Two recent studies showed that around half of the therapists participating in randomized controlled trials on the effectiveness of feedback did not actively use the feedback on their patients' progress, and as a result, outcomes were poorer for these therapists than for those using the feedback (De Jong, Nugter, Lambert, & Burlingame, 2012; Shimokawa, Lambert, & Smart, 2012). Feedback use was found to be predicted by therapists' attitude toward getting feedback (De Jong et al., 2012). Earlier studies revealed that therapists thought outcome monitoring was a waste of time (Aoun, Pennebaker, & Janca, 2002), and that therapists were not willing to use feedback, even if it would lead to demonstrably better outcomes (Walter, Cleary, & Rey, 1998). The aim of the current study is to explore why some therapists may have more trouble accepting outcome monitoring feedback than others.

Getting feedback that a patient is not progressing well might be stressful for therapists (De Jong,

2014). After all, information on how a patient is progressing also reflects on the effectiveness of the therapists, especially when (negative) feedback is provided on multiple cases. Given that most therapists do not receive feedback on their performance any more after finishing their training, it may not be surprising that some therapists fear that the outcome monitoring will reveal them to be ineffective (Youn, Kraus, & Castonguay, 2012). Within clinical psychology, not much knowledge is available on how therapists respond to feedback. However, feedback is a general principle that has been studied extensively in social and organizational psychology. In the current study, two concepts that have been studied extensively in these fields will be further explored in the context of in clinical psychology.

Research on regulatory focus theory (Gorman et al., 1997) from social psychology has shown that people who have a strong focus on preventing failures (referred to as prevention focus) tend to react poorly to negative feedback. By contrast, people who have a strong focus on achieving success (referred to as promotion focus) tend to be able to handle negative feedback better (Gardner, Reithel, Cogliser, Walumbwa, & Foley, 2012; Kristof-Brown, Zimmerman, & Johnson, 2012). Prevention focus is also associated with giving up sooner after negative feedback, and generating fewer alternative solutions than people with a high promotion focus (Crowe & Higgins, 1997; Lanaj, Chang, & Johnson, 2002). Ideal goals, such as hopes and aspirations, are pursued through the promotion system, whereas ought goals, such as obligations and responsibilities, are pursued through the prevention system (Simon, Lambert, Harris, Busath, & Vazquez, 2013).

Outcome monitoring feedback forces therapists to pay more attention to their negative cases. Based on regulatory focus theory it is assumed that therapists with a promotion focus will focus on achieving good treatment results. They may see a case that is not progressing well as a learning experience. This results in a positive attitude toward the feedback and better outcomes for NOT cases. In contrast, therapists with a prevention focus are more sensitive to negative information. For this group of practitioners the feedback may be a threat and they might get insecure when a patient is not progressing well. A strong prevention focus is therefore expected to result in more negative attitudes toward feedback and poorer outcomes in NOT patients.

Another factor important in order for feedback to work, is creating a team climate in which NOT patients can be openly discussed (De Jong, 2014). Given the feelings of insecurity that may arise after negative feedback, it is plausible therapists who feel that they have a good fit with their organization's values experience a safer team climate, and thus are more open to use feedback. Different people can have different experiences within the same organization, because they differ in their organizational culture preference. This fit between the organizational culture and the culture preference of an employee is referred to as the person–organization fit (PO fit). PO fit helps employees understand why the organization does what it does and how it intends to accomplish its long-term goals (Kristof, 1996). A good fit between person and organization is related to several positive work outcomes such as job satisfaction, loyalty to the organization, prosocial behavior, motivation, career success and well-being of employees (Cable & DeRue, 2002; Edwards, Cable, Williamson, Lambert, & Shipp, 2006; Kristof, 1996; Kristof-Brown, Zimmerman & Johnson, 2005; Strauman et al., 2002). People generally function better and are more loyal toward the organization if they fit within the organizational culture. Given that the implementation of feedback was an organizational goal, people with a better PO fit are expected to have a more positive attitude toward feedback, and subsequently better outcomes.

Since no research on these variables exists in the context of psychotherapy, the aim of the current feasibility study is to explore of the relationship between PO fit and regulatory focus on therapists' attitude, attitude changes and outcomes, to determine whether these concepts might be worth further exploring in future studies. Based on the literature from organizational psychology, it is expected that having a good PO fit and a strong promotion focus will result in more positive attitudes toward feedback and better outcomes in NOT patients. A strong prevention focus is expected to result in more negative attitudes toward feedback and poorer outcomes in NOT patients.

Method

Data

Data were collected in a sample of therapists who participated in the feedback study by De Jong et al. (2012). In the original study 57 therapists participated, treating a total of 544 patients, on three locations of outpatient mental health care centers in the Netherlands. In the current study, therapists working on one of the locations where the feedback study took place were asked to participate in the current add-on study. For the other two locations no permission to approach the therapists was obtained. Therapists participated in this study on a voluntary basis. Data on patients' progress and therapists' attitude to feedback were collected as part of the feedback study.

Therapists

A total of 34 therapists were approached to participate in the add-on study and were given the additional questionnaires on regulatory focus (RF) and PO fit in addition to the attitude scale, six months after the start of the study. Twenty therapists (59%) returned the RF and PO fit questionnaires. Two of these had missing data on the attitude scale at time 1 (at the start of the study), and one at time 2 (six months after the start of the study). The sample consisted of 14 females (70%) and 6 males, with a mean age of 45.3 ($SD = 8.8$). The therapists in the sample did not differ significantly from the therapists that did not participate in this study on sex, age, the number of patients in the feedback study, years of experience, years working in the institution, years working at the department, and their attitude toward feedback at time 1. Table I presents the characteristics of the final sample.

Patients

The participating therapists treated 178 patients, who had a total of 762 observations on the Outcome Questionnaire (OQ-45). The sample consisted of 66 males (37%) and 112 females, with a mean age of 38.7 ($SD = 11.8$). Forty percent of patients were single, 32% was married, 8% lived in co-habitation, 15% was divorced and 3% was widowed. A little more than half of the patients (n = 100, 56%) had had prior treatment. The most frequent main diagnoses were adjustment disorder (29%), mood disorder (24%), anxiety disorder (15%) and personality disorder (10%).

Table I. Therapist characteristics.

	N	*n* (%) or *M* (*SD*)
Sex (% female)	20	14 (70%)
Discipline	20	
Psychologist		12 (60%)
Psychiatric nurse		8 (40%)
Years of experience	19	15.7 (10.1)
Years in institution	15	10.0 (8.6)
Years at department	14	9.9 (9.3)
Number of clients per therapist	20	9.1 (6.7)
Attitude at start trial	20	41.7 (5.2)
Attitude after six months	20	39.6 (4.8)
Person–Organization fit	20	0.24 (0.3)
Prevention focus	20	3.47 (1.0)
Promotion focus	20	5.63 (0.9)

Instruments

PO fit. PO fit was operationalized as the level of congruence between therapists' preferences for organizational values and the values that characterize their institution as an organization. We used a shortened version of the Organizational Culture Profile (OCP; Chatman, 1989; O'Reilly et al., 1991), which contains 16 value statements (e.g., being innovative, team oriented) that could assess the extent to which the values are both preferred by the therapist and characterize the organization. Participants sorted the 16 values into 7 categories two times; first to describe their own value preferences, then to describe the characteristic values of their organization. Categories ranged from least desirable or least characteristic (=1), via neutral (=4), to most desirable or most characteristic (=7), with a specified number of values in each category (in the pattern 1–2–3–4–3–2–1. PO fit was estimated by correlating a participant's desired values profile with the characteristic values profile of their organization, referred to as profile comparison analysis (e.g., Caldwell, Chatman, & O'Reilly, 2007; Kristof, 1996).

Regulatory focus. To assess therapists' regulatory orientation we adapted the general regulatory focus questionnaire (Lockwood et al., 2002) to fit individuals in a work situation. This measure consists of two subscales representing promotion goals at work (6 items, e.g., "In general, I am focused on achieving positive outcomes in my work.") and prevention goals at work (8 items, e.g., "I am anxious that I will fall short of my responsibilities and obligations at work." Participants rated on a scale from 1 (e.g., *not at all true of me*) to 9 (e.g., *very true of me*) how well each item characterized them. Cronbach's alpha for the promotion scale was 0.52 and 0.63 for the prevention scale. The scales were moderately related ($r = 0.38$, n.s.).

Attitude toward feedback. The therapists attitude toward feedback was measured using two subscales of the CFIT User Survey (Riemer & Bickman, 2007), the perceived validity scale and commitment to use feedback. The items are scored on various five-point rating scales. The commitment to use the feedback was measured with a scale based on the Goal Commitment Scale (Hollenbeck & Klein, 1987) that consists of seven items. A sample item is "It is hard to take the idea of using these measures in my clinical practice seriously." Perceived validity of the feedback was measured by a six-item scale. A sample item is: "I think that feedback based on the OQ-45 will be helpful for my counseling." Given that the scales correlated strongly ($r = 0.65$, $p < .01$), they were combined into one attitude scale. The internal consistency for this scale was 0.82.

Outcome Questionnaire-45 item version (OQ-45). The Outcome Questionnaire-45 (OQ-45) was used to measure patient progress during treatment. The OQ-45 (Lambert et al., 2004) is a self-report instrument and has 45 items, 9 of which are reversed, asking how the respondent has felt over the last week on a 5 point rating scale, ranging from 0 (never) to 4 (almost always). The OQ-45 consists of three subscales: Symptom Distress, Interpersonal Relations and Social Role. The Symptom Distress domain consists of 25 items relating to psychological symptoms that are common in highly prevalent mental disorders. The Interpersonal Relations domain consists of 9 items that assess the functioning of the patient in interpersonal relationships, and the Social Role domain consists of 11 items that assess the patients functioning in social roles, such as work and school. The cutoff score for normal functioning is 55 for the Dutch OQ-45 and the reliable change index is 14. The internal consistency for the Dutch version of the OQ-45 is between 0.92 and 0.96 for the Total score in university, community, patients and community and patients combined samples. For the subscales the internal consistency is 0.90–0.95 for the Symptom Distress scale, 0.74-0.84 for the Interpersonal Relations subscale and 0.53-0.72 for the Social Role subscale (De Jong et al., 2009).

Feedback Intervention

In the feedback condition, the therapist received e-mails that contain a progress report after sessions 1, 3, 5 and subsequently every fifth session. The patient's progress on the OQ-45 Total score was shown in a graph. A table showed the patient's baseline score, the last available measurement, the change in scores on the OQ-45 and the clinical and reliable change status. Positive changes were shown in green, negative changes in red. A second graph and table displayed the subscale scores. The critical items on the OQ-45, which alert the therapist to suicidal thoughts, aggression and drugs and alcohol use, were presented if patients answered them with a score of 1 (seldom) or higher. Prior to the study, all therapists were given a training that explained how the feedback could be interpreted. They also received an instruction card that explained all elements of the feedback report.

Procedure

The procedure of the feedback study is described in more detail elsewhere (De Jong et al., 2012). Patients completed the OQ-45 on the computer prior to each of the first five sessions of therapy, and subsequently every fifth session for a maximum period of one year. Therapists completed the attitude questionnaire at two points in time: at the start of the feedback study, and six months later. Regulatory focus and PO fit were measured six months after the start of the study, together with the second attitude measurement.

Analysis

Data were analyzed using IBM SPSS Statistics, version 21, and R for Windows, 64-bits, release 3.0.2. Missing data on the therapist level were imputed using the Multiple Imputation procedure in IBM SPSS Statistics 21. The multiple imputation procedure is based on the Multiple Imputation by Chained Equations (MICE; van Buuren, Brand, Groothuis-Oudshoorn, & Rubin, 2006) algorithm. Since multiple imputation is not supported for three-level models yet, single imputation of the missing values was selected. Only missing values on the therapist variables were imputed.

The relationship of regulatory focus and PO fit with therapists' attitude was tested using multiple regression analysis. To test whether outcomes were affected by regulatory focus and PO fit, a three level, random intercept (at levels two and three), random slope (at level three) multilevel model was estimated using the lme4 package in R for Windows. Similar to the original outcomes paper of this study (see De Jong et al., 2012), time was modeled as the log10 of the session number. Provided that outcomes were collected in a feedback trial, the main effect of treatment condition (feedback vs. control) and whether patients were NOT (14 point deterioration compared to baseline at some point in therapy) was also included in the analysis.

Results

Correlations

Descriptive statistics on the attitude scale at time 1 and 2, the PO fit and the regulatory focus are presented in Table I. Table II presents the correlations between the constructs, as well as the correlation with sex, age and years of experience for each construct. Correlations were low to moderate, except for the correlation between the attitude scale at time 1 and prevention focus ($r = 0.51$, $p < .05$).

Prediction of Attitude Toward Feedback

Given the limited therapist sample size, and the relatively low correlations between therapists' sex, age

Table II. Correlations between therapist characteristics, attitude, regulatory focus and PO fit.

	AT1	ΔAT	POF	PREV	PROM
Attitude at start (AT1)	1				
Attitude change (ΔAT)	−0.60**	1			
Person–Organization Fit (POF)	0.00	−0.05	1		
Prevention focus (PREV)	0.51*	−0.31	−0.35	1	
Promotion focus (PROM)	−0.10	−0.18	−0.03	0.37	1
Sex	0.06	0.26	0.10	0.08	−0.14
Age	−0.35	0.21	−0.03	−0.20	−0.24
Years of experience	−0.18	0.05	−0.01	−0.15	−0.04

*$p < .05$.
**$p < .01$.
***$p < .001$.

and years of experience and the attitude measurements (see Table II), only regulatory focus and PO fit were included as predictors in the regression model to predict therapist attitude. First, a prediction model for therapists' attitude toward feedback at time 1 was postulated. Contrary to our expectations, only prevention focus significantly predicted the attitude at time 1. Therapists with a stronger prevention focus had a more positive attitude toward feedback at the start of the study. Promotion focus and PO fit did not predict the attitude. Second, the change in attitude between time 1 and 2 was examined. However, none of the variables significantly predicted the attitude change (see Table III).

Prediction of outcomes

To test whether regulatory focus and PO fit moderated the rate of change (e.g., would influence how fast patients treated by a certain therapists would improve over time), a three-level multilevel model was postulated. Table IV shows the resulting model. Both prevention and promotion focused interacted with feedback in NOT cases. Therapists with a stronger prevention focus achieved slower change in their NOT patients when they received feedback, whereas therapists with a stronger promotion focus achieved faster change in their NOT patients in the feedback condition. PO fit interacted with the feedback (in both on track and NOT patients). Surprisingly, a better PO fit resulted in slower change when feedback was provided.

Discussion

Despite a vast amount of research on the effectiveness of outcome monitoring and feedback tools in clinical practice, many therapists still seem reluctant to use it for their patients. It seems like therapists' negative attitudes toward getting feedback on patients' progress are an important factor in the implementation process. However, we know very little on what factors influence therapists attitude. This feasibility study aimed to explore how the perceived match between values of an individual (PO fit) and motivation to prevent failure or to achieve success (regulatory focus) are related to therapists' attitude, attitude changes over time, and outcomes. It was expected

Table III. Regression models for regulatory focus and PO fit on attitude.

					95% Confidence interval	
	B	SE	*β*	*p*	Lower bound	Upper bound
Model 1: Attitude to feedback at start						
Constant	39.1	6.4		.000	25.5	52.7
Prevention focus	3.6	1.1	0.72	.005	1.2	6.0
Promotion focus	−1.9	1.2	−0.35	.113	−4.4	0.5
Person–Organization fit	3.7	3.3	0.23	.276	−3.3	10.7
Model 2: Attitude change						
Constant	6.2	8.3		.468	−1.4	23.7
Prevention focus	−1.6	1.5	−0.31	.279	−4.7	1.5
Promotion focus	−0.4	1.5	−0.07	.785	−3.6	2.8
Person–Organization fit	−0.9	4.3	−0.05	.833	−10.0	8.1

Note: Model 1: $R^2 = 0.40$; Model 2: $R^2 = 0.33$.

Table IV. Multilevel model of change in outcomes.

	Parameter	Estimate	SE
Fixed effects			
Initial status	Intercept	77.9	1.7
Rate of change	Time	−8.8	10.3
	Feedback (Fb)	−14.0	18.8
	Not on Track (NOT)	17.7	21.5
	Feedback * NOT	56.7	42.8
	Prevention Focus	3.5	2.3
	Promotion Focus	−2.9	2.1
	PO Fit	4.8	6.6
	Fb * Prevention	−5.5[a]	3.3
	Fb * Promotion	5.9[a]	3.4
	Fb * PO Fit	−21.7*	10.7
	NOT * Prevention	−6.3[a]	3.8
	NOT * Promotion	4.2	4.7
	NOT * PO Fit	0.7	14.2
	Fb* NOT * Prevention	29.6**	8.8
	Fb * NOT * Promotion	−28.0*	11.3
	Fb *NOT * PO Fit	14.2	20.0
Variance components			
Level 1	Within-person	98.6	9.9
Level 2	Intercept	448.3	21.2
Level 3	Intercept	0.0	0.1
	Slope	0.7	0.8

Note: Time is modeled as the log10 of the session number. Negative values in the fixed part of the models correspond with a faster decrease of dysfunctioning over time. NOT and Feedback were coded as dummy variables (0 = no, 1 = yes).
$^{*}p < .05$.
$^{**}p < .01$.
$^{a}p < .10$.

that having a good PO fit would result in a more positive attitude toward feedback and better outcomes in NOT patients. This was only partially confirmed: PO fit did not predict attitude or attitude change, and contrary to our expectations, interacted with getting feedback in a negative way. Therapists who experienced a stronger PO fit achieved slower change when feedback was provided, regardless of whether patients were on track or NOT. With regard to regulatory focus it was expected that a strong prevention focus would result in more negative attitudes toward feedback and poorer outcomes in NOT patients, whereas a strong promotion focus was expected to have the opposite effect. Again, these hypotheses were only partially confirmed. Contrary to our expectations, therapists with a strong prevention focus had a more positive attitude toward feedback. However, as was expected, they did achieve slower symptom reduction in their NOT cases. A strong promotion focus was not significantly predictive of attitude, but did result in faster symptom reduction in at risk patients when feedback was provided. Attitudinal changes were not predicted by regulatory focus.

The effect of PO fit was not as expected. PO fit did not predict therapists' attitude, although the beta values in the regression model are in the right direction, but the standard error was relatively large, suggesting more variability in the relationship between PO fit and attitude compared to the other variables. Given that PO fit has not been studied in therapists before, it might be that PO fit works in a different way in therapists than in other types of employees. Perhaps there is a moderator variable unmeasured in this study that explains part of the variance in outcomes, such as personality traits (e.g., Edwards et al., 2006). The negative interaction between PO fit and feedback was not anticipated. One possible explanation is that the implementation of the feedback tool altered the local organizational culture, causing people who previously had a high PO fit to have a poorer PO fit toward the end of the study. Although PO fit was measured six months into the study, at that point most therapists had not received feedback on many of their cases. The study took three years in total, a time period in which organizational change is possible, and might have been reflected in outcomes, but not in the PO fit measurement.

Regulatory focus did not predict attitude toward feedback in the way that we anticipated. It seems like therapists with a stronger prevention focus had a more positive attitude toward feedback than therapists with a stronger promotion focus. In fact, although not significantly so, therapists with a promotion focus tended to have a more negative attitude on average. A possible explanation might be that therapists perceive outcome monitoring more as an obligation or responsibility, rather than a way to improve patient care. Given that participation in the study was mandatory for the therapists in the department and as such, it was an obligation, it makes sense that prevention focused therapists were more open to it.

It was confirmed that therapists with a stronger prevention focus achieved slower progress in their NOT cases, whereas therapists with a stronger promotion focus were better at achieving progress with these patients. As was mentioned earlier, prevention focused therapists may experience negative affect when being presented with NOT cases, as they may represent the risk of failure to the therapists, which is exactly what prevention focused people want to avoid. It would be interesting to investigate in a future study, what kind of attributions these therapists make about the cause of the lack of progress by the patient. One option why feedback is less effective in these cases might be that these therapists make external attributions (e.g., the patient is difficult) about the cause of the patient getting NOT—which is good for the therapists' mental health, but may not be ideal for obtaining better outcomes for these patients (De Jong, 2014).

An important limitation of the present study is that the number of therapists that participated in the study was restricted. We only got permission to approach one of the departments in the study, which resulted in a smaller sample size than would ideally be the case. Also, a fair amount of therapists approached did not complete a sufficient number of questionnaires to be included in the study (40%). Although that response rate is not uncommon, it is certainly not ideal in an already limited population. The small sample size limited the number of predictor variables that could be entered in the study, as well as power to detect effects for the predictor variables that were included. It also may have affected the multilevel model, in the sense that standard errors of the variances (random effects) are potentially underestimated in higher level sample sizes (number of therapists in this case) smaller than 100 (Lockwood, Jordan, & Kunda, 2005). Although this does not influence the estimation of the fixed effects, biased random effects would limit the generalizability of the results.

Another possible limitation to this study is that regulatory focus and PO fit were measured six months into the study. This was caused by having to spread the number of questionnaires to therapists over time, to decrease their burden, but it may have caused bias. Although regulatory focus and PO fit are supposed to be relatively stable traits, they also have certain state-like aspects that could have caused them to respond differently after six months than at the start of the study.

It should be noted that performance feedback in therapists may be different than performance feedback in, for instance, sales persons. A patient's progress is not entirely under the control of the therapist and some patients may have more chronic complaints. However, one could argue that sales are also not entirely under the control of a sales person. The difference is perhaps that therapists still have to deal with a patient who is not progressing, whereas sales people do not have to bother with a customer who does not want to make a purchase anymore. According to attribution theory, the combination of negative feedback and low perceived control may give rise to unpleasant feelings in the therapist.

This is the first study that investigated regulatory focus and PO fit in therapists. We can conclude that these constructs seem feasible to study in the context of psychotherapy. The results suggest that therapists' motivational approach to work and perceived match with the organization they work for can influence both their attitude toward outcome monitoring and their outcomes, although results would have to be replicated by future studies with larger samples in order to draw more definite conclusions. The current study adds to the conclusion by De Jong et al. (2012) that therapist characteristics is an important topic for further study within the context of feedback. Until recently, feedback effects at the level of the therapists were a black box, and these studies have contributed to the initial disentanglement of these effects. If these effects are confirmed by other studies, it may lead to recommendations to adapt the feedback to therapist characteristics or to train therapists with certain characteristics to better deal with (negative) feedback. In the end, it would be important to find a way to incorporate feedback in such a way that all therapists are able to use it to help prevent negative outcomes in patients.

Acknowledgements

The authors would like to thank Ella Dikkentman and Michel Handgraaf for their contributions to this study.

References

Aoun, S., Pennebaker, D., & Janca, A. (2002). Outcome measurement in rural mental health care: A field trial of rooming-in models. *Australian Journal of Rural Health, 10*, 302–307. doi:10.1046/j.1440-1584.2002.00484.x

van Buuren, S., Brand, J. P. L., Groothuis-Oudshoorn, K., & Rubin, D. B. (2006). Fully conditional specification in multivariate imputation. *Journal of Statistical Computation and Simulation, 76*, 1049–1064. doi:10.1080/10629360600810434

Cable, D. M., & DeRue, D. S. (2002). The convergent and discriminant validity of subjective fit perceptions. *Journal of Applied Psychology, 87*, 875–884. doi:10.1037/0021-9010.87.5.875

Caldwell, D. F., Chatman, J. A., & O'Reilly, C. A. (2007). Profile comparison methods for assessing person-situation fit. In C. Ostroff & T. A. Judge (Eds.), *Perspectives on organizational fit* (pp. 356–361). Mahwah, NJ: Erlbaum.

Chatman, J. A. (1989). Matching people and organizations: Selection and socialization in public accounting firms. *Academy of Management Proceedings 1*, 199–203. doi:10.5465/ambpp.1989.4980837

Crowe, E., & Higgins, E. T. (1997). Regulatory focus and strategic inclinations: Promotion and prevention in decision-making. *Organizational Behavior and Human Decision Processes, 69*, 117–132.

De Jong, K. (2014). Deriving implementation strategies for outcome monitoring feedback from theory, research and practice. *Administration and Policy in Mental Health and Mental Health Services Research*, 1–5. doi:10.1007/s10488-014-0589-6

De Jong, K., Nugter, M. A., Lambert, M. J., & Burlingame, G. M. (2009). *Handleiding voor afname en scoring van de outcome Questionnaire (OQ-45)*. Salt Lake City, UT: OQ Measures LLC.

De Jong, K., van Sluis, P., Nugter, M. A., Heiser, W. J., & Spinhoven, P. (2012). Understanding the differential impact of outcome monitoring: Therapist variables that moderate feedback effects in a randomized clinical trial. *Psychotherapy Research, 22*, 464–474. doi:10.1080/10503307.2012.673023

Edwards, J. R., Cable, D. M., Williamson, I. O., Lambert, L., & Shipp, A. J. (2006). The phenomenology of fit: Linking the person and environment to the subjective experience of person-environment fit. *Journal of Applied Psychology, 91*, 802–827.

Gardner, W. L., Reithel, B. J., Cogliser, C. C., Walumbwa, F. O., & Foley, R. T. (2012). Matching personality and organizational culture: Effects of recruitment strategy and the five-factor model on subjective person–organization fit. *Management Communication Quarterly*. doi:10.1177/0893318912450663

Gorman, C. A., Meriac, J. P., Overstreet, B. L., Apodaca, S., McIntyre, A. L., Park, P., et al. (2012). A meta-analysis of the regulatory focus nomological network: Work-related antecedents and consequences. *Journal of Vocational Behavior, 80*, 160–172.

Higgins, E. T. (1997). Beyond pleasure and pain. *The American psychologist, 52*, 1280–1300. doi:10.1037/0003-066X.52.12.1280

Hollenbeck, J. R., & Klein, H. J. (1987). Goal commitment and the goal-setting process: Problems, prospects, and proposals for future research. *Journal of Applied Psychology, 72*, 212–220. doi:10.1037/0021-9010.72.2.212

Kristof, A. L. (1996). Person-organization fit: An integrative review of its conceptualizations, measurement, and implications. *Personnel Psychology, 49*, 1–49. doi:10.1111/j.1744-6570.1996.tb01790.x

Kristof-Brown, A. L., Zimmerman, R. D., & Johnson, E. C. (2005). Consequence of individuals' fit at work: A meta-analysis of person-job, person-organization, and person-supervisor fit. *Personnel Psychology, 58*, 281–342. doi:10.1111/j.1744-6570.2005.00672.x

Lambert, M. J. (2007). Presidential address: What we have learned from a decade of research aimed at improving psychotherapy outcome in routine care. *Psychotherapy Research, 17*, 1–14. doi:10.1080/10503300601032506

Lambert, M. J., Morton, J. J., Hatfield, D. R., Harmon, C., Hamilton, S., Shimokawa, K., ... Reisinger, C. W. (2004). *Administration and scoring manual for the OQ-45.2 (Outcome Questionnaire)* (3 ed.). Wilmington, DE: American Professional Credentialling Services LLC.

Lanaj, K., Chang, C.-H. D., & Johnson, R. E. (2012). Regulatory focus and work-related outcomes: A review and meta-analysis. *Psychological Bulletin, 138*(5), 998–1034. doi:10.1037/a0027723

Lockwood, P., Jordan, C. H., & Kunda, Z. (2002). Motivation by positive or negative role models: Regulatory focus determines who will best inspire us. *Journal of Personality and Social Psychology, 83*, 854–864. doi:10.1037/0022-3514.83.4.854

Maas, C. J. M., & Hox, J. J. (2005). Sufficient sample sizes for multilevel modeling. *Methodology, 1*, 86–92.

O'Reilly, C. A., Chatman, J., & Caldwell, D. F. (1991). People and organizational culture: A profile comparison approach to assessing person-organization fit. *Academy of Management Journal, 34*, 487–516. doi:10.2307/256404

Riemer, M., & Bickman, L. (2007). *CFIT user survey—counselor version*. Nashville, TN: Vanderbilt University.

Shimokawa, K., Lambert, M. J., & Smart, D. W. (2010). Enhancing treatment outcome of patients at risk of treatment failure: Meta-analytic and mega-analytic review of a psychotherapy quality assurance system. *Journal of Consulting and Clinical Psychology, 78*, 298–311. doi:10.1037/a0019247

Simon, W., Lambert, M. J., Harris, M. W., Busath, G., & Vazquez, A. (2012). Providing patient progress information and clinical support tools to therapists: Effects on patients at risk of treatment failure. *Psychotherapy research, 22*, 638–647. doi:10.1080/10503307.2012.698918

Strauman, T. J., Detloff, A. M., Sestokas, R., Smith, D. V., Goetz, E. L., Rivera, C., & Kwapil, L. (2013). What shall I be, what must I be: Neural correlates of personal goal activation. *Frontiers in Integrative Neuroscience, 6*. doi:10.3389/fnint.2012.00123

Tepeci, M., & Bartlett, A. L. B. (2002). The hospitality industry culture profile: A measure of individual values, organizational culture, and person–organization fit as predictors of job satisfaction and behavioral intentions. *International Journal of Hospitality Management, 21*, 151–170. doi:10.1016/S0278-4319(01)00035-4

Walter, G., Cleary, M., & Rey, J. M. (1998). Attitudes of mental health personnel towards rating outcome. *Journal of Quality in Clinical Practice, 18*, 109–115.

Youn, S. J., Kraus, D. R., & Castonguay, L. G. (2012). The treatment outcome package: Facilitating practice and clinically relevant research. *Psychotherapy, 49*, 115–122. doi:10.1037/a0027932

The effect of implementing the Outcome Questionnaire-45.2 feedback system in Norway: A multisite randomized clinical trial in a naturalistic setting

INGUNN AMBLE[1,2], TORE GUDE[2], SVEN STUBDAL[1], BROR JUST ANDERSEN[3], & BRUCE E. WAMPOLD[2,4]

[1]*Outpatient Clinic, Modum Bad Psychiatric Center, Vikersund, Norway;* [2]*Research Institute, Modum Bad Psychiatric Center, Vikersund, Norway;* [3]*Baerum District Psychiatric Center, Vestre Viken HF, Drammen, Norway &* [4]*Department of Counseling Psychology, University of Wisconsin-Madison, Madison, WI, USA*

Abstract

It has been claimed that the monitoring of ongoing psychotherapy is of crucial importance for improving the quality of mental health care. This study investigated the effect of using the Norwegian version of the patient feedback system OQ®-Analyst using the Outcome Questionnaire-45.2. Patients from six psychiatric clinics in Southern Norway (N = 259) were randomized to feedback (FB) or no feedback (NFB). The main effect of feedback was statistical significant (p = .027), corroborating the hypothesis that feedback would improve the quality of services, although the size of the effect was small to moderate (d = 0.32). The benefits of feedback have to be considered against the costs of implementation.

Introduction

In general, psychotherapy is considered effective (Fonagy, Roth, & Higgitt, 2005; Lambert, 2013; Lambert & Ogles, 2004) and in manual-based clinical trials most patients improve (Hansen, Lambert, & Forman, 2002). However, there is definitely a need to improve the quality of services because it appears that in routine psychiatric care, not more than 50% improve (Hansen & Lambert, 2003) and about 5–10% actually get worse, being treatment failures or non-responders (Hansen et al., 2002; Lambert & Ogles, 2004; Mohr, 1995). The current efforts to improve the quality of services involve the dissemination of evidence-based treatments into practice settings (e.g., Shafran et al., 2009). However, the effectiveness of such transportation is not clear, as the superiority of evidence-based treatment to treatment-as-usual is not well established, especially when the treatment-as-usual provides adequate amounts of psychotherapy (Budge et al., 2013; Spielmans, Gatlin, & McFall, 2010; Wampold et al., 2011; Weisz, Jensen-Doss, & Hawley, 2006). Another method to improve the quality of services, not incompatible with the former, involves what has been called practice-based evidence (Barkham, Hardy, & Mellor-Clark, 2010; Lambert, 2010; Miller, Duncan, Sorrell, & Brown, 2005). Practice-based evidence involves utilizing evidence from practice to improve the quality of service. One way in which practice-based evidence is used is to provide feedback about patients' progress to therapists and/or patients.

A number of systems have been developed to implement practice-based evidence by providing feedback to therapists or feedback to both therapists and patients, including systems that use the Outcome Questionnaire-45.2 (OQ-45) (Lambert et al., 1996), the outcome rating scale (ORS) (Miller et al., 2005), the clinical outcomes in routine evaluation—outcome measure (CORE-OM) (Evans et al., 2002), the systemic therapy inventory of change (STIC) (Pinsof et al., 2009), and the counseling center assessment of psychological symptoms (C-CAP) (McAleavey et al., 2012). Of these, only the systems that use the OQ-45 and the ORS have been investigated with randomized clinical trials. Meta-analyses of trials that have compared feedback to treatment-as-usual (no feedback) have shown that the OQ-45 and the ORS feedback systems improve the quality of care, primarily by improving outcomes for cases that are at risk for deterioration, which are often called "signal cases" or "not-on-track" (Lambert & Shimokawa, 2011a, 2011b; Shimokawa, Lambert, & Smart, 2010). The OQ®-Analyst (OQ-Analyst) is the most widely tested system and the results have been particularly promising (Lambert & Shimokawa, 2011b; Shimokawa et al., 2010). In a comprehensive review of six trials of the OQ-45, Shimokawa et al. (2010) concluded, "The current state of evidence appears to support the efficacy and effectiveness of feedback interventions in enhancing treatment outcomes" (p. 298). Although the evidence is convincing, there are some caveats that limit the veridicality and generalizability of the results. First, classification of evidence-based treatments relies on evidence from two independent groups (Chambless et al., 1996), whereas all of the OQ-45 trials reviewed by Shimokawa et al. were conducted in collaboration with the team which originally developed the system. Second, with one exception (viz., Hawkins, Lambert, Vermeersch, Slade, & Tuttle, 2004), all patients in these trials were university college students receiving services at the same university college counseling center.

After publication of the meta-analyses, additional trials using the OQ-45 have been published. Five trials, involving patients who were not university students, including outpatients and specialty care, substance abuse outpatients, eating disorder patients, and psychosomatic inpatients, found that feedback using the OQ-45 was effective (Crits-Christoph et al., 2012; de Jong et al., 2014; Probst et al., 2013; Simon et al., 2013; Simon, Lambert, Harris, Busath, & Vazquez, 2012).

Despite the evidence to support feedback using the OQ-45, there is a need for independent replication of the effectiveness of OQ-45 feedback, particularly with more severely distressed patients. To our knowledge, only two OQ-45 trials have been conducted outside the USA. In a large study with more than 400 patients with diverse disorders from three outpatient clinics in the Netherlands, de Jong, van Sluis, Nugter, Heiser, & Spinhoven (2012) found no significant effect of OQ-45 feedback, even for patients who were not-on-track. However, not-on-track patients whose therapists actively used the feedback did achieve better outcomes than patients of the same therapists for whom feedback was not used and it appears that feedback was more effective with relatively shorter treatment (i.e., less than 35 sessions: de Jong et al., 2014). A study with 252 patients in psychosomatic in-patient treatment in Germany concluded that using OQ-45 feedback improved the outcome for patients at risk for treatment failure (Probst et al., 2013). However, because the OQ-45 is being adopted internationally (see Amble et al., 2013), it is critical that additional trials be conducted in non-US locations.

The purpose of the present study was to examine the effects of OQ-45 feedback in Norwegian inpatient and outpatient psychiatric clinics treating patients with moderate to severe dysfunction, by randomly assigning them to feedback (FB) or no feedback (NFB). We hypothesized that FB to therapists and patients about patient progress would improve the outcome of psychotherapy compared with NFB, particularly for patients who are at risk for deterioration or achieving less than expected change.

Method

Instrument and Feedback System

The Outcome Questionnaire-45.2. The OQ-45 is an instrument developed to examine patient progress (Hatfield & Ogles, 2004). The OQ-45 is a 45-item patient self-report instrument designed to assess experience of psychological distress, interpersonal functioning, and contentment with social role functioning (Lambert et al., 1996). The 45 items are assessed with a 5-point Likert scale (0 = never, 1 = rarely, 2 = sometimes, 3 = frequently, 4 = almost always), with nine of the items reverse scored to limit the likelihood of response bias. The OQ-45 is typically given prior to the first and each subsequent therapy session, in either paper/pencil or electronic formats, and takes 5–10 min to complete. The sum of all items gives a total distress (TD) score, ranging from zero to 180, with higher scores being indicative of greater levels of psychological distress.

The psychometric properties of the OQ-45 have been studied extensively in the USA and the instrument has been found to be reliable and valid (Beretvas et al. 2003; Bludworth et al. 2010; Chapman 2003; Kim, Beretvas, & Sherry, 2010; Lambert et al., 1996; Mueller et al., 1998). Due to promising studies in the USA, the OQ-45 has been translated into more than 20 languages and psychometric analyses have been conducted on translated versions in Germany (Lambert, Hannöver, Nisslmüller, Richard, & Kordy, 2002), the Netherlands (de Jong et al., 2007), Italy (Chiappelli, Coco, Gullo, Bensi, & Prestano, 2008; Lo Coco et al., 2008), Sweden (Wennberg, Philips & Jong, 2010), China (Qin & Hu, 2008), Poland (Simon et al., 2013), and Norway (Amble et al., 2013).

The Norwegian version of the OQ-45 used in this study has been shown to have adequate test–retest reliability and internal stability (r = .85 and α =

0.93, respectively) and validity with other international instruments (Amble et al., 2013). The clinical cut-off score for the Norwegian version is 62 and the reliable change index (RCI) is 16 (Amble et al., 2013).

The Feedback System. The OQ-Analyst software provides the therapist and patient with a report showing the session-by-session progress. The system compares a given patient's rate of improvement with normative and expected rates of improvements based upon samples with patients at the same initial level of distress. Patients who are predicted to eventually deteriorate (not-on-track for a positive outcome) are identified and corresponding feedback messages are given to the therapist and patient. The feedback reports include a graph of the patients' progress up to the current assessment and a colored alert determined by the empirical method (i.e., by comparing progress to normative trajectories; see Lambert, Kahler, Harmon, & Burlingame, 2011). A white alert indicates that the patient's score is similar to people in a state of normal functioning and termination of therapy could be considered. A green signal indicates that the progress is as expected but there is still need for more treatment. A yellow alert is given when there is concern about the patient's progress or that a positive outcome is in doubt. A red alert indicates serious concern about the final outcome and that there is risk of deterioration unless changes are made. If a patient has an OQ-45 score that generates a red or a yellow alert during therapy, the case is defined as a *signal case* (i.e., not-on-track).

Procedures

This RCT was developed in order to test the OQ-Analyst in Norwegian naturalistic psychiatric settings. The project was approved by the Norwegian regional ethics committee prior to inviting clinics in a local geographical region to participate. Twelve clinics were invited and six consented. Two of the clinics were inpatient clinics and four of the clinics were outpatient clinics, of which one was a substance abuse clinic (Table I). The clinics signed a cooperation agreement based on the research protocol and agreed to implement the randomization procedures and contribute data to the project.

A steering group, which included a project coordinator from each clinic as well as researchers from the University of Oslo and Modum Bad Psychiatric Center, was established for supervision and monitoring of the project progress. At each clinic, one information meeting (1.5 hr) and one therapist training course (2.5 hr) were conducted. At one of the clinics, where the project leader was employed, the therapist participation was obligatory and at the other clinic therapists participation was voluntary (Table I).

Because the aim of the trial was to examine the OQ-Analyst in the context of a naturalistic clinical setting, the therapists were not instructed to conduct treatment according to a specific protocol or using a particular clinical treatment method. A monthly OQ-forum was arranged at each clinic to address logistical, practical, and clinical issues, as well as to evaluate and share experiences with the use of OQ-Analyst. The project leader, the project coordinators, and two IT-consultants were available for personal supervision by telephone or by mail for all the participating therapists and office staffs during the entire project period.

After having signed and returned an informed consent, the patients were randomized into the FB or NFB condition in blocks of 8 and by gender. All the patients, in both conditions, filled in the OQ-45 online prior to each session. They were informed about their randomization condition after having completed the initial score. In this study, OQ-45 reports and alerts were generated by the OQ-Analyst software on a session-by-session basis each time a patient completed the measure. For the patients in the FB condition, the therapists were instructed to consider the feedback report, show it to the patient

Table I. Participants.

Clinic	Clinic description	Number of patients	Number of FB	Number of NFB	Female (%)	Number and % of the employed therapists participating
1	Outpatient	127	67	60	73	13/14 (93%)
2	Outpatient	40	26	14	63	13/60 (22%)
3	Outpatient	51	30	21	77	8/24 (33%)
4	Substance abuse, outpatient	11	5	6	46	5/16 (31%)
5	Inpatient	7	3	4	57	2/12 (17%)
6	Inpatient	23	13	10	52	4/9 (44%)
Total		259	144	115	69	45/135 (33%)

Note. FB = Feedback condition, NFB = No feedback condition.

every session, and discuss the report when useful or necessary. Although we do not know the extent to which therapists showed the reports to the patients, we have classified the trial as comparing FB to both therapists and patients to NFB (i.e., opposed to trials that restrict FB to the therapist only). No further specific instructions on how to use the feedback reports were given, but it was emphasized that the feedback reports should be opened, studied, shared, and used in a clinical useful way. The feedback reports on the NFB patients could not be opened by anyone other than the project leader.

Participants

Patients. During the inclusion period (June 2010–September 2013), a total of 377 adult patients referred to outpatient or inpatient treatment were invited to participate in the present study, as part of the clinic's intake procedures. No exclusion criteria other than the inability to complete the OQ-45, as determined by the therapist, were established. Of the eligible patients, 37 patients did not return a signed consent, either because they declined to participate, the therapist determined they were unable to complete the OQ-45, or the therapist forgot to ask them to complete the consent. The mean age of the patients was 35.8 years (*SD*: 11.66, range: 18–65) and 68% were female (Tables I and II).

The 340 patients initially consenting to participate were randomized to the FB or the NFB condition. At one of the sites, 19 patients were not randomized correctly and were therefore excluded from the sample, leaving 321 to be distributed to the two conditions. To be included in the analyses, a patient was required to have completed the OQ-45 for a minimum of two sessions representing the first and any subsequent session[1]. Over the course of the study, 14 patients in the FB and 15 in the NFB condition never completed the OQ-45; 16 patients in the FB and 17 in the NFB condition completed the OQ-45 only once. Thus, 259 patients constituted the sample used in this study with 144 in the FB and 115 in the NFB condition. Patient inclusion and exclusion are presented in Figure 1.

Patients seen in the clinics had a wide range of diagnoses and comorbidity, except in the substance abuse clinic where all patients had a substance abuse disorder as their primary diagnosis. All patients were diagnosed by their therapist using International Classification of Diseases (ICD-10). No inter-rater reliability procedures were conducted. The primary diagnoses, from the most frequent, were as follows: Various affective disorders (47%), anxiety disorders (33%), behavioral disorders (mainly Attention Deficit/Hyperactivity Disorder [ADHD], 7%), substance abuse (all from the substance abuse clinic, 4%), eating disorders (4%), personality disorders (3%), schizophrenia (1%), and no diagnosis (1%).

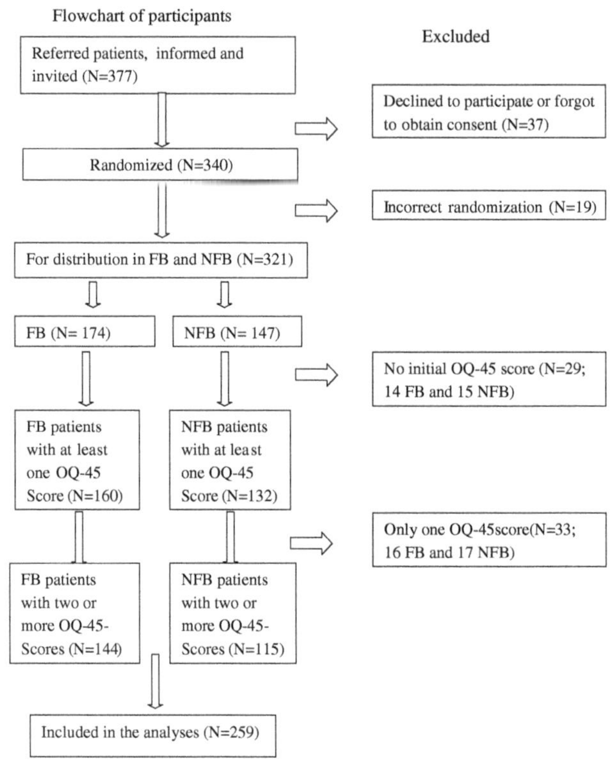

Figure 1. Flowchart of participants.

Therapists. In this study, 45 licensed therapists (Table I) employed at the six clinics participated. They provided a variety of theoretically guided treatments, including cognitive-behavioral, psychodynamic, and eclectic orientations. The mean age in the therapist group was 48.5 (*SD*: 9.54, range: 32–66), the mean years of experience as a therapist was 11.4 years (*SD*: 6.81, range: 1–31), 63% of the therapists were female and represented various professions, including psychologists (41%), medical doctors (18% psychiatrists and 15% MD in training), psychiatric nurses (16%), and others (10%). The participating therapists had between 1 and 39 patients in treatment, distributed on both FB and NFB condition with a mean number of patients of 6.1 (*SD*: 7.17).

Analyses

The primary analysis examined the effects of feedback (i.e., FB vs. NFB) with a general linear model, where the final OQ-45 score was the dependent variable and the first OQ-45 score was a covariate. To determine if the clinic affected the results, clinic was modeled as a random factor so that it could be determined whether the effects of feedback differed among clinics in general. It would not be surprising to find that the outcome of psychotherapy differed in the various clinics, given the differences in severity, diagnoses, and setting. To test whether effects of feedback differed among the clinics, the interaction of clinics and FB/NFB was tested. Because the effects of feedback have been found to be particularly apparent with signal cases (i.e., cases that received a yellow or red flag during the course of therapy), we examined signal cases and the interaction of signal cases and feedback.

Results

Demographics, means and standard deviations of the intake OQ-45 scores for the two conditions (FB and NFB), and percentage of signal cases are presented in Table II. There were no statistical differences between FB and NFB in the number of sessions ($t(257) = 0.41$, $p > .50$) nor in the proportion of signal cases ($\chi^2 = 0.12$, $p > .50$).

The results of the general linear model are presented in Table III. The main effect of feedback was statistical significant ($F = 3.80$, $p = .027$), corroborating the hypothesis that feedback would improve the quality of services. To assess the size of the effect for feedback, we calculated Cohen's *d* (Cohen, 1988; Durlak, 2009) for the post-test scores comparing FB to NFB for the entire sample and found that the effect size was 0.32 (Table II).

Not surprisingly, there was a main effect for clinic[2] and for signal cases, however no interaction effects occurred between sites and FB/NFB as well as between signal case/no signal case and FB/NFB, indicating that neither clinic or at risk status had a significant effect on whether feedback improved outcomes.

To illustrate the implications of the feedback effect, we classified all patients as recovered, improved, unchanged, or deteriorated. The clinical cut-off and the RCI were used to calculate how the patients in the FB and the NFB groups were distributed in these four different outcome groups. Patients were defined as recovered if their final OQ-45 score was in the non-clinical range (i.e., below 62) and the patients achieved reliable change (i.e., more than 16 points of change from initial to final OQ-45 score). Patients were classified as improved if their final OQ-45 score exhibited reliable change but remained in the clinical range. If the OQ-45 score increased by more than 16 points (i.e., reliable deterioration), the patient was classified as deteriorated. Patients who did not meet any of these criteria were defined as unchanged. The percentages in each category for FB and NFB are found in Table IV, where it is apparent that feedback increased the probability of improvement and reduced the probability of treatment failure.[3] There was no significant difference in the mean number of sessions between the two conditions (Table II, $p = .59$).

Table III. Results of general linear model predicting last OQ-45 score.

Variable	*F*	*df (n, d)*	*P*
Intercept	3.98	1,227	.047
OQ-45 first score	125.31	1,224	.000
Clinic (random)	5.55	5,5	.036
Signal case (vs. not signal case)	47.61	1,244	.000
Feedback (FB vs. NFB)	8.67	1,96	.004
Feedback × clinic	0.24	5,244	.947
Feedback × signal case	0.29	1,244	.588

Note. FB = Feedback condition, NFB = No feedback condition.

Discussion

The hypothesis that feedback would improve outcomes in psychotherapy was corroborated in a clinical trial that was conducted in a naturalistic setting in Norway. Not surprising, the main effect for clinic was statistically significant, indicating that some clinics exhibited more change than others, which is understandable given that some clinics were inpatient and one was a specialty clinic. However, the interaction of clinic and feedback was not significant, and importantly was negligible, indicating that the effect of feedback was not significantly different among the various clinics. Not surprising as well, there was a main effect for signal cases, with signal cases showing poorer outcomes than non-signal cases. The main finding of this study was consistent with the studies

Table II. Statistics for feedback and NFB conditions

	N	Female	Mean age	Mean first score	*SD*	Mean last score	*SD*	Mean number of sessions	SD	Signal cases (%)	Effect[a] FB vs. NFB
FB	144			91.0	18.0	75.5	28.6	9.7	8.6	41.0	
NFB	115			94.0	21.5	84.6	25.1	10.3	9.2	44.3	
Total	259	69%	35.8	92.3	20.2	79.5	27.4	9.9	8.9	42.5	0.32

[a]Cohen's *d*
Note. FB = Feedback condition, NFB = No feedback condition.

Table IV. Results classified by change status.

	FB-number	FB (%)	NFB-number	NFB (%)
Recovered	33	22.9	16	13.9
Improved	27	18.8	21	18.3
Unchanged	76	52.8	68	59.1
Deteriorated	8	5.6	10	8.7
Total	144	100.0	115	100.0

Note. FB = Feedback condition, NFB = No feedback condition.

reviewed by Shimokawa and Lambert (Lambert & Shimokawa, 2011b; Shimokawa et al., 2010)—that is, feedback improves outcomes. However, as opposed to many feedback trials, the feedback effect was present for patients making expected progress as well as for signal cases, as the interaction of signal cases and feedback was not significant. To our knowledge, only two OQ-45 studies have found a feedback effect for the entire sample and not just for the signal cases (e.g., Hawkins et al., 2004; Simon et al., 2013). The effect size of 0.32 would be classified as small to moderate and is less than the meta-analytic estimate of approximately 0.50 reported by Lambert and Shimokawa for not-on-track patients (Lambert & Shimokawa, 2011b; Shimokawa et al., 2010) but larger than the meta-analytic estimate (0.10) of Knaup, Koesters, Schoefer, Becker, and Puschner (2009), which was based on all patients (not restricted to signal cases). The effect from the present study was converted to a number needed to treat (NNT), which is the metric used in evidence-based medicine to judge the efficacy of a treatment (Kraemer & Kupfer, 2006). The NNT for this sample was six, which can be interpreted as follows: Six patients have to have been involved in a system of care with the OQ-Analyst to have one additional success in contrast to a system of care without the OQ-Analyst.

In the present study getting feedback did not change the mean session number, which could be interpreted in two ways: it does not change the retention rate or increases or reduces the necessary treatment length.

When comparing the results of the present study to other studies of the OQ-45 feedback, it is important to note several issues. First, the patients in the present sample were more distressed and diverse than was the case in other studies, particularly given that many OQ-45 feedback studies were conducted with students at a college counseling center. Interestingly, Hawkins et al. (2004) utilized a sample of patients with a similar level of distress as the present sample and found a significant effect for feedback to therapist and patients based on the entire sample, rather than only not-on-track patients. However, two other studies involving severely distressed patients (viz., Probst et al., 2013, with psychosomatic inpatients and Crits-Christoph et al., 2012 with substance abuse patients) found effects only for at-risk patients. Second, one of the two OQ-45 trials conducted outside the USA in a naturalistic outpatient setting found no effect for feedback for the system of care (de Jong et al., 2012), although they did find greater effects for feedback to both therapists and patients for not-on-track cases in short-term therapies (viz., treatments less than 35 weeks; de Jong et al., 2014), which would be treatments more comparable to the treatment provided in the present study. Third, the only other feedback study conducted in Norway found that feedback using the ORS also was effective (Anker et al., 2009).

At Clinic 1 (where the project leader and main coordinator worked), three times as many patients were included compared to Clinic 2 (127 vs. 40) (Table I), although the number of therapists participating was almost equal (13 vs. 12). This probably underlines the importance of having a dedicated local advocate monitoring and following up the procedures for using a feedback system and secure the daily operation of the system to succeed in implementing a feedback system in routine care.

Strengths of this study are the multisite design with ordinary psychiatric patients, the sample size, and the low attrition rate. We did not establish control routines to secure the therapists' adherence with the protocol. This can be regarded as a strength as this is the naturalistic setting using the system as it would be in usual care, but also as a limitation as we do not know how compliant the therapists were when it comes to opening and using the reports. Recall that de Jong et al. (2012) found that only patients of therapists who opened and used the reports benefited from feedback. On the other hand, the clinic where the project leader and the main project coordinator were employed and daily involved with the therapists did not produce greater feedback effects relative to clinics with more limited resources and less leader involvement.

At one of the clinics, there were short periods with an unstable Internet function (approximately 10 days in the 2 years in which data were collected), which had as a consequence that the patients were presented the paper/pencil format of the OQ-45, causing increased work load and delays in feedback for the FB condition, which might have attenuated the effects of feedback during this time period. The IT interruptions also may have limited the inclusion of patients at this clinic. A system like the OQ-Analyst is dependent on a stable and well-functioning Internet connection, and the availability of IT expertise is crucial when implementing an online feedback system.

There are also other limitations to the present study. First, as is the case in all feedback trials, blinding is not possible. In the present study that utilized a crossed design (i.e., therapists had patients in both conditions), the therapist is well aware of whether a particular patient was in the feedback condition or not. As well, patients were informed of their assignment and were involved in reviewing reports when their therapists followed the feedback protocol. Consequently, the effects of feedback may have been due to a Hawthorne effect (Jones, 1992) of being in the experimental condition. Not knowing how the therapists used the feedback precludes investigating mechanisms underlying the observed effect—that is, we do not know what happened in therapy that created improved outcomes. The diversity of the clinics renders the results of this study generalizable yet limits knowledge about how feedback might be used in various contexts. Of course, the lack of differences in the effects of feedback across clinics supports generalizability across various types of mental health services, although it is not clear that the manner in which feedback is used in one context (say outpatient) is similar to the way feedback is used in another context (say inpatient). Another limitation is that the trajectories used in this study were based on American samples and it is possible that Norwegian trajectories would have been different, although what seems to matter most in terms of trajectories is not related to much other than initial severity (Lambert et al., 2011; Wampold & Brown, 2005).

At five of the clinics, the therapists' participation was voluntary. All therapists were introduced to the OQ-Analyst and the related research results at an information meeting. Strikingly only about 25% of the therapists employed at the clinics (30 of 121, Table I) agreed to participate. It is possible that the research design deterred them from participating, and that they might have used the OQ-Analyst under routine care conditions, but it could also underline the experience that the implementation of a new tool is difficult and that therapists choose not to use feedback tools even if they are informed that this could help their patients getting a better outcome from therapy (Aoun, Pennebaker, & Janca, 2002; Walter, Cleary, & Rey, 1998; Willis, Deane, & Coombs, 2009). The relatively low participation rate of therapists limits understanding of how mandatory implementation in a system of care might fare, particularly when there is not an advocate of feedback leading the system (as was the case in the clinic in this study where use of the system was mandatory). Last, a limitation might be the lack of reliable diagnostic procedures excluding us from testing our hypothesis within different diagnostic groups.

Use of the OQ-Analyst as a monitoring system in psychotherapy with ordinary in- and outpatient psychiatric patients, many of whom were severely distressed, showed a significant effect for feedback to both patients and therapists compared with NFB. No differences between sites and on-track versus not-on-track patients (signal cases) were detected. This implies that a monitoring feedback system for psychotherapy with ordinary psychiatric patients appears to be viable regardless of setting and selection of patients. Nevertheless, the benefits of feedback have to be considered against the costs of implementation, including financial costs of the system, the costs of training, including opportunity costs, the time burden, the effects on the therapists within the system, reducing the therapists' fear and mistrust and the establishment of a necessary "local champion" to be responsible for the daily running of the system (Boswell, Kraus, Miller, & Lambert, 2013). Nevertheless, it should be noted that feedback is the only quality improvement strategy that has shown demonstrable benefits in rigorous clinical trials and thus should be considered an evidence-based strategy for improving the quality of mental health care (Laska, Gurman, & Wampold, 2013).

Notes

1 It could be asserted that feedback would not have an effect by session 2, as no progress has been measured, and therefore patients with only two sessions should be removed. The mechanisms of feedback have not been investigated sufficiently to claim that the patient would not benefit from the participating in feedback, due to the fact, for example, that they are encouraged by a therapist who cares about their progress. As well, previous studies have used patients with two observations (e.g., Hawkins et al., 2004). Nevertheless, we removed the 22 patients who had only two sessions and the results were essentially the same (viz., conclusions about statistical significance did not change for any effect tested).

2 An issue related to clinics is whether the outpatients and inpatients benefited from feedback differently. Because this contrast is not orthogonal from the primary analysis involving clinics, it is not reported here. However, we did conduct the analysis and the results showed no interaction effect of inpatient/outpatient and feedback.

3 We did not perform statistical tests of these proportions because they are redundant with the primary analysis that involved continuously distributed OQ-45 scores.

References

Amble, I., Gude, T., Stubdal, S., Oktedalen, T., Skjorten, A. M., Andersen, B. J., ... Wampold, B. E. (2013). Psychometric properties of the Outcome Questionnaire-45.2: The Norwegian version in an international context. *Psychotherapy Research*, 504–513. doi:10.1080/10503307.2013.849016

Anker, M. G., Duncan, B. L. et al. (2009). Using client feedback to improve couple therapy outcomes: A randomized clinical trial in a naturalistic setting. *Journal of Consulting and Clinical Psychology, 77*, 693–704. doi:10.1037/a0016062

Aoun, S., Pennebaker, D., & Janca, A. (2002). Outcome measurement in rural mental health care: A field trial of rooming-in models. *Australian Journal of Rural Health, 10*, 302–307. doi:10.1046/j.1440-1584.2002.00484.x

Barkham, M., Hardy, G. E., & Mellor-Clark, J. (2010). *Developing and delivenng practice-based evidence: A guide for the psychological therapies*. Chichester: Wiley Blackwell. doi:10.1002/9780470687994

Beretvas, S., Kearney, L. et al. (2003). A shortened form of the Outcome Questionnaire: A validation of scores across ethnic groups. *Published on line by the Counseling and Mind Health Center of Texas University.*

Bludworth, J. L., Tracey, T. J. G. et al. (2010). The bilevel structure of the Outcome Questionnaire–45. *Psychological Assessment, 22*, 350–355. doi:10.1037/a0019187

Boswell, J. F., Kraus, D. R., Miller, S. D., & Lambert, M. J. (2013). Implementing routine outcome monitoring in clinical practice: Benefits, challenges, and solutions. *Psychotherapy Research* (ahead-of-print), 1–14. doi:10.1080/10503307.2013.817696

Budge, S. L., Moore, J. T., Del Re, A. C., Wampold, B. E., Baardseth, T. P., & Nienhuis, J. B. (2013). The effectiveness of evidence-based treatments for personality disorders when comparing treatment-as-usual and bona fide treatments. *Clinical Psychology Review, 33*, 1057–1066. doi:10.1016/j.cpr.2013.08.003

Chambless, D. L., Sanderson, W. C., Shoham, V., Johnson, S. B., Pope, K. S., Crits-Christoph, P., ... McCurry, S. (1996). An update on empirically validated therapies. *The Clinical Psychologist, 49*(2), 5–18.

Chapman, J. E. (2003). *Reliability and validity of the progress questionnaire: An adaptation of the outcome questionnaire* (Doctoral dissertation), Drexel University, Philadelphia.

Chiappelli, M., Coco, G. L., Gullo, S., Bensi, L., & Prestano, C. (2008). The Outcome Questionnaire 45.2. Italian validation of an instrument for the assessment of phychological treatments. *Epidemiologia e Psichiatria Sociale* [Epidemiology and Social Psychiatry], *17*(2), 152–161.

Cohen, J. (1988). *Statistical power analysis for the behavioral sciencies*. East Sussex: Psychology Press.

Crits-Christoph, P., Ring-Kurtz, S., Hamilton, J. L., Lambert, M. J., Gallop, R., McClure, B., ... Rotrosen, J. (2012). A preliminary study of the effects of individual patient-level feedback in outpatient substance abuse treatment programs. *Journal of Substance Abuse Treatment, 42*, 301–309. doi:10.1016/j.jsat.2011.09.003

de Jong, K., Nugter, M. A., Polak, M. G., Wagenborg, J. E. A., Spinhoven, P., & Heiser, W. J. (2007). The Outcome Questionnaire (OQ-45) in a Dutch population: A cross-cultural validation. *Clinical Psychology & Psychotherapy, 14*, 288–301. doi:10.1002/cpp.529

de Jong, K., Timman, R., Hakkaart-Van Roijen, L., Vermeulen, P., Kooiman, K., Passchier, J., & van Busschbach, J. (2014). *The effect of outcome monitoring feedback to clinicians and patients in short and long-term psychotherapy: A randomized controlled trial. Psychotherapy Research*. doi:10.1080/10503307.2013.871079

de Jong, K., van Sluis, P., Nugter, M. A., Heiser, W. J., & Spinhoven, P. (2012). Understanding the differential impact of outcome monitoring: Therapist variables that moderate feedback effects in a randomized clinical trial. *Psychotherapy Research, 22*, 464–474. doi:10.1080/10503307.2012.673023

Durlak, J. A. (2009). How to select, calculate, and interpret effect sizes. *Journal of Pediatric Psychology, 34*, 917–928. doi:10.1093/jpepsy/jsp004

Evans, C., Connell, J., Barkham, M., Margison, F., McGRATH, G., Mellor-Clark, J., & Audin, K. (2002). Towards a standardised brief outcome measure: Psychometric properties and utility of the CORE—OM. *The British Journal of Psychiatry, 180*(1), 51–60. doi:10.1192/bjp.180.1.51

Fonagy, P., Roth, A., & Higgitt, A. (2005). The outcome of psychodynamic psychotherapy for psychological disorders. *Clinical Neuroscience Research, 4*, 367–377. doi:10.1016/j.cnr.2005.03.005

Hansen, N. B., & Lambert, M. J. (2003). An evaluation of the dose–response relationship in naturalistic treatment settings using survival analysis. *Mental Health Services Research, 5*(1), 1–12. doi:10.1023/A:1021751307358

Hansen, N. B., Lambert, M. J., & Forman, E. M. (2002). The psychotherapy dose-response effect and its implications for treatment delivery services. *Clinical Psychology: Science and Practice, 9*, 329–343. doi:10.1093/clipsy.9.3.329

Hatfield, D. R., & Ogles, B. M. (2004). The use of outcome measures by psychologists in clinical practice. *Professional Psychology: Research and Practice, 35*, 485–491. doi:10.1037/0735-7028.35.5.485

Hawkins, E. J., Lambert, M. J., Vermeersch, D. A., Slade, K. L., & Tuttle, K. C. (2004). The therapeutic effects of providing patient progress information to therapists and patients. *Psychotherapy Research, 14*, 308–327. doi:10.1093/ptr/kph027

Jones, S. R. G. (1992). Was there a Hawthorne effect? *American Journal of Sociology, 98*, 451–468. doi:10.1086/230046

Kim, S.-H., Beretvas, S. N., & Sherry, A. R. (2010). A validation of the factor structure of OQ-45 scores using factor mixture modeling. *Measurement and Evaluation in Counseling and Development, 42*, 275–295. doi:10.1177/0748175609354616

Knaup, C., Koesters, M., Schoefer, D., Becker, T., & Puschner, B. (2009). Effect of feedback of treatment outcome in specialist mental healthcare: Meta-analysis. *The British Journal of Psychiatry, 195*(1), 15–22. doi:10.1192/bjp.bp.108.053967

Kraemer, H. C., & Kupfer, D. J. (2006). Size of treatment effects and their importance to clinical research and practice. *Biological Psychiatry, 59*, 990–996. doi:10.1016/j.biopsych.2005.09.014

Lambert, M. J. (2010). *Prevention of treatment failure: The use of measuring, monitoring, and feedback in clinical practice*. Washington, DC: American Psychological Association.

Lambert, M. J. (2013). *Bergin and Garfield's handbook of psychotherapy and behavior change*. New York, NY: John Wiley & Sons.

Lambert, M., & Ogles, B. (2004). The efficacy and effectiveness of psychotherapy. In M. J. Lambert (Ed.), *Bergin and Garfield's handbook of psychotherapy and behaviour change* (pp. 139–193). Chichester: John Wiley & Sons.

Lambert, M. J., & Shimokawa, K. (2011a). Measuring client outcome. In J. C. Norcross (Ed.), *Psychotherapy relationships that work: Evidence-based responsiveness* (2nd ed., pp. 203–223). New York, NY: Oxford University Press.

Lambert, M. J., & Shimokawa, K. (2011b). Collecting client feedback. *Psychotherapy, 48*(1), 72–79. doi:10.1037/a0022238

Lambert, M. J., Kahler, M., Harmon, C., Burlingame, G. M. (2011). Administration and Scoring Manual Outcome Questionnaire OQ-45.2. (OQ Measures L.L.C.).

Lambert, M. J., Burlingame, G. M., Umphress, V., Hansen, N. B., Vermeersch, D. A., Clouse, G. C., & Yanchar, S. C. (1996). The reliability and validity of the Outcome Questionnaire. *Clinical Psychology & Psychotherapy, 3*, 249–258. doi:10.1002/(SICI)1099-0879(199612)3:4<249::AID-CPP106>3.0.CO;2-S

Lambert, M. J., Hannöver, W., Nisslmüller, K., Richard, M., & Kordy, H. (2002). Fragebogen zum Ergebnis von Psychotherapie [Questionnaire on the results of psychotherapy: Reliability and validity of the German translation of the Outcome Questionnaire 45.2 (OQ-45.2)]. *Zeitschrift für klinische Psychologie und Psychotherapie* [Journal of Clinical Psychology and Psychotherapy], *31*(1), 40–46. doi:10.1026//1616-3443.31.1.40

Laska, K. M., Gurman, A. S., & Wampold, B. E. (2013). Expanding the lens of evidence-based practice in psychotherapy:

A common factors perspective. *Psychotherapy* [Epub ahead of print].

Lo Coco, G., Chiappelli, M., Bensi, L., Gullo, S., Prestano, C., & Lambert, M. J. (2008). The factorial structure of the outcome questionnaire-45: A study with an Italian sample. *Clinical Psychology & Psychotherapy, 15*, 418–423. doi:10.1002/cpp.601

McAleavey, A. A., Nordberg, S. S., Hayes, J. A., Castonguay, L. G., Locke, B. D., & Lockard, A. J. (2012). Clinical validity of the Counseling Center Assessment of Psychological Symptoms-62 (CCAPS-62): Further evaluation and clinical applications. *Journal of Counseling Psychology, 59*, 575–590. doi:10.1037/a0029855

Miller, S. D., Duncan, B. L., Sorrell, R., & Brown, G. S. (2005). The partners for change outcome management system. *Journal of Clinical Psychology, 61*(2), 199–208.

Mueller, R. M., Lambert, M. J. et al. (1998). Construct validity of the Outcome Questionnaire: A confirmatory factor analysis. *Journal of Personality Assessment, 70*, 248–262. doi:10.1207/s15327752jpa7002_5

Mohr, D. C. (1995). Negative outcome in psychotherapy: A critical review. *Clinical Psychology: Science and Practice, 2*(1), 1–27. doi:10.1111/j.1468-2850.1995.tb00022.x

Pinsof, W. M., Zinbarg, R. E., Lebow, J. L., Knobloch-Fedders, L. M., Durbin, E., Chambers, A., … Friedman, G. (2009). Laying the foundation for progress research in family, couple, and individual therapy: The development and psychometric features of the initial Systemic Therapy Inventory of Change. *Psychotherapy Research, 19*(2), 143–156. doi:10.1080/10503300802669973

Probst, T., Lambert, M. J., Loew, T. H., Dahlbender, R. W., Göllner, R., & Tritt, K. (2013). Feedback on patient progress and clinical support tools for therapists: Improved outcome for patients at risk of treatment failure in psychosomatic in-patient therapy under the conditions of routine practice. *Journal of Psychosomatic Research, 75*, 255–261. doi:10.1016/j.jpsychores.2013.07.003

Qin, Y.-f., & Hu, S.-j. (2008). Usability report of outcome Questionnaire-45 in part of Chinese sample. *Chinese Journal of Clinical Psychology, 16*, 138–140.

Shafran, R., Clark, D. M., Fairburn, C. G., Arntz, A., Barlow, D. H., Ehlers, A., … Wilson, G. T. (2009). Mind the gap: Improving the dissemination of CBT. *Behaviour Research and Therapy, 47*, 902–909. doi:10.1016/j.brat.2009.07.003

Shimokawa, K., Lambert, M. J., & Smart, D. W. (2010). Enhancing treatment outcome of patients at risk of treatment failure: Meta-analytic and mega-analytic review of a psychotherapy quality assurance system. *Journal of Consulting and Clinical Psychology, 78*, 298–311. doi:10.1037/a0019247

Simon, W., Lambert, M. J., Busath, G., Vazquez, A., Berkeljon, A., Hyer, K., … Berrett, M. (2013). Effects of providing patient progress feedback and clinical support tools to psychotherapists in an inpatient eating disorders treatment program: A randomized controlled study. *Psychotherapy Research, 23*, 287–300. doi:10.1080/10503307.2013.787497

Simon, W., Lambert, M. J., Harris, M. W., Busath, G., & Vazquez, A. (2012). Providing patient progress information and clinical support tools to therapists: Effects on patients at risk of treatment failure. *Psychotherapy Research, 22*, 638–647. doi:10.1080/10503307.2012.698918

Spielmans, G. I., Gatlin, E. T., & McFall, J. P. (2010). The efficacy of evidence-based psychotherapies versus usual care for youths: Controlling confounds in a meta-reanalysis. *Psychotherapy Research, 20*, 234–246. doi:10.1080/10503300903311293

Walter, G., Cleary, M., & Rey, J. (1998). Attitudes of mental health personnel towards rating outcome. *Journal of Quality in Clinical Practice, 18*(2), 109.

Wampold, B. E., & Brown, G. S. (2005). Estimating therapist variability: A naturalistic study of outcomes in managed care. *Journal of Consulting and Clinical Psychology, 73*, 914–923. doi:10.1037/0022-006X.73.5.914

Wampold, B. E., Budge, S. L., Laska, K. M., Del Re, A. C., Baardseth, T. P., Flückiger, C., … Gunn, W. (2011). Evidence-based treatments for depression and anxiety versus treatment-as-usual: A meta-analysis of direct comparisons. *Clinical Psychology Review, 31*, 1304–1312. doi:10.1016/j.cpr.2011.07.012

Weisz, J. R., Jensen-Doss, A., & Hawley, K. M. (2006). Evidence-based youth psychotherapies versus usual clinical care: A meta-analysis of direct comparisons. *American Psychologist, 61*, 671–689. doi:10.1037/0003-066X.61.7.671

Wennberg, P., Philips, B., & Jong, K. (2010). The Swedish version of the Outcome Questionnaire (OQ-45): Reliability and factor structure in a substance abuse sample. *Psychology and Psychotherapy: Theory, Research and Practice, 83*, 325–329. doi:10.1348/147608309X478715

Willis, A., Deane, F. P., & Coombs, T. (2009). Improving clinicians' attitudes toward providing feedback on routine outcome assessments. *International Journal of Mental Health Nursing, 18*, 211–215. doi:10.1111/j.1447-0349.2009.00596.x

Feedback mechanisms of change: How problem alerts reported by youth clients and their caregivers impact clinician-reported session content

SUSAN R. DOUGLAS[1†], BAE JONGHYUK[2], ANA REGINA VIDES DE ANDRADE[2], M. MICHELE TOMLINSON[3], RYAN PAMELA HARGRAVES[4], & LEONARD BICKMAN[1]

[1]*Department of Psychology and Human Development, Vanderbilt University, Nashville, TN, USA;* [2]*Department of Economics, Vanderbilt University, Nashville, TN, USA;* [3]*Hope Network, Grand Rapids, Michigan &* [4]*Emma, Nashville, Tennessee*

Abstract

Objective. This study explored how clinician-reported content addressed in treatment sessions was predicted by clinician feedback group and multi-informant cumulative problem alerts that appeared in computerized feedback reports for 299 clients aged 11–18 years receiving home-based community mental health treatment. *Method.* Measures included a clinician report of content addressed in sessions and additional measures of treatment progress and process (e.g., therapeutic alliance) completed by clinicians, clients, and their caregivers. Item responses in the top 25th percentile in severity from these measures appeared as "problem alerts" on corresponding computerized feedback reports. Clinicians randomized to the feedback group received feedback weekly while the control group did not. Analyses were conducted using the Cox proportional hazards regression for recurrent events. *Results.* For all content domains, the results of the survival analyses indicated a robust effect of the feedback group on addressing specific content in sessions, with feedback associated with shorter duration to first occurrence and increased likelihood of addressing or focusing on a topic compared to the non-feedback group. *Conclusion.* There appears to be an important relationship between feedback and cumulative problem alerts reported by multiple informants as they influence session content.

While not yet widespread, there is growing evidence that providing clinicians with feedback about client treatment progress improves outcomes for youth and adult clients (e.g., Bickman, Douglas Kelley, Breda, de Andrade, & Riemer, 2011; Bickman et al., 2015; Chorpita, Bernstein, & Daleiden, 2011; Chorpita, Bernstein, Daleiden, & the Research Network on Youth Mental Health, 2008; Knaup, Koesters, Schoefer, Becker, & Puschner, 2009; Lambert, Harmon, Slade, Whipple, & Hawkins, 2005; Lambert et al., 2003; Shimokawa, Lambert, & Smart, 2010). In comparison, the use of systematic feedback to improve outcomes has been a proven quality improvement tool for decades in related fields, such as management, education, and health care (e.g., Kluger & DeNisi, 1996). Based on the available evidence to date, it has been recommended that greater use of outcome monitoring and feedback should occur in everyday mental health practice (APA Presidential Task Force on Evidence-Based Practice, 2006; Kazdin, 2008; Weisz, Ng, & Bearman, 2014).

Feedback is a foundational element of an evidence-based practice approach, which calls for the integration of research evidence with clinical decision-making and contextual factors associated with the client and setting (APA Presidential Task Force on Evidence-Based Practice, 2006). The current position in psychotherapy research generally

[†]Note: Susan Douglas has been previously published as Susan Douglas Kelley.

supports the benefits of routine outcome monitoring and feedback (e.g., Shimokawa et al., 2010; Youn, Kraus, & Castonguay, 2012), albeit with some caveats because the challenges in implementation may be substantial. For example, in addition to practical considerations like time burden and resources, mental health clinicians may overestimate their own abilities to assess treatment progress and outcomes based on clinical judgment leading to lower utilization of outcome management systems (Boswell, Kraus, Miller, & Lambert, 2015). Importantly, we do not yet know enough about the mechanisms of action and role-relationship implications of using routine outcome monitoring and feedback to inform performance evaluations (Evans, 2012; Noell & Gansle, 2014).

While the concept of using feedback to influence behavior makes intuitive sense, the design and implementation of feedback interventions must be approached with caution to avoid detrimental effects. For example, over a third of feedback interventions in Kluger and DeNisi's (1996) meta-analysis actually resulted in poorer performance. Comprehensive theories of feedback interventions integrate information from social and cognitive psychology, organizational theory, and management (Kluger & DeNisi, 1996; Riemer & Bickman, 2011; Riemer, Rosof-Williams, & Bickman, 2005). However, there is little research evidence about what characteristics of feedback interventions in mental health are most effective in influencing behavior. Critical issues to explore further are feedback delivery schedules and procedures (e.g., actual mechanisms like technology or mixed technology and paper, the visual presentation like graphics, etc.), to whom feedback is provided, and the sources of data that inform the feedback (Kluger & DeNisi, 1996; Noell & Gansle, 2014). In addition, there are also client, clinician, and setting characteristics to consider, particularly as they influence implementation (de Jong, 2014).

Promising characteristics of feedback include greater frequency of feedback (weekly or biweekly) and the inclusion of information on treatment progress. In addition, it has been recommended that feedback is most effective when data collection is simple, flexible, and transparent and the feedback is specific, accepted as valid, and actionable (Boswell et al., 2015; Cannon & Witherspoon, 2005; Knaup et al., 2009; Riemer & Bickman, 2011). By actionable, we mean that specific feedback elements are linked to actions that can be taken in response, as in a clinical support tool or a recommended behavior by a supervisor.

Feedback is intended to improve the accuracy of clinicians' judgments about client progress thus enabling them to better tailor treatment activities consistent with the client's progress (or lack thereof). For example, Worthen and Lambert (2007) hypothesized that feedback from clients influenced clinical outcomes by providing clinicians with information that they may have unintentionally overlooked or underemphasized while also identifying problems within domains that could jeopardize progress. This is a particularly important feature of feedback, given the poor accuracy of clinicians in predicting or identifying client deterioration (Hannan et al., 2005; Hatfield, McCullough, Frantz, & Krieger, 2009) and low agreement between clinicians and clients on the focus of treatment (Hawley & Weisz, 2003). As Kazdin (2008) stated, clinicians are "researchers in the sense of hypothesizing that a particular treatment combination will have particular effects and testing this hypothesis with the individual case" (p. 155). Feedback can provide systematic data to enhance, not replace, clinical decision-making.

We know little about how feedback affects clinical decision-making and clinician behavior in treatment sessions (Lambert et al., 2003) or in supervision (Sparks, Kisler, Adams, & Blumen, 2011; Worthen & Lambert, 2007). Thus, we can only speculate about how feedback influences outcomes. As a result of feedback, clinicians may address the feedback directly with the client; change their case conceptualization and resulting interventions to introduce into treatment; delay discharge due to new concerns; become more attentive to a client; discuss feedback within supervision sessions in order to increase awareness of the treatment process; or they may ignore the feedback altogether. What these actions have in common is that the clinician is central to linking feedback to client outcomes. Understanding how clinician behavior is influenced by feedback is an important next step in advancing the use of feedback to improve client outcomes.

For youth clients, it is unknown how clinicians may change their behavior based on feedback from different sources about the same client. While clinicians generally value the client's and family's perspectives, there can be doubts about the perceived validity of their feedback due to competing motives (e.g., an adolescent understates symptoms in order to discontinue treatment) or lack of insight into one's own problems (Riemer & Bickman, 2011; Sapyta, Riemer, & Bickman, 2005). A better understanding of how session content may be correlated with problems reported by the youth and caregiver should provide some insight into how feedback influences clinician behavior.

The current study was intended as the next step to build on previous findings (Douglas Kelley, Vides de Andrade, Bickman, & Robin, 2012; Douglas Kelley,

Vides de Andrade, Sheffer, & Bickman, 2010) and is part of a larger study investigating the effects of feedback to clinicians on clinician behavior and client outcomes in community youth mental health treatment. The intervention is called Contextualized Feedback Systems (CFS). The effectiveness of CFS has been established in two longitudinal randomized experiments, one where randomization occurred at the site level (Bickman et al., 2011) and other where randomization occurred at the client level (Bickman et al., 2015). Both studies found an effect of feedback on client outcomes for youths receiving home-based and outpatient mental health services, respectively. The purpose of this study was to explore how clinician-reported content addressed in treatment sessions was predicted by clinician feedback group and multi-informant cumulative problem alerts that appeared in computerized feedback reports.

The current study has three aims: To explore whether feedback impacts (i) the likelihood of addressing content in sessions per clinician's report; (ii) the timeliness of addressing content in sessions; and (iii) session content differentially based on the presence of dynamic problem-specific severity. Two hypotheses were proposed. First, it is anticipated that the relative likelihood of addressing content will be higher for clients whose clinicians were in the feedback condition compared to the non-feedback condition. Second, it is hypothesized that the time to addressing content will be shorter for clients whose clinicians were in the feedback condition compared to the non-feedback condition. Both of these hypotheses are predicated on the possibility of increased awareness of client problems based on viewing related problem alerts in the feedback reports. The third aim is exploratory and was partially based on previous findings from the Douglas Kelley et al. (2012) study, which found session content correlated differently based on type of problem and reporter.

Methods

Feedback Intervention

CFS has been described in detail elsewhere (Bickman et al., 2011, 2015). Feedback intervention characteristics included weekly clinical feedback to clinicians on youth treatment progress (e.g., symptoms and functioning) and treatment process (e.g., therapeutic alliance) intended to alert clinicians to youth or caregiver problems they may not have perceived or ignored, to assist in assessing client progress so as to inform treatment plans and goals, and to enhance dialogue and case understanding in clinical supervision. In training and ongoing support for clinicians in the feedback group, clinicians were taught how to interpret feedback reports where problem alerts were present. Specifically, they were asked to consider the clinical utility of incorporating the feedback in the very next session by addressing any alerts that were unexpected or indicated a decline in treatment progress or process. The development and refinement of CFS was a user-centered collaboration between researchers and practitioners (Bickman, Douglas Kelley, & Athay, 2012; Riemer, Douglas Kelley, Casey, & Taylor Haynes, 2012). CFS implementation training and support was designed to emphasize integration with clinical values and workflow, promote administrative leadership, and facilitate sustainability by encouraging innovation (Douglas, Button, & Casey, 2014).

Procedures

The Peabody Treatment Progress Battery (PTPB; Bickman et al., 2010) measures were administered using paper and pencil forms at the close of treatment sessions. Respondents were instructed to complete measures privately, which were then placed into an envelope that was then sealed. Thus, the administration was designed so that problem alerts and other feedback would not be accessible except to clinicians in the feedback group when they viewed feedback reports on their computers. As soon as an administrative assistant data entered the measures into a computer, feedback reports became automatically available for viewing by clinicians in the feedback condition. Feedback viewing was recorded within the CFS application, with approximately one-third (35%) of the clinicians in the feedback group who did not view any feedback reports. On average, clinicians in the feedback group who viewed at least one report viewed 41% ($SD = 27\%$) of reports, with viewing rates ranging from 2% to 100%.

Clinicians completed the Session Report Form (SRF; Douglas Kelley et al., 2010) at the close of each session, documenting whether they addressed, focused on, or did not address SRF topics as part of that treatment encounter. In addition, all participants in the session (clients, caregivers, and clinicians) completed the scheduled PTPB measures relevant to treatment progress and process resulting in item-level problem alerts corresponding to specific SRF topics. Notably, the problem alerts that were contained in feedback reports were lagged, meaning that they included all previous item alerts up to but not including that session when the SRF was completed. However, because of the possibility the completion of measures spurred conversation in the session, a conservative approach was used where the cumulative problem alert variables were created to include all previous item alerts up to and including that session. The Vanderbilt University Institutional Review Board approved all procedures with a waiver of informed consent.

Participants

Participants were drawn from the larger study that first evaluated the effects of CFS on youth outcomes (Bickman et al., 2011). They are the same subsample used in the previous study (Douglas Kelley et al., 2012) that explored the relationship between clinician-reported session content and concurrent multi-informant problem alerts. All clients had presenting problems encompassing a range of common youth mental health issues (e.g., mood and anxiety disorders, school problems, oppositional behavior, and impulsivity/attention deficit disorders) and were receiving "treatment as usual" mental health care, typically in home-based settings.

Twenty-eight sites in 10 states were included in the larger study, with randomization to the feedback or non-feedback conditions occurring at the site level. There were no baseline differences between the feedback and non-feedback conditions on demographic and background characteristics for clinicians, with one significant finding for youths and caregivers (there were more black and fewer white youths and caregivers in the feedback group compared to the control condition; Bickman et al., 2011). To be included in the current study, youths from the larger evaluation sample had to be new clients receiving home-based counseling with at least one session where the clinician completed the SRF measure. A total of 299 clients aged 11–18 years were included, with a total of 3143 sessions with SRFs completed by 133 clinicians. Table I shows client's background characteristics by randomized condition. Similar to the initial evaluation study there were no significant differences at the adjusted p-value (< 0.01) with the exception of client and caregiver race (see Bickman et al., 2011, for more details on caregiver and clinician background characteristics).

Measures

The SRF (Douglas Kelley et al., 2010) is a 25-item self-report measure developed collaboratively by a team of clinicians and researchers. Previous analyses of the SRF indicate some evidence of a distinct subscale of treatment process using principal components analysis (Cronbach's alpha = 0.81). There is also evidence of content validity with an adequate range of topics related to session content as well as discrimination in patterns of client and clinician topics addressed. The SRF was completed by clinicians as part of the documentation associated with a specific treatment session (e.g., progress notes), and is intended to be completed at the end of each session. It is part of the larger *PTPB* of measures of youth treatment process and progress (Bickman et al., 2010). In addition to items describing session characteristics (i.e. who participated, length and location of the session, rating of the session, and time spent in crisis), the SRF contains 20 content domains that could be addressed as part of the session. For each content domain (e.g., emotional issues and family issues) the clinician reported whether the topic was not addressed, addressed in, or a focus of the session. For this study, responses were recoded as binary variables (not addressed vs. addressed/focus).

Almost all topics corresponded to other measures in the PTPB. For example, the SRF topic "emotional issues" is a content domain that related to 13 items related to internalizing symptoms reported by the youth, caregiver, and clinician on the measure of youth symptoms and functioning shown in Table II. All of the PTPB measures have excellent psychometric properties with strong evidence of reliability, evidence for construct validity including estimates of factorial and discriminant validity for all measures and concurrent validity for the Symptoms and Functioning Severity Scale (SFSS) (Bickman & Athay, 2012; Bickman et al., 2010). Internal consistency statistics are provided in the footnotes for Table II. Table II presents the PTPB measures that were sources for multi-informant problem alerts. Items were rated as "problem alerts" when the response was in the top 25% of the distribution of item severity from the psychometric sample (Bickman et al., 2010). Problem alerts are item- and informant-specific. Thus, where there were multiple informants of a measure, whether or not an item counted as a problem alert could differ by respondent.

Analytic Approach

Data were available at the session level. Because feedback reports included item alerts prior to the session, the analytic models had to account for cumulative item alerts as a lagged time-varying covariate. Cumulative item alerts was coded as 1 where one or more item alerts existed for sessions prior and up to that particular SRF administration and 0 for no previous item alerts. The other independent variable, feedback group, was constant, coded as 0 for the non-feedback condition and 1 for the feedback condition. The

Table I. Baseline characteristics of clients ($N = 299$) participating in the study.

	Control group ($N = 149$)		Feedback group ($N = 150$)	
Characteristic	*N*	%	*N*	%
Gender				
Female	75	52	68	46
Male	68	48	81	54
Ethnicity				
Hispanic or Latino	11	10	19	16
Not Hispanic or Latino	104	90	99	84
Race				
White	83	67	64	47
Nonwhite	41	33	71	53
American Indian or Alaska Native	3	2	1	1
Black or African-American	22	18	37	27
More than one race	13	11	21	16
Other	3	2	12	9
Age (mean ± *SD* years)	15.03 ± 1.82		14.52 ± 1.75	
Baseline SFSS (mean ± *SD* score)[a]				
Youth	2.33 ± 0.64		2.37 ± 0.71	
Caregiver	2.53 ± 0.74		2.59 ± 0.73	
Clinician	2.26 ± 0.56		2.41 ± 0.52	
Number of sessions (mean ± *SD*)	10.88 ± 9.70		10.15 ± 8.07	
Number of weeks in CFS (mean ± *SD*)	19.74 ± 15.35		16.93 ± 10.61	

[a]Possible scores for the SFSS range from 1 to 5, with higher scores indicating greater severity.

interaction term was the product of multiplying the two variables. The dependent variables of interest were the 18 SRF topic variables that were coded as 0 for not addressed and 1 for addressed in or a focus of the session. Although clinicians could discriminate topics that were simply addressed from those that were a focus of the session, these responses were combined to create a binary variable to simplify the statistical models.

Since the dependent variable could be considered as recurrent events that may or may not occur repeatedly throughout the observation period, we used survival analysis of repeated events (Hosmer, Lemeshow, & May, 2008; Twisk, Smidt, & de Vente, 2005). The estimation method used was the Cox proportional hazards for recurrent events model, which is a common method used to analyze time to success or failure (i.e. occurrence of the event) separately for repeated events, adjusted for the clustering of time periods within clients. This model is a multivariate approach and treats each recurrent event as identical. The counting approach was used, where each time period was analyzed separately with the assumption that clients were at risk each time irrespective of whether the event occurred in the prior time period (Twisk et al., 2005). The robust standard error was reported to account for the nesting of recurrent events within clients. Each model results in output that includes a regression coefficient and a hazard ratio. The regression coefficient represents the duration to occurrence of a failure event, defined here as the topic being addressed/focused upon in the session.[1] A positive coefficient means a shorter duration and a negative coefficient means a longer duration. The hazard ratio is the exponent of the coefficient, with hazard ratios above 1.0 representing increased likelihood of addressing/focusing on a topic and those below 1.0 representing reduced likelihood.

For each independent variable, five models were estimated. The first was the simple model, which estimated the relative likelihood of addressing/focusing on a topic based on randomized condition of clinicians to the feedback group or the non-feedback group. The second was the adjusted model with two covariates, which estimated the relative likelihood of addressing/focusing on a topic for feedback group adjusting for cumulative problem alerts and vice versa. The third was the interaction model with the two covariates and their interaction. The null group is the non-feedback condition with a value of 0 (feedback group = 0 times cumulative problem alerts = 0). The treatment group is the feedback condition with a value equal to the cumulative problem alerts (feedback group = 1 times cumulative problem alerts = cumulative problem alerts). As per Hosmer et al.'s (2008) recommendations, the three models were compared and the most complete model that reached significance was chosen for interpretation (shaded in grey in the tables in the results section). The second and third models were run with two sets of variables (clinician-reported

Table II. PTPB measure sources of session problem alerts by SRF topic and informant.

SRF Topic	Informant[a]	Measure[b]	Administration schedule	# Problem alert items[c]	Likert scale for items[c]
Emotional issues	Y, Cg, Cl	SFSS	Even weeks	13	1–5 (high)
Behavioral issues	Y, Cg, Cl	SFSS	Even weeks	16	1–5 (high)
Family issues	Y, Cg, Cl	SFSS	Even weeks	4	1–5 (high)
School/work issues	Y, Cg, Cl	SFSS	Even weeks	3	1–5 (high)
Friends/peer issues	Y, Cg, Cl	SFSS	Even weeks	6	1–5 (high)
Problems w/delinquent behavior	Y, Cg, Cl	SFSS	Even weeks	3	1–5 (high)
Alcohol/substance use	Y, Cg, Cl	SFSS	Even weeks	2	1–5 (high)
Harm to self or others	Cl	SFSS	Even weeks	1	1–5 (high)
Client hope for future	Y	CHS-PTPB	Once/quarter	4	1–6 (low)
Client motivation for treatment	Y	MYTS	Twice/quarter	4	1–5 (low)
Therapeutic relationship w/client	Y	TAQS	Odd weeks	5	1–5 (low)
Client perceptions on counseling impact	Y	YCIS	Odd weeks	6	1–5 (low)
Client satisfaction w/services	Y	SSS	Once/quarter	4	1–4 (low)
Caregiver strain	Cg	CGSQ-SF7	Once/quarter	7	1–5 (high)
Caregiver satisfaction w/life	Cg	SWLS	Twice/quarter	5	1–7 (low)
Caregiver motivation for youth treatment	Cg	MYTS	Twice/quarter	7	1–5 (low)
Therapeutic relationship w/caregiver	Cg	TAQS	Odd weeks	5	1–5 (low)
Caregiver satisfaction w/services	Cg	SSS	Once/quarter	4	1–4 (low)

[a]Y, Youth; Cg, caregiver; Cl, clinician.
[b]SFSS, *Symptoms and Functioning Severity Scale* (Cronbach's alpha = 0.92–0.94 depending on informant; Athay, Riemer, & Bickman, 2012); CHS-PTPB, *Children's Hope Questionnaire-Revised PTPB edition* (Cronbach's alpha = 0.87; Dew-Reeves, Athay, & Kelley, 2012); MYTS, *Motivation for Youth's Treatment Scale* (Cronbach's alpha = 0.82–0.84 depending on informant; Breda & Riemer, 2012); TAQS, *Therapeutic Alliance Quality Scale* (Cronbach's alpha = 0.85; Bickman et al., 2012); YCIS, *Youth Counseling Impact Scale* (Cronbach's alpha = 0.90; Kearns, Athay, & Riemer, 2012); SSS, *Service Satisfaction Scale* (Cronbach's alpha = 0.85–0.86 depending on informant; Athay & Bickman, 2012); CGSQ, *Caregiver Strain Questionnaire-SF7* (Cronbach's alpha=0.89; Brannan, Athay, & Vides de Andrade, 2012); SWLS, *Satisfaction with Life Scale* (Cronbach's alpha = 0.89; Athay, 2012).
[c]Problem alert are items rated at the top 25% of the distribution of item severity from the psychometric sample described in the PTPB manual (Bickman et al., 2010). For all measures, response choices were Likert-type items with varied scales. The directionality of the Likert scales for each measure is indicated by low (lower scores are more severe) or high (higher scores are more severe).

problem alerts, combined client/caregiver-reported problem alerts) for a total of five models per variable. To adjust for the number of models, the p-value was adjusted to $<0.05/5$ or < 0.01. Kaplan–Meier plots were produced to aid in interpreting the regression coefficients that were used to determine the effect of feedback on time to first addressing/focusing on a topic.

Results

Table III presents descriptive information for all clients on both session content that was addressed or focused upon in sessions and cumulative problem alerts (reported by the clinician and the combined client/caregiver) by the SRF topic. As can be seen in the first column on session content by topic, there were very few clients with missing data points for the dependent variable (1–3% of clients had a missing SRF topic). The frequency of session content being addressed/focused on in sessions varied by topic. Of note, there was wide variation in missing data for problem alerts. While the large majority of clients (90–94% depending on reporter) had data for the first 9 topics that corresponded to the SFSS, the percentage of clients with non-missing data for treatment process and caregiver-related topics (the last 9 topics) ranged from 32% to 90%. This was largely because those measures were typically scheduled less frequently (Table II).

A series of independent samples t-tests (equal variances not assumed) were conducted to determine whether there were any significant differences by feedback group for the cumulative problem alert variables. None approached significance at the adjusted p-value of < 0.01.

The regression coefficients were significantly positive ($p < 0.05$) for almost all topics with the exception of problems with delinquent behavior and alcohol/substance use. This means that for 16 of the 18 topics, the time to addressing content was shorter for clients whose clinicians were in the feedback condition compared to the non-feedback condition. To

Table III. Descriptive information for all clients ($N = 299$) on session content addressed/focused upon and cumulative problem alerts (reported by clinician or combined client and/or caregiver) by SRF topic.

	Session content by topic			Clinician-reported problem alerts			Combined client/caregiver problem alerts		
SRF topic	No. of clients with non-missing data	% Clients with any addressed/ focused	% sessions with addressed/ focused	No. of clients with non-missing data	% Clients with any alert	Median # alerts	No. of clients with non-missing data	% Clients with any alert	Median # alerts
Emotional issues	295	98	82	280	96	17.0	269	97	19.0
Behavioral issues	295	97	82	280	95	15.5	269	96	23.0
Family issues	295	97	83	280	83	4.0	269	84	6.0
School/work issues	295	94	69	280	85	3.0	269	87	5.0
Friends/peer issues	295	92	66	280	95	8.0	269	93	8.0
Problems w/ delinquent behavior	291	52	23	280	79	2.5	269	85	3.0
Alcohol/ substance use	290	51	19	280	42	0.0	269	52	1.0
Harm to self or others	293	58	20	280	45	0.0			
Client hope for future	291	88	58				173	43	0.0
Client motivation for treatment	293	84	46				121	41	0.0
Therapeutic relationship w/client	293	67	27				268	60	1.0
Client perceptions on counseling impact	292	79	39				132	61	1.5
Client satisfaction w/services	293	73	32				184	23	0.0
Caregiver strain	292	75	38				124	78	3.0
Caregiver satisfaction w/life	292	63	25				151	54	1.0
Caregiver motivation for youth treatment	291	69	32				97	38	0.0
Therapeutic relationship w/caregiver	291	49	17				208	59	1.0
Caregiver satisfaction w/services	290	58	23				130	5	0.0

provide a visual example, Figure 1 shows the Kaplan–Meier survival estimates for the topic of behavioral issues. The graph shows that clients whose clinicians were in the feedback group have a lower survival rate than clients whose clinicians were in the control condition. In other words, the duration to event is shorter. For example, at 20 weeks the survival rate is 0.25 for the feedback group and 0.35 for the non-feedback group, which means behavioral issues have been addressed/focused on for 75% of the clients in the feedback group compared to 65% of the clients in the non-feedback group. For the two exceptions

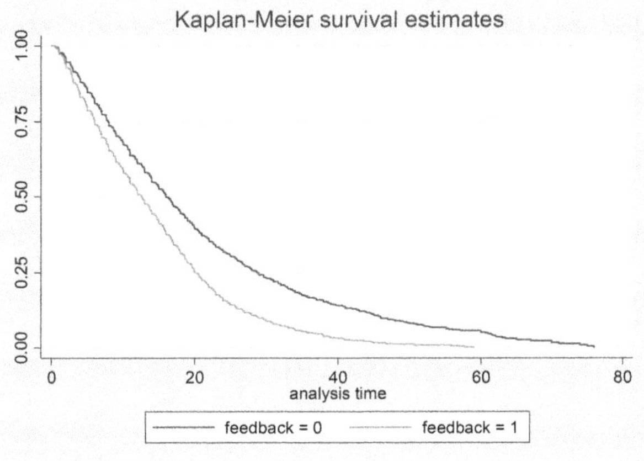

Figure 1. Kaplan–Meier survival plot for the SRF topic addressing behavioral issues by randomized group (feedback = 1, non-feedback = 0). Note. The feedback group was coded as 1, with the non-feedback group coded as 0.

(problems with delinquent behavior and alcohol/substance use) where feedback did not shorten time to addressing content, both were typically addressed infrequently (for about half the clients) with the first occurrence after several weeks in treatment (average time was about seven weeks).

There was a significant effect of feedback on the likelihood of addressing and/or focusing on every SRF topic. A summary of the significant model results from the survival analyses can be found in Figure 2 (note that the results for all models are presented in the appendix). As recommended (Hosmer et al., 2008), we compared the three models per reporter per topic and chose the most complete model for interpretation that was significant at an adjusted p-value of < 0.01. The figure shows the hazard ratio and the 95% confidence interval for each selected model by reporter (clinician, client and/or caregiver combined) and SRF topic. All hazard ratios were above 1.0, indicating significantly increased likelihood of addressing/focusing on a topic. Hazard ratios can be interpreted by subtracting 1.0 then converting the result into the percent increased likelihood. In order of increasing complexity, the three models were the simple (S) model, the adjusted (A) model, and the interaction (I) model.

The simple model is most consistent with the first hypothesis that the relative likelihood of addressing content will be higher for clients whose clinicians were in the feedback condition compared to the non-feedback condition. Six of the SRF topics were best explained by this model. For example, for client-reported perceptions of counseling impact the simple model was the best explanatory model, indicating that clinicians in the feedback group were on average 66% (Hazard ratio of 1.66) more likely to address/focus on client-reported counseling impact problems than clinicians in the control condition. Other topics where the simple model provided the best explanation were clinician-rated family issues, client and/or caregiver-rated emotional issues, client-rated satisfaction with services, caregiver strain, and caregiver satisfaction with services (respectively, 33%, 39%, 65%, 95%, and 134% more likely to be addressed/focused on by clinicians in the feedback group than the control condition).

There were six topics where the adjusted model provided the best explanatory fit, indicating that feedback increased the relative likelihood of addressing or focusing on a topic even after adjusting for cumulative problem alerts. For example, after adjusting for clinician-reported cumulative problem alerts related to client harm to self or others, the model in Figure 2 indicates that clinicians in the feedback group were 64% more likely to address/focus on harm as a topic in the next session than were clinicians in the non-feedback condition. The other topics all included combined client/caregiver-reported problem alerts in the adjusted models as shown in Figure 2, including family issues, client hope for the future, therapeutic relationship with the client and the caregiver separately, and caregiver satisfaction with life (respectively, 46%, 24%, 63%, 73%, and 104% more likely).

The interaction between feedback group and problem alerts provided the best explanatory model for eight of the topics (a total of 13 of the models differing by reporter). For all of these topics, the interaction of cumulative problem alerts heightened the impact of feedback. To interpret the interaction models, the hazard ratio presented in Figure 2 represent the sum of hazard ratios for feedback plus the interaction term where there were cumulative problem alerts present prior to the clinician's completion of the SRF. For example, the alcohol/ substance use topic is significant for the interaction

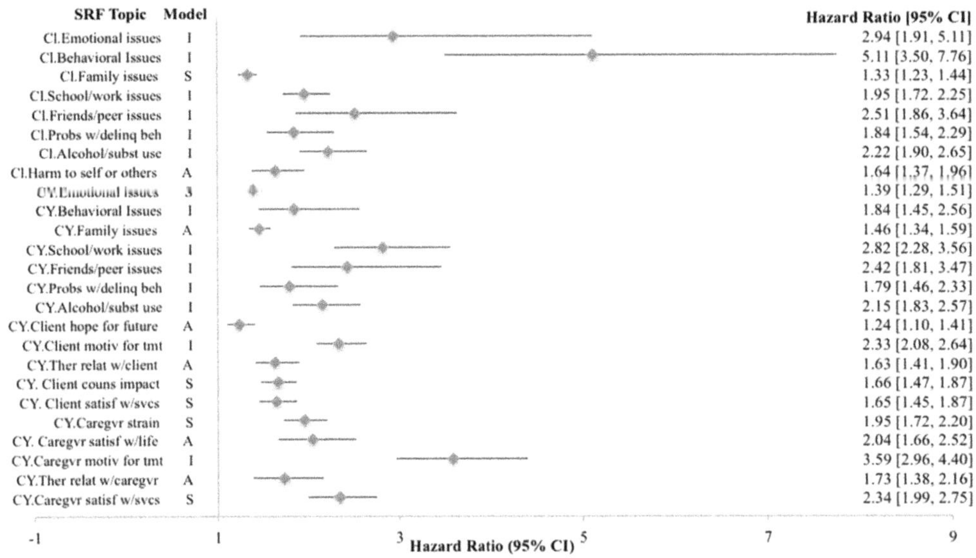

Figure 2. Forest plot summarizing results of Cox regression for recurrent events where addressing content in sessions was predicted by feedback group, clinician- or client/caregiver-reported dynamic problem-specific severity, and their interaction.
Note: This table only includes the simplest model chosen for interpretation for each topic by reporter (Cl, Clinician, CY, Client and/or caregiver). The results for all models including statistics are presented in the appendix (Table AI for clinician-reported measures and Table AII for client and/or caregiver-reported measures). All reported models were significant at an adjusted p-value of <0.01. S, Simple model (likelihood of addressing/focusing on content was higher for clients whose clinicians were in the feedback condition compared to the non-feedback condition); A, adjusted model (relative likelihood that feedback increased addressing/focusing on content after adjusting for cumulative problem alerts); I, interaction model (the relative likelihood for the feedback condition of addressing/focusing on content where cumulative problem alerts were present). Where the interaction model was significant, the hazard ratio of feedback was calculated by summing the hazard ratios for feedback plus the interaction term where the cumulative problem alert = 1.

model for both clinician-reported and combined client/caregiver-reported problem alerts (hazard ratio for the feedback group were 2.22 and 2.15, respectively). This indicates that for clients with reported alcohol or substance use problems, the clinicians in the feedback condition were over two times more likely to address and/or focus on this issue in a following session than were clinicians in the control condition.

Discussion

This study represents an important next step in exploring how feedback provided to clinicians may influence their behavior in sessions with youths receiving treatment in community mental health settings. The findings show that the duration to first occurrence and relative likelihood of clinicians addressing content related to specific domains of youth treatment progress and process was significantly improved for clinicians randomized to the feedback group compared to the non-feedback group. For a few topics, there appears to be a simple relationship between feedback group and increased likelihood of addressing or focusing on content. However, for most content areas there is an important relationship between feedback group and the cumulative problem alerts reported by multiple informants. In other words, the effect of feedback group is enhanced by the presence of problem alerts.

Previous research on the SRF found that clinicians had a general style in their approach to treatment, accounting for more of the variance than did clients on several topics related to youth symptoms and functioning (Douglas Kelley et al., 2010). A follow-up study on the relationship between clinician-reported content addressed in sessions and concurrent multi-informant problem alerts found several differences in session content based on type of problem alert and reporter. Clinicians reported addressing content related to emotional, family, and friend/peer problems more when reported by youths, while content related to youth behavioral problems occurred more when reported by caregivers (Douglas Kelley et al., 2012). High-risk problems (alcohol/substance use, harm to self or others) were strongly correlated with session content when reported by anyone (clinician, youth, or caregiver). Problems with the treatment process (e.g., therapeutic alliance) and caregiver strain were not associated with session content regardless of reporter.

The results presented here showed that several treatment process- and caregiver-related content domains do increase in likelihood in relation to feedback group, but are not influenced by matching problem alerts (e.g., the simple model). It is possible that there is an activating effect of feedback, where clinicians become more generally attuned to issues of importance to clients and their caregivers. Furthermore, it is clear that the client and the caregiver are bringing issues of importance to the fore through their completion of PTPB measures. Notably, there were no differences in the distribution of problem alerts by treatment condition between clients whose clinicians were in the feedback group compared to the non-feedback group. Yet, there remained an effect of feedback on the likelihood of addressing and/or focusing on those problems either after accounting for cumulative problem alerts or including it as an interaction term in the models.

Although this study did not include outcome data in analyses, there are two separate randomized clinical trials of the same feedback system (one with the same dataset) that both show faster improvements in youth symptoms and functioning for clients whose clinicians were in the feedback group compared to the control condition (Bickman et al., 2011, 2015). The present study showed that for all but two of the content areas, clinicians in the feedback group addressed topics earlier in treatment than did clinicians in the control group. In regard to clinical significance, hazard ratios are used to express the effects associated with the relative differences between treatment conditions (Hosmer et al., 2008), which can be more useful than simply considering statistical significance. Nine of the SRF topics had hazard ratios between 2.15 and 5.11, which can be interpreted as clinicians in the feedback group being 115–411% more likely to address a topic than clinicians in the comparison group. Hazard ratios for the remaining nine topics ranged between 1.33 and 1.95, indicating smaller but still potentially clinically meaningful effects.

The practice implications suggested by the study findings seem clear. Routine outcome monitoring and feedback may increase clinicians' responsiveness to common problems reported by clients and caregivers in youth psychotherapy, at least in terms of self-reported content addressed in sessions. This is consistent with a common factors approach to psychotherapy, where non-model-specific factors such as motivation for treatment or the therapeutic alliance have been found to be associated with improved outcomes (e.g., Lambert & Barley, 2002; Wampold, 2001). It is also consistent with the research on client-centered clinician communication behaviors, which typically include active use of the client's own language for problems and treatment goals and partnering in collaborative treatment planning (Levinson, Lesser, & Epstein, 2010; Makoul, 2001).

This is not an argument against specific treatment modalities (e.g., cognitive-behavioral therapy). Common factors of treatment and client-centered communication interventions can be combined with specific treatment modalities (e.g., cognitive-behavioral therapy) to enhance outcomes. Rather, these findings provide evidence to support the importance of a broad-based common factors approach to the selection of measures for inclusion in routine outcome monitoring and feedback (Douglas Kelley, Bickman, & Norwood, 2010). The present study was conducted in community mental health centers with "treatment as usual". It would be interesting to explore how the effects of feedback on addressing session content changed in the context of an evidence-based treatment, where fidelity to the treatment model is valued.

In an effort to gain greater understanding of clinician behavior in sessions, several researchers have focused on specific treatment strategies or techniques (Bearsley-Smith, Sellick, Chesters, & Francis, 2008; Chorpita et al., 2011, 2008; Garland, Hurlburt, Brookman-Frazee, Taylor, & Accurso, 2009). An alternate approach taken here was to focus on content rather than techniques, since content is more universally understood and less likely to be subject to misinterpretation or require extensive training for form completion. As a clinician self-reported measure, the SRF holds practical value in ease of use; however, other methods of measuring content of sessions may be more accurate, such as observational coding systems. Hurlburt, Garland, Nguyen, and Brookman-Frazee (2010) compared ratings of the occurrence and intensity of clinical strategies as reported by clinicians to standardized coding of session videotapes. They found that clinicians were 2.5 times more likely to overestimate the number of goals and strategies pursued in each session compared to trained observers. Furthermore, correspondence on specific goals and strategies was low. It is quite possible that clinicians may self-report intended behaviors that may not be perceptible to others.

It should be noted that these session-based data are highly complex with multiple measures, multiple informants, and time-varying effects on clinician-reported content addressed in sessions. While the recurrent events survival analysis techniques used here offer a sophisticated approach to dealing with this type of data structure, two analytic limitations remain to be explored. First, while the use of the robust standard error accounted for clustering of events within clients (Twisk et al., 2005), these models did not adjust for clustering of clients within clinicians. Second, the Cox proportional hazards regression model assumes that recurrent events are identical, resulting in the hazard ratio being constant. The stratified Cox model is an alternative model that can address this issue (Hosmer et al., 2008).

This study was intended to investigate a vast, complex dataset that has been collected in a real-life clinical setting. While the results provide evidence supporting the hypothesis that one mechanism of action for feedback to clinicians about clients' problems is that it increases the likelihood of addressing these problems in sessions, further research is needed. In addition to the analytic limitations mentioned here, there are also important relationships that were not modeled. There are potential client, setting, and clinician characteristics that may influence the impact of feedback on addressing or focusing on session content. In addition, we know that a third of the clinicians in the feedback group did not view a single feedback report for any of their clients (Bickman et al., 2011). Both of the evaluation studies linked to this study have shown a strong dose–response relationship between implementation (defined as rates of measure completion and feedback viewing). This would be an important area to explore since better implementation may improve even further the relationship between feedback, multi-informant problem alerts, and addressing/focusing on session content.

Acknowledgements

The content is solely the responsibility of the authors and does not necessarily represent the official views of the National Institutes of Health.

Funding

Preparation of this article was partially supported by the National Institute of Mental Health of the National Institutes of Health under Award Number R01087814.

Note

[1] In survival analyses most commonly reported in the medical literature, the failure event is a negative one, such as death, relapse, or other treatment failure. In this study, the failure event is positive (the addressing or focusing on a topic). Thus, the desired direction of effect is positive (we want the event to happen) rather than what is typically seen in the medical literature (where the failure event is not desired).

References

APA Presidential Task Force on Evidence-Based Practice. (2006). Evidence-based practice in psychology. *American Psychologist, 61*, 271–285.

Athay, M. M. (2012). Satisfaction with Life Scale (SWLS) in caregivers of clinically-referred youth: Psychometric properties and mediation analysis. *Administration and Policy in Mental Health and Mental Health Services Research, 39*(1–2), 41–50. doi:10.1007/s10488-011-0390-8.

Athay, M. M., & Bickman, L. (2012). Development and psychometric evaluation of the youth and caregiver Service Satisfaction Scale. *Administration and Policy in Mental Health and Mental Health Services Research, 39*(1–2), 71–77. doi:10.1007/s10488-012-0407-y.

Athay, M. M., Riemer, M., & Bickman, L. (2012). The Symptoms and Functioning Severity Scale (SFSS): Psychometric evaluation and discrepancies among youth, caregiver, and clinician ratings over time. *Administration and Policy in Mental Health and Mental Health Services Research, 39*(1–2), 13–29. doi:10.1007/s10488-012-0403-2.

Bearsley-Smith, C., Sellick, K., Chesters, J., & Francis, K. (2008). Treatment content in child and adolescent mental health services: Development of the treatment recording sheet. *Administration and Policy in Mental Health and Mental Health Services Research, 35*(5), 423–435.

Bickman, L., & Athay, M. M. (Eds.). (2012). *Youth mental health measurement [special issue] Administration and policy in mental health and mental health services research, 39*(1–2), 1–146.

Bickman, L., Athay, M. M., Riemer, M., Lambert, E. W., Kelley, S. D., Breda, C., ... Vides de Andrade, A. R. (Eds.). (2010). *Manual of the Peabody Treatment Progress Battery* (2nd ed.). Nashville, TN: Vanderbilt University.

Bickman, L., Douglas Kelley, S., & Athay, M. (2012). The technology of measurement feedback systems. *Journal of Couple & Family Psychology: Research and Practice, 1*(4), 274–284.

Bickman, L., Douglas Kelley, S., Breda, C., de Andrade, A. R., & Riemer, M. (2011). Effects of routine feedback to clinicians on mental health outcomes of youths: Results of a randomized trial. *Psychiatric Services, 62*, 1423–1429.

Bickman, L., Douglas, S., Vides de Andrade, A. R., Tomlinson, M., Gleacher, A., Olin, S., & Hoagwood, K. (2015). Implementing a measurement feedback system: A tale of two sites. *Administration and Policy in Mental health and Mental Health Services Research.* doi:10.1007/s10488-015-0647-8.

Bickman, L., Vides de Andrade, A. R., Athay, M. M., Chen, J. I., De Nadai, A. S., Jordan-Arthur, B., & Karver, M.S. (2012). The relationship between change in therapeutic alliance and improvement in youth symptom severity: Whose ratings matter the most? *Administration and Policy in Mental Health and Mental Health Services Research, 39*(1–2), 78–89. doi:10.1007/s10488-011-0398-0.

Boswell, J. F., Kraus, D. R., Miller, S. D., & Lambert, M. J. (2015). Implementing routine outcome monitoring in clinical practice: Benefits, challenges, and solutions. *Psychotherapy Research, 25*(1), 6–19.

Brannan, A. M., Athay, M. M., & Vides de Andrade, A. R. (2012). Measurement quality of the Caregiver Strain Questionnaire-Short Form 7 (CGSQ-SF7). *Administration and Policy in Mental Health and Mental Health Services Research, 39*(1–2), 51–59. doi:10.1007/s10488-012-0412-1

Breda, C. S., & Riemer, M. (2012). Motivation for Youth's Treatment Scale (MYTS): A new tool for measuring motivation among youths and their caregivers. *Administration and Policy in Mental Health and Mental Health Services Research, 39*(1–2), 118–132. doi:10.1007/s10488-012-0408-x

Cannon, M. D., & Witherspoon, R. (2005). Actionable feedback: Unlocking the power of learning and performance improvement. *The Academy of Management Executive, 19*(2), 120–134.

Chorpita, B. F., Bernstein, A. D., & Daleiden, E. L. (2011). Empirically guided coordination of multiple evidence-based treatments: An illustration of relevance mapping in children's mental health services. *Journal of Consulting and Clinical Psychology, 79*, 470–480.

Chorpita, B. F., Bernstein, A. D., Daleiden, E. L., & the Research Network on Youth Mental Health. (2008). Driving with roadmaps and dashboards: Using information resources to structure the decision models in service organizations. *Administration and Policy in Mental Health and Mental Health Services Research, 35*, 114–123.

Dew-Reeves, S. E., Athay, M. M., & Kelley, S. D. (2012). Validation and use of the Children's Hope Scale-Revised PTPB Edition (CHS-PTPB): High initial youth hope and elevated baseline symptomatology predict poor treatment outcomes. *Administration and Policy in Mental Health and Mental Health Services Research, 39*(1–2), 60–70. doi:10.1007/s10488-012-0411-2.

Douglas, S., Button, S., & Casey, S. E. (2014). Implementing for sustainability: Promoting use of a measurement feedback system for innovation and quality improvement. *Administration and Policy in Mental Health and Mental Health Services Research.* Advance online publication. doi:10.1007/s10488-014-0607-8

Douglas Kelley, S., Bickman, L., & Norwood, E. (2010). Evidence-based treatments and common factors in youth psychotherapy. In B. L. Duncan, S. D. Miller, B. E. Wampold, & M. A. Hubble (Eds.), *The heart and soul of change: What works in therapy* (2nd ed., pp. 325–355). Washington, DC: American Psychological Association.

Douglas Kelley, S., Vides de Andrade, A. R., Bickman, L., & Robin, A. V. (2012). The Session Report Form (SRF): Are clinicians addressing concerns reported by youth and caregivers? *Administration and Policy in Mental Health and Mental Health Services Research, 39*(1–2), 133–145.

Douglas Kelley, S., Vides de Andrade, A. R., Sheffer, E., & Bickman, L. (2010). Exploring the black box: Measuring youth treatment process and progress in usual care. *Administration and Policy in Mental Health and Mental Health Services Research. Special Issue: Psychotherapy Practice in Usual Care, 37*(3), 287–300.

Evans, C. (2012). Cautionary notes on power steering for psychotherapy. *Canadian Psychology/Psychologie Canadienne, 53* (2), 131–139.

Garland, A. F., Hurlburt, M. S., Brookman-Frazee, L., Taylor, R. M., & Accurso, E. C. (2009). Methodological challenges of characterizing usual care psychotherapeutic practice. *Administration and Policy in Mental Health and Mental Health Services, 37*, 208–220.

Hannan, C., Lambert, M. J., Harmon, C., Nielson, S., Smart, D., Shimokawa, K., & Sutton, S. W. (2005). A lab test and algorithms for identifying clients at risk for treatment failure. *Journal of Clinical Psychology, 61*(2), 155–163.

Hatfield, D., McCullough, L., Frantz, S. H. B., & Krieger, K. (2009). Do we know when our clients get worse? An investigation of therapists' ability to detect negative client change. *Clinical Psychology and Psychotherapy, 17*(1), 25–32.

Hawley, K. M., & Weisz, J. R. (2003). Child, parent and therapist (dis)agreement on target problems in outpatient therapy: The therapist's dilemma and its implications. *Journal of Consulting and Clinical Psychology, 71*(1), 62–70.

Hosmer, D. W., Lemeshow, S., & May, S. (2008). *Applied survival analysis: Regression modeling of time-to-event data* (2nd ed.). Hoboken, NJ: John Wiley & Sons.

Hurlburt, M. S., Garland, A. F., Nguyen, K., & Brookman-Frazee, L. (2010). Child and family therapy process: Concordance of therapist and observational perspectives. *Administration and Policy in Mental Health and Mental Health Services Research, 37*, 230–244.

de Jong, K. (2014). Deriving effective implementation strategies for outcome monitoring from feedback theory. *Administration and Policy in Mental Health and Mental Health Services Research.* Advance online publication. doi: 10.1007/s10488-014-0589-6

Kazdin, A. E. (2008). Evidence-based treatment and practice: New opportunities to bridge clinical research and practice, enhance the knowledge base, and improve patient care. *American Psychologist, 63*(3), 146–159.

Kearns, M. A., Athay, M. M., & Riemer, M. (2012). Measuring youths' perceptions of counseling impact: Description, psychometric evaluation, and longitudinal examination of the Youth Counseling Impact Scale v.2. *Administration and Policy in Mental Health and Mental Health Services Research, 39*(1-2), 104–117. doi:10.1007/s10488-012-0414-z.

Kluger, A. N., & DeNisi, A. (1996). The effects of feedback interventions on performance: A historical review, a meta-analysis, and a preliminary feedback intervention theory. *Psychological Bulletin, 119*, 254–284.

Knaup, C., Koesters, M., Schoefer, D., Becker, T., & Puschner, B. (2009). Effect of feedback of treatment outcome in specialist mental healthcare: Meta-analysis. *The British Journal of Psychiatry, 195*(1), 15–22.

Lambert, M. J., & Barley, D. E. (2002). Research summary on the therapeutic relationship and psychotherapy outcome. In J. C. Norcross (Ed.), *Psychotherapy relationships that work: Therapist contributions and responsiveness to patients* (pp. 17–32). Oxford: Oxford University Press.

Lambert, M. J., Harmon, C., Slade, K., Whipple, J. L., & Hawkins, E. J. (2005). Providing feedback to psychotherapists on their patients' progress: Clinical results and practice suggestions. *Journal of Clinical Psychology, 61*(2), 165–174.

Lambert, M. J., Whipple, J. L., Hawkins, E. J., Vermeersch, D. A., Nielsen, S. L., & Smart, D. W. (2003). Is it time for clinicians to routinely track patient outcome? A meta-analysis. *Clinical Psychology, 10*(3), 288–301.

Levinson, W., Lesser, C. S., & Epstein, R. M. (2010). Developing physician communication skills for patient-centered care. *Health Affairs, 29*, 1310–1318.

Makoul, G. (2001). Essential elements of communication in medical encounters: The Kalamazoo consensus statement. *Academic Medicine, 76*, 390–393.

Noell, G. H., & Gansle, K. A. (2014). The use of performance feedback to improve intervention implementation in schools. In L. M. Hagermoser Sanetti & T. R. Kratochwill (Eds.), *Treatment integrity: A foundation for evidence-based practice in applied psychology* (pp. 161–184). Washington, DC: American Psychological Association.

Riemer, M., & Bickman, L. (2011). Using program theory to link social psychology and program evaluation. In M. M. Mark, S. I. Donaldson, & B. Campbell (Eds.), *Social psychology and program/policy evaluation* (pp. 104–139). New York, NY: Guilford.

Riemer, M., Douglas Kelley, S., Casey, S., & Taylor Haynes, K. (2012). Developing effective research-practice partnerships for creating a culture of evidence-based decision making. *Administration and Policy in Mental Health and Mental Health Services Research. Special Issue: Research Practice Partnerships, 39* (4), 248–257.

Riemer, M., Rosof-Williams, J., & Bickman, L. (2005). Theories related to changing clinician practice. *Child and Adolescent Psychiatric Clinics of North America, 14*, 241–254, viii.

Sapyta, J., Riemer, M., & Bickman, L. (2005). Feedback to clinicians: Theory, research and practice. *Journal of Clinical Psychology*, *61*, 145–153.

Shimokawa, K., Lambert, M. J., & Smart, D. (2010). Enhancing treatment outcome of patients at risk of treatment failure: Meta-analytic and mega-analytic review of a psychotherapy quality assurance system. *Journal of Consulting and Clinical Psychology*, *78*, 298–311.

Sparks, J. A., Kisler, T. S., Adams, J. F., & Blumen, D. G. (2011). Teaching accountability: Using client feedback to train effective family therapists. *Journal of Marital and Family Therapy*, *37*, 452–467.

Twisk, J. W. R., Smidt, N., & de Vente, W. (2005). Applied analysis of recurrent events: A practical overview. *Journal of Epidemiological Community Health*, *59*, 706–710.

Wampold, B. E. (2001). *The great psychotherapy debate: Models, methods, and findings*. Mahwah, NJ: Lawrence Erlbaum Associates.

Weisz, J. R., Ng, M. Y., & Bearman, S. K. (2014). Odd couple? Reenvisioning the relation between science and practice in the dissemination-implementation era. *Clinical Psychological Science*, *2*(1), 58–74.

Worthen, V. E., & Lambert, M. J. (2007). Outcome oriented supervision: Advantages of adding systematic client tracking to supportive consultations. *Counseling and Psychotherapy Research*, *7*(1), 48–53.

Youn, S. J., Kraus, D. R., & Castonguay, L. G. (2012). The treatment outcome package: Facilitating practice and clinically relevant research. *Psychotherapy*, *49*, 115–122.

Appendix

Table AI. Results of Cox regression for recurrent events for simple, adjusted, and interaction models where addressing content was predicted by feedback group, clinician-reported dynamic problem-specific severity, and their interaction.

Topic	Survival analysis model	Reg. coeff. (b)	SE (b)	*p*-Value	Hazard ratio	95% CI for hazard ratio
Emotional issues	*Simple model*—Feedback group	0.33	0.04	0.000	1.39	1.29, 1.51
	Adjusted model—Feedback group			0.000	1.44	1.33, 1.57
	Cumulative problem alerts (clinician)			0.086	1.07	0.99, 1.15
	Interaction model—Feedback group			0.086	1.93	0.91, 4.09
	Cumulative problem alerts (clinician)			0.231	1.05	0.97, 1.15
	Feedback * Cumulative alerts			0.008	1.01	1.00, 1.02
Behavioral issues	*Simple model*—Feedback group	0.44	0.04	0.000	1.55	1.43, 1.68
	Adjusted model—Feedback group			0.000	1.61	1.48, 1.75
	Cumulative problem alerts (clinician)			0.000	1.05	1.03, 1.08
	Interaction model—Feedback group			0.000	4.10	2.50, 6.74
	Cumulative problem alerts (clinician)			0.009	1.04	1.01, 1.06
	Feedback * Cumulative alerts			0.001	1.01	1.01, 1.02
Family issues	*Simple model*—Feedback group	0.29	0.04	0.000	1.33	1.23, 1.44
	Adjusted model—Feedback group			0.000	1.36	1.26, 1.48
	Cumulative problem alerts (clinician)			0.827	1.00	0.99, 1.01
	Interaction model—Feedback group			0.948	1.00	0.83, 1.20
	Cumulative problem alerts (clinician)			0.841	1.00	0.99, 1.01
	Feedback * Cumulative alerts			0.183	1.01	1.00, 1.02
School/work issues	*Simple model*—Feedback group	0.22	0.04	0.000	1.25	1.15, 1.36
	Adjusted model—Feedback group			0.000	1.28	1.17, 1.39
	Cumulative problem alerts (clinician)			0.007	1.03	1.01, 1.05
	Interaction model—Feedback group			0.604	0.93	0.71, 1.22
	Cumulative problem alerts (clinician)			0.074	1.02	1.00, 1.04
	Feedback * Cumulative alerts			0.000	1.02	1.01, 1.03

(Continued)

Table AI. Continued.

Topic	Survival analysis model	Reg. coeff. (b)	SE (b)	p-Value	Hazard ratio	95% CI for hazard ratio
Friends/peer issues	*Simple model*—Feedback group	0.15	0.04	0.000	1.17	1.07, 1.27
	Adjusted model—Feedback group			0.000	1.23	1.12, 1.34
	Cumulative problem alerts (clinician)			0.376	1.02	0.98, 1.05
	Interaction model—Feedback group			0.168	1.49	0.85, 2.61
	Cumulative problem alerts (clinician)			1.000	1.00	0.96, 1.04
	Feedback * Cumulative alerts			0.000	1.02	1.01, 1.03
Problems w/delinquent behavior	*Simple model*—Feedback group	0.18	0.08	0.027	1.20	1.02, 1.41
	Adjusted model—Feedback group			0.060	1.17	0.99, 1.39
	Cumulative problem alerts (clinician)			0.011	1.04	1.01, 1.07
	Interaction model—Feedback group			0.277	0.78	0.50, 1.22
	Cumulative problem alerts (clinician)			0.208	1.02	0.99, 1.05
	Feedback * Cumulative alerts			0.000	1.06	1.04, 1.07
Alcohol/substance use	*Simple model*—Feedback group	−0.01	0.09	0.904	0.99	0.83, 1.17
	Adjusted model—Feedback group			0.850	0.99	0.82, 1.17
	Cumulative problem alerts (clinician)			0.508	1.01	0.99, 1.03
	Interaction model—Feedback group			0.313	1.17	0.87, 1.58
	Cumulative problem alerts (clinician)			0.213	0.99	0.97, 1.01
	Feedback * Cumulative alerts			0.000	1.05	1.03, 1.07
Harm to self or others	*Simple model*—Feedback group	0.43	0.09	0.000	1.54	1.30, 1.82
	Adjusted model—Feedback group			0.000	1.64	1.37, 1.96
	Cumulative problem alerts (clinician)			0.000	0.96	0.95, 0.98
	Interaction model—Feedback group			0.000	1.71	1.28, 2.28
	Cumulative problem alerts (clinician)			0.000	0.96	0.94, 0.98
	Feedback * Cumulative alerts			0.855	1.00	0.98, 1.02

Note. Significance determined at an adjusted p-value of <0.01. CI, confidence interval.

Table AII. Results of Cox regression for recurrent events for simple, adjusted, and interaction models where addressing content was predicted by feedback group, client and/or caregiver-reported dynamic problem-specific severity, and their interaction.

Variable	Topic	Reg. coeff. (b)	SE (b)	p-Value	Hazard ratio	95% CI for hazard ratio
Emotional issues	*Simple model*—Feedback group	0.33	0.04	0.000	1.39	1.29, 1.51
	Adjusted model—Feedback group			0.000	1.48	1.36, 1.61
	Cumulative problem alerts (cl/cg)			0.809	1.10	0.93, 1.10
	Interaction model—Feedback group			0.000	4.72	2.08, 10.7
	Cumulative problem alerts (cl/cg)			0.280	0.95	0.87, 1.04
	Feedback * Cumulative alerts			0.025	1.01	1.00, 1.02
Behavioral issues	*Simple model*—Feedback group	0.44	0.04	0.000	1.55	1.43, 1.68
	Adjusted model—Feedback group			0.000	1.61	1.48, 1.75
	Cumulative problem alerts (cl/cg)			0.032	1.06	1.01, 1.11
	Interaction model—Feedback group			0.559	0.83	0.45, 1.54
	Cumulative problem alerts (cl/cg)			0.259	1.03	0.98, 1.09
	Feedback * Cumulative alerts			0.005	1.01	1.00, 1.02
Family issues	*Simple model*—Feedback group	0.29	0.04	0.000	1.33	1.23, 1.44
	Adjusted model—Feedback group			0.000	1.46	1.34, 1.59
	Cumulative problem alerts (cl/cg)			0.000	1.01	1.00, 1.02
	Interaction model—Feedback group			0.000	2.00	1.53, 2.62
	Cumulative problem alerts (cl/cg)			0.789	1.00	0.99, 1.01
	Feedback * Cumulative alerts			0.124	1.01	1.00, 1.02

(*Continued*)

Table AII. Continued.

Variable	Topic	Reg. coeff. (b)	SE (b)	*p*-Value	Hazard ratio	95% CI for hazard ratio
School/work issues	*Simple model*—Feedback group	0.22	0.04	0.000	1.25	1.15, 1.36
	Adjusted model—Feedback group			0.000	1.41	1.29, 1.54
	Cumulative problem alerts (cl/cg)			0.001	1.02	1.01, 1.04
	Interaction model—Feedback group			0.001	1.80	1.27, 2.54
	Cumulative problem alerts (cl/cg)			0.063	1.01	1.00, 1.03
	Feedback * Cumulative alerts			0.000	1.02	1.01, 1.02
Friends/peer issues	*Simple model*—Feedback group	0.15	0.04	0.000	1.17	1.07, 1.27
	Adjusted model—Feedback group			0.000	1.27	1.16, 1.39
	Cumulative problem alerts (cl/cg)			0.837	1.00	0.98, 1.03
	Interaction model—Feedback group			0.242	1.40	0.80, 2.44
	Cumulative problem alerts (cl/cg)			0.669	1.00	0.97, 1.02
	Feedback * Cumulative alerts			0.000	1.02	1.01, 1.03
Problems w/delinquent behavior	*Simple model*-Feedback group	0.18	0.08	0.027	1.20	1.02, 1.41
	Adjusted model—Feedback group			0.002	1.31	1.10, 1.55
	Cumulative problem alerts (cl/cg)			0.000	1.12	1.05, 1.19
	Interaction model-Feedback group			0.269	0.74	0.43, 1.27
	Cumulative problem alerts (cl/cg)			0.005	1.09	1.03, 1.16
	Feedback * Cumulative alerts			0.000	1.05	1.03, 1.06
Alcohol/substance use	*Simple model*—Feedback group	−0.01	0.09	0.904	0.99	0.83, 1.17
	Adjusted model—Feedback group			0.159	1.14	0.95, 1.37
	Cumulative problem alerts (cl/cg)			0.016	1.03	1.01, 1.06
	Interaction model—Feedback group			0.619	1.09	0.79, 1.50
	Cumulative problem alerts (cl/cg)			0.363	1.01	0.99, 1.04
	Feedback * Cumulative alerts			0.000	1.06	1.04, 1.07
Client hope for future	*Simple model*—Feedback group	0.16	0.05	0.001	1.18	1.07, 1.29
	Adjusted model—Feedback group			0.001	1.24	1.10, 1.41
	Cumulative problem alerts (client)			0.000	0.98	0.97, 0.99
	Interaction model—Feedback group			0.000	1.39	1.19, 1.62
	Cumulative problem alerts (client)			0.000	0.98	0.96, 0.99
	Feedback * Cumulative alerts			0.230	0.98	0.97, 1.01
Client motivation for treatment	*Simple model*—Feedback group	0.32	0.06	0.000	1.38	1.24, 1.54
	Adjusted model—Feedback group			0.000	1.53	1.30, 1.79
	Cumulative problem alerts (client)			0.000	1.04	1.02, 1.05
	Interaction model—Feedback group			0.016	1.27	1.05, 1.54
	Cumulative problem alerts (client)			0.000	1.03	1.02, 1.05
	Feedback * Cumulative alerts			0.000	1.06	1.03, 1.10
Therapeutic relationship w/ client	*Simple model*—Feedback group	0.44	0.07	0.000	1.55	1.34, 1.79
	Adjusted model—Feedback group			0.000	1.63	1.41, 1.90
	Cumulative problem alerts (client)			0.006	1.02	1.01, 1.04
	Interaction model—Feedback group			0.000	2.89	2.25, 3.70
	Cumulative problem alerts (client)			0.089	1.02	1.00, 1.03
	Feedback * Cumulative alerts			0.242	0.99	0.97, 1.01
Client perceptions on counseling impact	*Simple model*—Feedback group	0.50	0.06	0.000	1.66	1.47, 1.87
	Adjusted model—Feedback group			0.000	2.14	1.82, 2.52
	Cumulative problem alerts (client)			0.171	0.99	0.97, 1.01
	Interaction model—Feedback group			0.000	2.79	2.15, 3.62
	Cumulative problem alerts (client)			0.333	0.99	0.98, 1.01
	Feedback * Cumulative alerts			0.065	0.98	0.96, 1.00

(*Continued*)

Table AII. Continued.

Variable	Topic	Reg. coeff. (b)	SE (b)	*p*-Value	Hazard ratio	95% CI for hazard ratio
Client satisfaction w/services	*Simple model*—Feedback group	0.50	0.07	0.000	1.65	1.45, 1.87
	Adjusted model—Feedback group			0.000	1.91	1.61, 2.26
	Cumulative problem alerts (client)			0.030	0.98	0.96, 1.00
	Interaction model—Feedback group			0.000	1.89	1.57, 2.28
	Cumulative problem alerts (client)			0.587	1.00	0.97, 1.02
	Feedback * Cumulative alerts			0.054	0.96	0.92, 1.00
Caregiver strain	*Simple model*—Feedback group	0.67	0.06	0.000	1.95	1.72, 2.20
	Adjusted model—Feedback group			0.000	2.05	1.71, 2.46
	Cumulative problem alerts (caregiver)			0.050	1.03	1.00, 1.06
	Interaction model—Feedback group			0.126	1.49	0.89, 2.47
	Cumulative problem alerts (caregiver)			0.058	1.03	1.00, 1.06
	Feedback * Cumulative alerts			0.484	1.00	0.99, 1.02
Caregiver satisfaction w/life	*Simple model*—Feedback group	0.78	0.08	0.000	2.18	1.88, 2.53
	Adjusted model—Feedback group			0.000	2.04	1.66, 2.52
	Cumulative problem alerts (caregiver)			0.000	1.02	1.00, 1.04
	Interaction model—Feedback group			0.000	2.57	1.83, 3.61
	Cumulative problem alerts (caregiver)			0.513	1.01	0.98, 1.03
	Feedback * Cumulative alerts			0.125	1.02	1.00, 1.04
Caregiver motivation for youth treatment	*Simple model*—Feedback group	0.63	0.07	0.000	1.88	1.65, 2.15
	Adjusted model—Feedback group			0.000	2.17	1.76, 2.69
	Cumulative problem alerts (caregiver)			0.017	1.02	1.00, 1.04
	Interaction model—Feedback group			0.000	2.52	1.93, 3.29
	Cumulative problem alerts (caregiver)			0.953	1.00	0.98, 1.02
	Feedback * Cumulative alerts			0.000	1.07	1.03, 1.11
Therapeutic relationship w/ caregiver	*Simple model*—Feedback group	0.73	0.10	0.000	2.08	1.71, 2.53
	Adjusted model—Feedback group			0.000	1.73	1.38, 2.16
	Cumulative problem alerts (caregiver)			0.004	1.04	1.01, 1.07
	Interaction model—Feedback group			0.111	0.78	0.58, 1.06
	Cumulative problem alerts (caregiver)			0.017	1.04	1.01, 1.07
	Feedback * Cumulative alerts			0.034	1.03	1.00, 1.05
Caregiver satisfaction w/ services	*Simple model*—Feedback group	0.85	0.08	0.000	2.34	1.99, 2.75
	Adjusted model—Feedback group			0.000	2.83	2.18, 3.66
	Cumulative problem alerts (caregiver)			0.576	1.01	0.97, 1.06
	Interaction model—Feedback group			0.000	3.00	2.31, 3.89
	Cumulative problem alerts (caregiver)			0.410	1.07	0.91, 1.26
	Feedback * Cumulative alerts			0.775	0.98	0.82, 1.16

Note. Significance determined at adjusted *p*-value of <0.01. CI, confidence interval.

Predicting outcome of substance abuse treatment in a feedback study: Can recovery curves be improved upon?

PAUL CRITS-CHRISTOPH[1], HANNAH M. MARKELL[1], ROBERT GALLOP[2], MARY BETH CONNOLLY GIBBONS[1], BRIDGET MCCLURE[3], & JOHN ROTROSEN[4]

[1]*Department of Psychiatry, University of Pennsylvania, Philadelphia, PA, USA;* [2]*Department of Mathematics, West Chester University, West Chester, PA, USA;* [3]*Joint Clinical Trials Office, Weill Cornell Medical College, New York, NY, USA &* [4]*Department of Psychiatry, New York University School of Medicine, New York, NY, USA*

Abstract

Objective: The goal of the study was to evaluate whether enhanced normative feedback recovery curves are needed for treatment of substance use problems. **Method:** Patient predictors of outcome were examined using data from four substance abuse treatment clinics. **Results:** Baseline severity of symptoms/functioning, employment, and craving were found to be associated with rate of change in symptoms/functioning. Several other variables were associated with rate of change in alcohol use, although in the opposite direction than found in efficacy trials. **Conclusions:** The results point to the complexity of designing feedback systems using normative recovery curves for those with substance use problems and highlight the important differences between real-world treatment of those with substance use problems compared to data from efficacy trials.

Substantial evidence has accumulated that providing feedback on patient's progress to clinicians can enhance treatment outcomes (Shimokawa, Lambert, & Smart, 2010). In the Lambert et al. (2003) feedback system (Lambert & Hawkins, 2001; Lambert, Hansen, & Finch, 2001; Lambert et al., 2001) in which clinicians are provided with data based on patient self-assessments using the Outcome Questionnaire-45 (OQ-45; Lambert, Lunnen, Umphress, Hansen, & Burlingame, 1994), feedback reports incorporate warnings for patients who are not demonstrating expected treatment responses. Expected treatment response is based on normative "recovery curves" derived from large naturalistic treatment samples in which expected rate of change over time is calculated for patients at various levels of initial distress/functioning (Finch, Lambert, & Schaalje, 2001; Lambert et al., 2002). In the OQ-45 feedback studies, patients not progressing as expected are termed *off-track*. Patients who are progressing as expected are referred to as *on-track*.

In an effort to define normative recovery curves for outpatient psychotherapy using an outcome measure similar to the OQ-45, Lueger et al. (2001) created a prediction model based on seven intake variables including subjective well-being, symptoms, life functioning, clinician-rated severity, chronicity, previous treatment, and treatment expectations. However, no information was provided regarding the strength of this predictive model and the amount of variance accounted for by the selected variables. Another approach to feedback is based on a model predicting good/bad outcomes used multiple variables (Kordy, Hannöver, & Richard, 2001). For those predicted to achieve poor outcome ("signal cases"), 30% actually achieved poor outcome and

10% achieved relatively better outcome. The authors conclude that "The predictive value of the whole model is not overwhelming" (Kordy et al., 2001, p. 180). When designing the OQ-45 feedback system, recovery curves for patients at different initial levels of the OQ-45 total score were calculated because initial level was a strong predictor of rate of improvement over time. The exact predictive model that is used for the OQ-45 feedback system has not been published, but Lambert et al. (2002) report an R^2 of .17 for a model that contains both initial level and change after one session of therapy predicting final outcome status. For standard outpatient samples, typically mostly comprised of patients with complaints centering on depression, anxiety, and/or interpersonal difficulties, the use of initial level to define normative recovery curves has worked exceptional well, as evidenced by results of feedback studies showing statistically significant and clinically meaningful benefits from feedback based on deviation from such normative recovery curves (Shimokawa et al., 2010). Nevertheless, the clinical usefulness of a feedback system might be enhanced by using normative recovery curves based on greater precision of predictive models for change over time.

In the treatment of substance use problems in particular, there are a couple of reasons to believe that other predictor variables, besides initial OQ level, might be relevant to expected rate of improvement. For one, many patients beginning a course of substance abuse treatment are not at their peak level of distress. Patients who arrive for substance abuse treatment have often been clean from drug or alcohol for some period of time before beginning treatment. Whether treatment is mandated, following a driving under the influence or driving while intoxicated conviction, is the result of pressure from family/friends to reduce/stop using drug or alcohol or is simply a personal decision that it is time to address alcohol/drug use, stopping use in the weeks before an initial treatment session is common. For example, in a recent four-site substance abuse feedback intervention study, more than 75% of patients reported no days of drug or alcohol use in the past seven days at baseline (Crits-Christoph et al., 2012). Similarly, in the Crits-Christoph et al. (2010) study involving 20 substance abuse treatment clinics, 77% of those who began treatment reported no alcohol use and 83% reported no drug use, in the past week. When a patient is currently using, the focus of treatment is typically to stop/reduce use of drugs/alcohol. After usage has stopped, treatment often enters a phase of relapse prevention. Because many patients are "clean" from drugs/alcohol at baseline, the goal of treatment for such patients would typically move directly to prevent relapse rather than to focus on stopping current use or reduce immediate distress associated with heavy use. There might be other baseline variables associated with the course of improvement when the focus on relapse prevention rather than stopping current use.

A second reason to expect that other variables besides initial level of use might be important to consider in understanding the typical course of improvement for those with substance use disorders is that a variety of studies have successfully identified predictors of outcome of substance use treatment. In a review of the literature on predictors of substance use outcomes, Haaga, Hall, and Haas (2005) identified three consistent findings in the literature: (i) patients who are employed have better outcomes than those who are unemployed, (ii) the presence of comorbid antisocial personality disorder is associated with poorer outcomes, and (iii) psychiatric severity is associated with worse outcomes. In a comprehensive study of predictors of the outcome of treatment for cocaine dependence, four baseline variables were identified as significant predictors of outcome (Crits-Christoph et al., 2007). These were craving, acuity of biomedical problems, expectations for improvement, and belief in the drug counseling recovery (primarily 12-step) philosophy. The joint effect of these predictors was clinically meaningful: for patients with none of the four positive prognostic attributes, the probability of achieving 2 or more months of consecutive abstinence was 11%; and for those with three or more of the prognostic attributes, the probability of achieving 2 or more months of consecutive abstinence was 62%. Although Crits-Christoph et al. (2007)'s predictive results were obtained in the context of a randomized efficacy trial for cocaine dependence, the robustness of the findings across a range of psychosocial treatments (individual and group drug counseling, cognitive therapy, and supportive-expressive psychotherapy) in the trial suggests that such predictors might also apply to naturalistically delivered substance abuse treatment (i.e., drug counseling with a 12-step and/ or relapse prevention focus).

The current study, therefore, was designed to examine predictors of the outcome of naturalistic substance use treatment in order to inform the development of recovery curves for feedback reports within a substance using population. Based on the Haaga et al. (2005) review, we examined employment status and psychiatric severity (as captured by OQ-45 total scores) as predictors. Based on the Crits-Christoph et al. (2007) study, we examined craving, acuity of biomedical problems, belief in the drug counseling/recovery philosophy, and expectations for improvement as predictors of change. Given the emphasis on initial severity for defining

OQ-45 recovery curves, we also examined baseline levels of drug/alcohol use as predictors for comparison purposes. These analyses were conducted within the context of an OQ-45 feedback study conducted with patients and clinicians in real-world substance abuse treatment facilities. The impact of these predictor variables on rate of change in OQ-45 scores over the course of 12 treatment sessions was investigated for the group of patients whose clinicians did not receive feedback. Because alcohol and drug use outcomes are especially important among those seeking help with substance use problems, we also investigated prediction of these outcomes.

We hypothesized that each of the predictor variables would be associated with rate of change in OQ-45 scores, alcohol use, and drug use. Although normative recovery curves should be evaluated within a nonfeedback condition, we also examined the same predictor variables within the context of a feedback condition to explore any potential impact of feedback on the predictor-outcome relations.

Methods

The current study uses data from a previously reported feedback study (Crits-Christoph et al., 2012) that used a modified version of the OQ-45 feedback system in three real-world clinics that treat patients with substance use problems. There were two phases in the intervention study. In Phase I, patients exclusively were assessed via the modified OQ-45 instrument, administered at the beginning of treatment sessions. In Phase II, different patients at the same clinics completed the modified OQ-45 at their treatment sessions, and their counselors immediately received feedback reports based upon the patient's OQ-45 assessment. Additionally, if a patient went off-track (according to the OQ-45), Phase II counselors were granted access to clinical support tools in addition to feedback. Affiliated university and clinic Institutional Review Boards approved the study protocol.

Participants

Clinics. Four clinics participated in the study, two in New York City, Philadelphia, and Salt Lake City. Each was a community-based outpatient substance abuse treatment clinic (nonmethadone maintenance).

Clinicians. Clinician eligibility requirements at the participating clinics were as follows: clinicians needed to be providing individual counseling to adult (age 18 or older) clients, work a minimum of 20% of time at the given clinic, and provide their written informed consent.

Patients. Eligible patients (aged 18 years or above) presented at the clinic in search of a new course of individual outpatient treatment were enrolled within 2 weeks of their intake session. Additionally, patients could only participate if their individual counseling appointments were scheduled at a minimum of twice monthly. All participating patients gave their written informed consent.

Assessments

Modified OQ-45. The OQ-45 was used to track patient's progress in this study. The OQ-45 is a 45-item self-report scale which was created specifically for tracking and assessing patient outcomes in a therapeutic setting. The OQ-45 is scored on a 5-point scale (0 = *never*, 1 = *rarely*, 2 = *sometimes*, 3 = *frequently*, 4 = *almost always*), yielding scores ranging from a possible 0 to 180. Higher scores on the OQ-45 are indicative of greater levels of symptoms and/or poorer functioning. The OQ-45 was modified in one key way for the purposes of the current study, which entailed adding two items which measure the number of days in the past week that the patient used (i) alcohol and (ii) drugs. In this study, the total score and the individual alcohol and drug use items were used as outcome measures.

A well-established instrument, the OQ-45 has been validated across a wide array of healthy and clinical populations. The OQ-45's internal consistency reliability (Cronbach's alpha), as reported by Lambert et al. (2004), is .93 with a 3-week test–retest reliability value of .84 for the OQ-45 total score. The concurrent validity of the OQ-45 total score has been investigated via correlations with the Symptom Checklist-90 (SCL-90; Derogatis & Cleary, 1977), Beck Depression Inventory (BDI; Beck, Steer, & Carbin, 1988), Zung Depression Scale (Zung, Richards, & Short, 1965), and the State-Trait Anxiety Inventory (STAI; Spielberger, 1983). Each of these concurrent validity correlations was significant at the .01 level with *r*'s ranging from .50 to .85 (Lambert et al., 2004). Perhaps most importantly, the OQ-45 has demonstrated sensitivity to the effects of treatment on patients' functioning (Vermeersch, Lambert, & Burlingame, 2000; Vermeersch et al., 2004).

In both the phases (I and II), the OQ-45 was administered right before every treatment session. Patients could have up to a maximum of 12 post-baseline treatment sessions or 6 months (whichever came first). Electronically captured data were sent (via encrypted wireless connection) to a computer where it was stored in a database. During Phase II, reports were available to be viewed by clinicians immediately after the patient completed measures via a handheld computer or computer kiosk. The reports were viewed electronically, via a secure, password-protected computer system. Feedback reports generated from OQ-45 scores were the same as reports described in previous studies (Slade, Lambert, Harmon, Smart, & Bailey, 2008), except that patient scores on the alcohol and drug use questions were also included in reports and tracked over time to make changes in drug or alcohol use apparent to the counselor.

During Phase II, when the OQ-45 identified certain patients as being off-track based upon their scores, therapists were given the chance to employ clinical support tools which provided ideas for ways to improve treatment. Upon their identification of being off-track, patients were asked to fill out the Assessment for Signal Clients (ASC; Lambert et al., 2007), a 40-item self-report measure that is intended to evaluate the severity of certain problems which could be hindering progress in treatment—specifically, problems with therapeutic alliance, social support systems, motivation, and stressful life events.

Addiction recovery scale. The Addiction Recovery Scale (ARS) is a self-report scale that was developed for the NIDA Cocaine Collaborative Treatment Study (CCTS). Certain items on the scale reflect the drug counseling/12-step philosophical system, while other items assess involvement in the suggested behaviors. The total score for the ARS is calculated by summing the items (each rated on a 1–5 scale). A high score indicates greater endorsement of the philosophy and behaviors encouraged in 12-step-oriented drug counseling. The original scale had 40 items. A 10-item version of the scale, used in the current project, was created by selecting the items with the highest item-total correlations (two of the 10 items are reverse scored). Internal consistency (Cronbach's alpha) for the 10-item scale using baseline data in the current project was .75. Baseline ARS total scores have been found to predict sustained abstinence (Crits-Christoph et al., 2007), and change in the ARS total score has been found to be a partial statistical mediator of drug use outcomes of individual (plus group) drug counseling (Crits-Christoph et al., 2003).

Expectations for improvement. We used one item that directly measured expectations for improvement, "Overall, how much improvement do you expect to experience as a result of treatment here?" This item was rated on a 1 ("I expect to feel worse") to 7 ("I expect to feel much better") scale. Although this was only a single-item assessment of expectations for improvement, we used this item as a predictor because a meta-analysis found that the ratings of expectations for improvement were consistently related to the outcome of psychosocial treatment across 46 studies, with many of the studies employing a single-item scale (Constantino et al. 2011).

Craving. Craving for drug/alcohol was assessed each week with a three-item adapted from the Cocaine Craving Scale (Weiss et al., 1997, 2003) used in the NIDA CCTS. The three items were the following: (i) "Please rate how strong your desire was to use drugs or alcohol during the last 24 hours," (ii) "Please imagine yourself in the environment in which you previously used drugs and/or alcohol. If you were in this environment today, what is the likelihood that you would use drugs or alcohol?", and (iii) "Please rate how strong your urges are for drugs or alcohol when something in the environment reminds you of it." Response options ranged from 0 for "no desire/likelihood of use" to 9 for "strong desire/likelihood of use," and the final score was the sum of the three items. Internal consistency of this scale at baseline was .74 in the current study.

Acuity of biomedical problems. This scale was taken from the Recovery Attitude and Treatment Evaluator Questionnaire (Mee-Lee, Hoffmann, & Smith 1992). The three items of this scale include the following: (i) "Do you have any physical or medical problems whatsoever?", (ii) "Do your physical problems require you to see a health care professional such as a doctor, nurse or rehabilitation specialist?", and (iii) "Do your physical problems interfere with your treatment or recovery efforts from drugs/alcohol?" Each item is rated on a scale of 1 (e.g., "None—no need for medical visits") to 4 (e.g., "Very Much—Hospital care is needed"). The scale score is an average of the three items. Internal consistency of this scale at baseline was .74 in the current study.

Procedures

Counselors were given an orientation to the study goals and procedures and trained to interpret feedback reports. If a patient was identified as off-track based upon his rate of improvement indicated by OQ-45 scores, the ASC was administered via handheld computers or computer kiosks. Once electronically captured, the data were sent to and stored in a computer database via an encrypted wireless connection. In Phase II, the ASC was only completed once—the first time the patient went off-track.

Further details of the original feedback study are provided in Crits-Christoph et al. (2012).

Statistical Analysis

Primary outcome analyses included all patients who had at least a baseline and one treatment session's OQ-45 assessment in the Phase I (no-feedback) condition. Because feedback during Phase II influenced outcomes (Crits-Christoph et al., 2012), it was thought that it was more appropriate to primarily examine the relations of predictors to outcome in a treatment-as-usual cohort without feedback, as was done in the original OQ-45 recovery curve study (Lambert et al., 2002), though we also conducted exploratory analyses examining whether predictions varied for no feedback vs. feedback conditions.

The predictor analysis involved a longitudinal analysis of all OQ-45 data collected from Session 1 through to Session 12. The longitudinal analysis used a random-effects multilevel regression model (Goldstein, 1995) with a random slope and random intercept for each subject. Due to nonlinear change of individual patient profiles over time, a logarithmic transformation of time was performed. Separate analyses were initially conducted for each predictor variable. The following terms were included in the model: the predictor variable, time, baseline OQ-45 total score, and predictor by time interaction. The latter term was our focus to examine the relation of the predictor to rate of change in OQ-45 scores over time. To test for differential prediction in the feedback and no-feedback conditions, data from both Phase I (no-feedback) and Phase II (feedback) were used, and the weighted averages of subject-specific slope estimates were compared between the feedback and no-feedback groups by including a Predictor by Time by Phase interaction (in addition to the terms listed above, plus Phase and Phase by Time terms).

Drug and alcohol use items of the OQ-45 were analyzed in the same way as OQ-45 total scores. We used PROC MIXED in SAS (Littell, Milliken, Stroup, Wolfinger, & Schbenberger, 2006) to conduct the random-effects hierarchical regression analyses.

Effect sizes (converted to r), derived from the F-test for mixed-effects model, were calculated r = square root of $[F/(F + DF)]$, where F is the F-test statistic for the effect of interest in the multilevel design (Rosenthal & Rosnow, 1991; Verbeke & Molenberg, 2000). We used likelihood-ratio testing to assess the simultaneous effect of all predictors on change, compared to simple model with no predictors. The likelihood ratio test uses a chi-square distribution based on the difference of the log-likelihood functions, referred to as the deviance, with the degrees of freedom equal to the difference in number of fixed parameters estimated between the two nested models (Neter, Wasserman, & Kutner, 1989). An effect size (converted to η^2) was calculated from the likelihood ratio test.

Results

Baseline Characteristics of Sample

Across all the three sites, a total of 391 patients attended an intake session, and 304 patients had both intake data and a minimum of one post-baseline assessment in either Phase I or Phase II of the investigation (142 in Pennsylvania; 107 in Utah; 2 in one NY clinic, and 53 patients in a second NY clinic). Of these 304 individuals with at least one post-baseline assessment, 165 were from Phase I and 139 were from Phase II.

The 87 patients who attended intake but had no treatment sessions were largely comparable to the 304 patients who had at least one treatment session. Results of chi-square or t-test analyses comparing these two groups of patients revealed no significant differences on gender, education, Hispanic ethnicity, marital status, age, baseline alcohol use, or baseline OQ-45. However, there was evidence that those who attended intake only, compared to those who attended at least one treatment session, were more likely to be Black compared to White or Other race ($\chi^2[2] = 17.6$, $p < .001$), were less likely to be employed ($\chi^2[1] = 4.5$, $p = .043$; 8.0% of those who attended intake only were employed; 17.3% of those who attended at least one treatment session were employed), and were more likely to report drug use in the past 7 days at intake (intake only group, M = .97 days, SD = 1.9; at least one treatment session group, M = .46 days, SD = 1.3; unequal variance t-test: $t[111] = 2.3$, $p = .021$).

Overall, the demographic breakdown of these 304 patients (combining Phase I and Phase II) with baseline assessment and at least one post-baseline assessment was as follows: 55.9% were male and 36.5% were Caucasian. At baseline, 84.2% of patients reported no drug use and 78.6% reported no alcohol use. Alcohol had been a problem for about 11 years for the average patient, while drug use had been a problem for approximately 13 years. No significant differences existed between the Phase I (no-feedback) and Phase II (feedback) samples on any baseline characteristic variables (Table I).

A total of 38 clinicians across three sites had at least one patient that completed at least one post-baseline assessment. These clinicians were 60.5% female, 28.9% African-American, and 7.9% self-identified as Hispanic or Latino. On average,

Table I. Characteristics of patients.

Characteristic	No-feedback (Phase I) N = 165	Feedback (Phase II) N = 139	Total N = 304
Gender (women), n/N (%)	64/165 (38.8%)	58/139 (41.7%)	122/304 (40.1%)
Age, M, N (SD)	39.3, 163 (10.9)	39.0, 139 (9.9)	38.9, 302 (10.4)
Race, n/N (%)			
Caucasian	65/163 (39.9%)	55/138 (39.9%)	120/301 (39.9%)
Black	66/163 (40.5%)	64/138 (46.4%)	130/301 (43.2%)
Other race	32/163 (19.6%)	19/138 (13.8%)	51/301 (16.9%)
Ethnicity (Latino), n/N (%)	25/159 (15.7%)	16/136 (11.8%)	41/295 (13.9%)
Marital status, n/N (%) (married or cohabitating)	29/162 (17.9%)	27/135 (20.0%)	56/297 (18.9%)
Years of school, n/N (%) (HS diploma and further)	110/163 (67.5%)	101/136 (74.3%)	211/299 (70.6%)
Employment status, n/N (%) (Employed full or part-time)	27/162 (16.7%)	25/138 (18.1%)	52/300 (17.3%)
Alcohol use in past week, n/N (%) at baseline (1 or more days of use)	30/165 (18.2%)	35/139 (25.2%)	65/304 (21.4%)
Drug use in past week, n/N (%) at baseline (1 or more days of use)	27/165 (16.4%)	21/139(15.1%)	48/304 (15.8%)
Mean OQ45 total score at baseline, M, N (SD)	70.6, 165 (28.7)	68.6, 139 (28.3)	69.7, 304 (28.5)

Note. Sample sizes reflect small amounts of missing data for some variables.

participating clinicians were 44.5 years old. Regarding education, 63.2% of the clinicians had a master's degree, 15.8% had a bachelor's degree, and 15.8% had a doctoral degree. More than half (57.8%) reported having at least 5 years of experience as a counselor.

At baseline, the OQ-45 total scores correlated .14 (N = 304; p = .008) with alcohol use and .09 (N = 304; p = .06) drug use. Alcohol use and drug use were correlated .42 (N = 304; p < .001) at baseline.

Prediction of Rate of Change in OQ-45

Shown in Table II are parameter estimates and the statistical significance of predictor by time interactions (examined individually), representing the prediction of slope over time from Session 1 to Session 12, for patients in the no-feedback condition. Also shown are effect sizes expressed as correlations (r).

As expected, baseline level on the OQ-45 total score was a significant predictor of rate of change in the OQ-45 total score from Session 1 to Session 12 (r = .27, p = .005). However, two other variables, employment and craving at baseline, also significantly predicted rate of change in OQ-45 total scores at nearly the same level of strength (r's of .21 [p = .024], and .26 [p = .009], respectively). Employed patients had a faster rate of change; high craving at baseline was associated with a faster rate of change in OQ-45 total scores. Testing a model in which all three predictor variables were included (main effects plus interactions with time) versus a model without the three interactions with time (only main effects), yielded a highly significant effect for the addition of the three interactions with time (χ^2[3] = 16.9, p = .00073; effect size: η^2 = .112). However, the individual influence of each was attenuated in the model that contained all three predictors, suggesting that overlap between these variables was partly responsible for their predictive strength (in the model with all three predictors: Baseline OQ-45 total score by Time: r = 18, p = .064; Employment by Time: r = .19, p = .057; Craving by Time: r = .13, p = .205). Of note was that the effect of employment was comparable to that for baseline OQ-45 total score.

Within the feedback condition (Table III), baseline OQ-45 total score also significantly predicted rate of change in OQ-45 total scores, though the r was slightly lower (r = .24, p = .015). Restricting the sample in the feedback condition to only those who went off-track also revealed a significant relationship between baseline OQ-45 scores and rate of change in the OQ-45 total score (r = .34, p = .03, N = 54). Employment and craving, however, no longer significantly predicted rate of change in OQ-45 scores in the feedback condition (r's of .01 and .16, respectively). To test for the difference in these predictive relations in no-feedback vs. feedback, we examined statistical models that included a Predictor by Time by Phase interaction. Recognizing that statistical power was limited for testing three-way interactions, we note that no significant results were evident (for Employment, F[1, 256] = 2.3, p = .13; for Craving, F[1, 248] = 0.1, p = .80).

Prediction of Rate of Change in Alcohol and Drug Use

In the no-feedback condition, baseline OQ-45 total score was not associated significantly with rate of change in alcohol use or drug use (Table II). Rate of change in alcohol use, however, was predicted by several other variables in the no-feedback condition. Baseline level of alcohol use strongly predicted rate of change in alcohol use (r = .49, p < .001). In addition, craving (r = .31, p < .001), acuity of biomedical

Table II. Significance testing for predictors of outcome: no-feedback condition.

	Rate of change in OQ-45 total score				Rate of change in alcohol use				Rate of change in drug use			
Predictor	Estimate (se)	*F (DF)*	*p*	*r*	Estimate (se)	*F (DF)*	*p*	*r*	Estimate (se)	*F (DF)*	*p*	*r*
Employed by time	−12.497 (5.470)	5.2 (109)	.024	.21	−.646 (.330)	3.8 (161)	.052	.15	−.087 (.283)	0.1 (96)	.759	.03
Expectations for improvement by time	−.752 (2.269)	0.1 (110)	.741	.03	−.015 (.134)	0.0 (185)	.908	.00	−.007 (.111)	0.0 (106)	.951	.00
Acuity of biomedical problems by time	−1.884 (3.052)	0.4 (108)	.538	.06	−.371 (.184)	4.1 (165)	.045	.16	.259 (.152)	2.9 (96)	.092	.17
Craving by time	−.837 (.314)	7.1 (96)	.009	.26	−.074 (.018)	17.0 (163)	<.001	.31	−.018 (.016)	1.2 (90)	.275	.12
Addiction recovery scale by time	3.452 (3.094)	1.2 (100)	.267	.11	.485 (.189)	6.6 (171)	.011	.19	.093 (.158)	0.3 (98)	.559	.06
Baseline OQ-45 total score by time	−.214 (.075)	8.1 (106)	.005	.27	−.008 (.005)	3.2 (177)	.075	.13	−.003 (.004)	0.8 (97)	.387	.09
Baseline level of alcohol use by time	−2.783 (1.666)	2.8 (87)	.098	.18	−.601 (.092)	42.5 (135)	<.001	.49	−.062 (.084)	0.5 (78)	.466	.08
Baseline level of drug use by time	−1.295 (1.831)	0.5 (118)	.481	.07	−.201 (.106)	3.6 (195)	.060	.13	−.177 (.090)	3.8 (102)	.052	.19

Note. Separate models were calculated for each predictor. The Predictor by Time term examines the prediction of rate of change over time (slope), using a log transformation of session number. The baseline score on the dependent variable, obtained at intake, is also included in the model. The dependent variables are scores from Session 1 (which occurs subsequently to baseline) to Session 12 (or earlier end point for those who terminate). Alcohol and drug use are days using the past 7 days.

Table III. Significance testing for predictors of outcome: feedback condition.

	Rate of change in OQ45 total score				Rate of change in alcohol use				Rate of change in drug use			
Predictor	Estimate (se)	*F (DF)*	*p*	*r*	Estimate (se)	*F (DF)*	*p*	*r*	Estimate (se)	*F (DF)*	*p*	*r*
Employed	1.073 (8.474)	0.0 (107)	.900	.01	−.218 (369)	0.4 (109)	.556	.06	−.631 (.427)	2.2 (116)	.142	.14
Expectations for improvement by time	2.617 (2.471)	1.1 (109)	.292	.10	.021 (.114)	0.2 (125)	.857	.04	−.124 (.129)	0.9 (126)	.336	.01
Acuity of biomedical problems by time	−6.484 (4.579)	2.0 (92)	.160	.15	−.284 (.199)	2.0 (93)	.157	.15	−.299 (.229)	1.7 (91)	.195	.14
Craving by time	−.692 (.429)	2.6 (95)	.110	.16	−.041 (.019)	5.0 (97)	.028	.22	−.045 (.022)	4.4 (100)	.039	.20
Addiction recovery scale by time	9.350 (4.205)	4.9 (106)	.028	.21	.510 (178)	8.2 (106)	.005	.27	.531 (.212)	6.2 (114)	.014	.23
Baseline OQ-45 total score by time	−.279 (.113)	6.1 (96)	.015	.24	−.006 (.005)	1.6 (103)	.203	.13	−.001 (.006)	0.0 (105)	.841	.02
Baseline level of alcohol use by time	.490 (2.446)	0.0 (127)	.842	.02	−.375 (.101)	13.8 (104)	.000	.33	−.113 (.128)	1.0 (124)	.379	.08
Baseline level of drug use by time	.165 (2.413)	0.0 (98)	.946	.01	−.206 (.103)	4.0 (88)	.049	.21	−.265 (.121)	4.8 (95)	.031	.22

Note. Separate models were calculated for each predictor. The Predictor by Time term examines the prediction of rate of change over time (slope), using a log transformation of session number. The baseline score on the dependent variable, obtained at intake, is also included in the model. The dependent variables are scores from Session 1 (which occurs subsequently to baseline) to Session 12 (or earlier endpoint for those who terminate). Alcohol and drug use are days using the past 7 days.

problems ($r = .16$, $p = .045$), and the ARS ($r = .19$, $p = .011$) all significantly predicted rate of change in alcohol use. In addition, a marginally significant ($r = .15$, $p = .052$) effect was evident for employment. Relatively greater rate of change in alcohol use was associated with relatively high craving, low acuity of biomedical problems, less belief in the drug counseling/12-step philosophy of recovery, and being employed. In a model that included all of these predictors, baseline alcohol use ($r = .42$, $p < .001$) and craving ($r = .19$, $p = .015$) remained significant, while the effects of acuity of biomedical problems ($r = .09$, $p = .255$) and the ARS ($r = .12$, $p = .131$) were attenuated.

No significant predictor relations were apparent for rate of change in drug use in the no-feedback group, though a marginally significant ($r = .19$, $p = .052$) effect was evident for baseline level of drug use as a predictor.

Within the feedback group, craving ($r = .22$, $p = .028$), the ARS ($r = .27$, $p = .005$), and baseline level of alcohol use ($r = .33$, $p < .001$) all continued to be significant predictors of rate of change in alcohol use. While not significant, the relation of Acuity of Biomedical Problems to rate of change in alcohol use was of similar magnitude ($r = .15$) to that found in the no-feedback group. Craving ($r = .20$, $p = .039$) and the ARS ($r = .23$, $p = .014$) also predicted rate of change in drug use, as did baseline level of drug use ($r = .22$, $p = .031$). No significant interactions of predictors by phase (feedback vs. no-feedback) were apparent for rate of change in alcohol or drug use.

Discussion

The results of the current study have several implications for the use feedback systems in a substance using population. First, we found that baseline levels on the OQ-45 total score were associated with rates of change in OQ-45 total scores. This finding appears to validate, within a substance using population, the use of normative recovery curves for the OQ-45 that are based on initial level of the OQ-45 total score. However, initial level on the OQ-45 was not the only significant predictor of rate of change in the OQ-45, Two other variables, employment and craving, also predicted rate of change in the OQ-45. These findings therefore potentially suggest that more accurate normative OQ-45 recovery curves for a substance using population could be generated by incorporating multiple variables into models for recovery curves. Although the current OQ-45 feedback system produced positive results within a substance using population (Crits-Christoph et al., 2012), it is possible that more accurate normative recovery curves would allow for a feedback system that targets clinicians' attention more successfully to those patients who are deviating from the rate of change that one would expect for similar patients.

Our finding for employment is consistent with the Haaga et al. (2005) review that found that employment was a consistent predictor of the outcome of substance abuse treatments. Based on the consistency of this finding, it would seem useful for feedback systems to alert clinicians to whether a particular patient is improving as expected, or not, relative to other patients with the same employment status. However, the finding for craving seems to be inconsistent with the Crits-Christoph et al. (2007) study conducted using a cocaine-dependent sample. In the current study, high levels of craving were associated with a faster rate of change. In the Crits-Christoph et al. (2007) study, high rates of craving at baseline was associated with less duration of sustained abstinence over the course of treatment. Two factors are important to consider in understanding these discrepant findings in regard to craving. One is that, given that in the current sample about 80% of patients were not using drugs or alcohol in the past week at baseline, craving was relatively low for the sample as a whole. In fact, 21.3% of patients reported no craving or desire to use at all (score of 0 summing across three 0–9 craving items) in the current sample. The relatively low levels of craving may have created a "floor" effect, where those at the low end had little room to improve on the OQ-45 and no room to improve on the alcohol and drug use outcomes (zero use). Thus, high levels of craving could not be associated with relatively poor outcome in the current context. Second, it may be that craving is a stronger predictor of poor outcome within a cocaine-dependent (or opioid-dependent) sample compared to a mixed substance use sample (many with alcohol as the primary problem) that may be more characteristic of patients seeking treatment in some real-world substance abuse treatment facilities.

Also of interest in the current study was that craving, acuity of biomedical problems, and belief in the drug counseling/12-step philosophy were all predictive of rate of change in alcohol use. Each of these variables, however, predicted outcome in the opposite direction as was found in the Crits-Christoph et al. (2007) cocaine study. In addition, higher baseline levels of alcohol use were associated with a faster rate of change in alcohol use in the current study. In Project MATCH, a higher level of alcohol involvement prior to treatment was related to more drinks per day during follow-up (Project Match Research Group, 1997). As with craving predicting rate of change in the OQ-45, the current results for predictors of change in alcohol use are likely a function of the low level of baseline alcohol use for many patients, and the impact of this "floor" effect on predictive relationships. In addition, although those with relatively higher alcohol use at baseline may change more in the short run, such patients may also be more vulnerable to relapse at follow-up. Thus, predictors of short-term and long-term outcomes in the treatment of substance use disorders may differ.

The nature of the results of the current study, with multiple variables statistically significant in opposite directions than found previously, highlight the important distinction between the population and context of randomized clinical trials compared to naturalistic real-world clinics in the treatment of individuals with substance use problems. For randomized clinical trial efficacy studies, patients are preselected to have a predetermined degree of severity of the target problem at baseline so that change can be detected on that problem over the course of treatment. This typically translates into selecting patients who qualify for a DSM diagnosis of abuse/dependence and/or have used drugs/alcohol recently. As we have seen in the current study and other studies, many patients in real-world substance abuse treatment clinics have not used drug/alcohol recently. This may be a key factor in influencing the role of predictor variables.

Beyond the problem of low levels of substance use at baseline, patients seeking help at substance abuse treatment programs are heterogeneous on a variety of meaningful variables. Some patients are mandated to treatment, and the incentives connected to this process likely override the influence of other variables that normally would be associated with treatment outcome. In addition, individuals seek help in community clinics for problems with a wide range of drugs of abuse, including alcohol, opioids (both prescription medications and heroin), cocaine, methamphetamine, marijuana, club drugs, hallucinogens, and inhalants. The course of recovery from these different drugs, as well as polydrug abuse, may be somewhat different. Course of recovery is also likely to vary as a function of whether a patient is currently using or has been abstinent for a period of time. In addition, antisocial personality disorder has been consistently linked to poor outcome of substance abuse treatment (Haaga et al., 2005). Genetic variability may also play a role in terms of responsiveness to treatment for substance use problems (e.g., Anton et al., 2008). Because of the potential influence of all of these variables, identifying "normative recovery curves" in the context of such patient heterogeneity for those seeking help at substance abuse treatment programs would seem to be a major challenge.

An alternative to a single set of recovery curves based on multiple variables that would apply to all patients seeking treatment at substance abuse programs would be to develop recovery curves for separate subpopulations (e.g., young marijuana users; current heavy alcohol users). Obtaining adequate (large sample) databases for each subgroup, and then programming a feedback system to incorporate a diverse set of recovery curves for identifying off-track patients, is not likely to occur in the short run. Even if successful, the resultant system, tied to various recovery curves depending on a large number of baseline patient characteristics, might be so complicated that clinical use is limited.

Ideally, a study would be done to test whether feedback based on enhanced recovery curves leads to clinically significant improvement compared to feedback based on recovery curves developed only based on one predictor (i.e., initial OQ total score level). Although such finely tuned recovery curves may not be feasible, our results indicate that some adaptation of recovery curves based on certain findings (i.e., employment status) may improve the predictive validity of current feedback systems. It is likely that the clinical usefulness of more refined recovery curves is dependent on the size of the predictor–outcome relations on which such recovery curves are based; however, it is not known how high an effect is needed to have a meaningful impact when more refined recovery curves are used as the basis for feedback reports. Though the strength of individual predictors in the current study, as typically in other studies, is relatively small, if the joint effect of multiple predictors reaches a moderate or larger effect, it may well be worth generating recovery curves based on these predictors.

In addition to their potential role as part of the generation of recovery curves, it may also be of interest to examine the effects of feedback within subgroups defined by certain clinically relevant baseline variables. It may be, for example, that feedback has little impact among patients who have a long history of substance use. Such possible moderators of feedback effects should be tested in future studies with large samples sizes so that adequate statistical power exists for examining feedback effects within subgroups.

A number of limitations to the current study need mention. One limitation of this study is the lack of diagnostic information on patients. This makes it difficult to fully characterize the sample. Another limitation is that only certain potential predictor variables were available for analysis. A wider range of variables need to be examined in future research to more thoroughly investigate the potential predictors of rate of change in a naturalistic sample of patients seeking help at substance abuse treatment programs. Although data were collected at four clinics in separate areas of the USA, the generalizability of the current results to other locations is not known. Another limitation was that the sample that attended intake only was different on three variables from the sample of patients who attended at least one treatment session. Thus, the generalizability of the results to all patients who initially present to a substance abuse treatment facility is not known. However, it may be that it is more appropriate to generalize data on recovery curves only to the subset of individuals who actually receive any treatment.

Despite these limitations, the results support that recovery curves based on initial level are valid but might be improved based on other important baseline variables like employment. Substantial further research would be needed to fine-tune the accuracy of recovery curves for specific subgroups; though whether this would be clinically useful remains to be determined.

References

Anton, R. F., Oroszi, G., O'Malley, S., Couper, D., Swift, R., Pettinati, H., & Goldman, D. (2008). An evaluation of mu-opioid receptor (OPRM1) as a predictor of naltrexone response in the treatment of alcohol dependence: Results from the Combined Pharmacotherapies and Behavioral Interventions for Alcohol Dependence (COMBINE) study. *Archives of General Psychiatry, 65*, 135–144. doi:10.1001/archpsyc.65.2.135

Beck, A. T., Steer, R. A., & Carbin, M. G. (1988). Psychometric properties of the Beck Depression Inventory: Twenty-five years of evaluation. *Clinical Psychology Review, 8*(1), 77–100. doi:10.1016/0272-7358(88)90050-5

Constantino, M. J., Arnkoff, D. B., Glass, C. R., Ametrano, R. M., & Smith, J. Z. (2011). Expectations. *Journal of Clinical Psychology, 67*, 184–192.

Crits-Christoph, P., Connolly Gibbons, M. B., Barber, J. P., Hu, B., Hearon, B., Worley, M., & Gallop, R. (2007). Predictors of sustained abstinence during psychosocial treatments for cocaine dependence. *Psychotherapy Research, 17*, 240–252. doi:10.1080/10503300600818210

Crits-Christoph, P., Gibbons, M. B., Barber, J. P., Gallop, R., Beck, A. T., Mercer, D., ... Frank, A. (2003). Mediators of outcome of psychosocial treatments for cocaine dependence. *Journal of Consulting and Clinical Psychology, 71*, 918–925.

Crits-Christoph, P., Ring-Kurtz, S., Hamilton, J., Lambert, M., Gallop, R., McClure, B., ... & Rotrosen, R. (2012). A preliminary study of the effects of individual patient-level feedback in outpatient substance abuse treatment programs. *Journal of Substance Abuse Treatment, 42*, 301–309. doi:10.1016/j.jsat.2011.09.003

Crits-Christoph, P., Ring-Kurtz, S., McClure, B., Temes, C., Kulaga, A., Gallop, R., ... & Rotrosen, J. (2010). A randomized controlled study of a web-based performance improvement system for substance abuse treatment providers. *Journal of Substance Abuse Treatment, 38*, 251–262.

Derogatis, L. R., & Cleary, P. A. (1977). Confirmation of the dimensional structure of the SCL-90: A study in construct validation. *Journal of Clinical Psychology, 33*, 981–989. doi:10.1002/1097-4679(197710)33:4<981::AID-JCLP2270330412>3.0.CO;2-0

Finch, A. E., Lambert, M. J., & Schaalje, B. G. (2001). Psychotherapy quality control: The statistical generation of expected recovery curves for integration into an early warning system. *Clinical Psychology and Psychotherapy, 8*, 231–242. doi:10.1002/cpp.286

Goldstein, H. (1995). *Multilevel statistical models* (2nd ed.), London: Edward Arnold.

Haaga, D. A. F., Hall, S. M., & Haas, A. (2005). Participant factors in substance use disorders. In L. Castonguay & L. Beutler (Eds.). *Principle of therapeutic change that work.* New York, NY: Oxford University Press.

Kordy, H., Hannöver, W., & Richard, M. (2001). Computer assisted feedback driven active quality management for psychotherapy provision: The Stuttgart-Heidelberg model. *Journal of Consulting and Clinical Psychology, 69*, 173–183. doi:10.1037/0022-006X.69.2.173

Lambert, M. J., Bailey, R., Kimball, K., Shimokawa, K., Harmon, S. C., & Slade, K. (2007). *Clinical support tool manual – Brief version-40.* Salt Lake City, UT: OQMeasures.

Lambert, M. J., Hansen, N., & Finch, A. (2001). Patient-focused research: Using patient outcome data to enhance treatment effects. *Journal of Consulting and Clinical Psychology, 69*, 159–172. doi:10.1037/0022-006X.69.2.159

Lambert, M. J., & Hawkins, E. J. (2001). Using information about patient progress in supervision: Are outcomes enhanced? *Australian Psychologist, 36*(2), 131–138. doi:10.1080/00050060108259645

Lambert, M. J., Lunnen, K., Umphress, V., Hansen, N., & Burlingame, G. M. (1994). *Administration and scoring manual for the Outcome Questionnaire (OQ-45.1).* Salt Lake City, UT: IHC Center for Behavioral Healthcare Efficacy.

Lambert, M. J., Morton, J. J., Hatfield, D., Harmon, C., Hamilton, S., Reid, R. C., ... Burlingame, G. B. (2004). *Administration and scoring manual for the Outcome Questionnaire-45.* Orem, UT: American Professional Credentialing Services.

Lambert, M. J., Whipple, J. L., Bishop, M. J., Vermeersch, D. A., Gray, G. V., & Finch, A. E. (2002). Comparison of empirically derived and rationally derived methods for identifying clients at risk for treatment failure. *Clinical Psychology and Psychotherapy, 9*, 149–164. doi:10.1002/cpp.333

Lambert, M. J., Whipple, J. L., Hawkins, E. J., Vermeersch, D. A., Nielsen, S. L., & Smart, D.W. (2003). Is it time for clinicians to routinely track patient outcome? A meta-analysis. *Clinical Psychology, 10*, 288–301.

Lambert, M. J., Whipple, J. L., Smart, D. W., Vermeersch, D. A., Nielsen, S. L., & Hawkins, E. J. (2001). The effects of providing therapists with feedback on patient progress during psychotherapy: Are outcomes enhanced? *Psychotherapy Research, 11*(1), 49–68. doi:10.1080/713663852

Littell, R. C., Milliken G. A., Stroup, W. W., Wolfinger, R. D., & Schabenberger, O. (2006). *SAS system for mixed models* (2nd ed.). Cary, NC: SAS Institute.

Lueger, R. J., Howard, K. I., Martinovich, Z., Lutz, W., Anderson, E. E., & Grissom, G. (2001). Assessing treatment progress with individualized models of expected response. *Journal of Consulting and Clinical Psychology, 69*, 150–158. doi:10.1037/0022-006X.69.2.150

Mee-Lee, D., Hoffmann, N. G., Smith, M. B. (1992). *Recovery Attitude and Treatment Evaluator (RAATE) manual.* St. Paul, MN: CATOR/New Standards.

Neter, J., Wasserman, W., & Kutner, M.H. (1989). *Applied linear regression models* (2nd ed.). Burr Ridge, IL: Irwin. (See p. 604)

Project MATCH Research Group. (1997). Matching alcoholism treatments to client heterogeneity: Project MATCH posttreatment drinking outcomes. *Journal of Studies on Alcohol, 58*, 7–29.

Retrieved from http://www.jsad.com/jsad/downloadarticle/Matching_Alcoholism_Treatments_to_Client_Heterogeneity_Project_MATCH_Postt/440.pdf

Rosenthal, R., & Rosnow, R. L. (1991). *Essentials of behavioral research: Methods and data analysis* (2nd ed.). New York, NY: McGraw-Hill.

Shimokawa, K., Lambert, M. J., & Smart, D. W. (2010). Enhancing treatment outcome of patients at risk of treatment failure: Meta-analytic and mega-analytic review of a psychotherapy quality assurance system. *Journal of Consulting and Clinical Psychology*, *78*, 298–311. doi:10.1037/a0019247

Slade, K., Lambert, M. J., Harmon, S. C., Smart, D. W., & Bailey, R. (2008). Improving psychotherapy outcome: The use of immediate electronic feedback and revised clinical support tools. *Clinical Psychology & Psychotherapy*, *15*, 287–303. doi:10.1002/cpp.594

Spielberger, C. D. (1983). *Manual for the State-Trait Anxiety Inventory (STAI)*. Palo Alto, CA: Consulting Psychologists Press.

Verbeke, G., & Molenberg, G. (2000). *Linear mixed models for longitudinal data*. New York, NY: Springer.

Vermeersch, D. A., Lambert, M. J., & Burlingame, G. M. (2000). Outcome questionnaire: Item sensitivity to change. *Journal of Personality Assessment*, *74*, 242–261. doi:10.1207/S15327752JPA7402_6

Vermeersch, D. A., Whipple, J. L., Lambert, M. J., Hawkins, E. J., Burchfield, C. M., & Okiishi, J.C. (2004). Outcome Questionnaire: Is it sensitive to changes in counseling center clients? *Journal of Counseling Psychology*, *51*(1), 38–49. doi:10.1037/0022-0167.51.1.38

Weiss, R. D., Griffin, M. L., Hufford, C., Muenz, L. R., Najavits, L. M., Jansson, S. B., ... & Thompson, H. J. (1997). Early prediction of initiation of abstinence from cocaine. *The American Journal on Addictions*, *6*, 224–231.

Weiss, R. D., Griffin, M. L., Mazurick, C., Berkman, B., Gastfriend, D. R., Frank, A., ... & Moras, K. (2003). The relationship between cocaine craving, psychosocial treatment, and subsequent cocaine use. *American Journal of Psychiatry*, *160*, 1320–1325. doi:10.1176/appi.ajp.160.7.1320

Zung, W. W., Richards, C. B., & Short, M. J. (1965). Self-rating depression scale in an outpatient clinic: Further validation of the SDS. *Archives of General Psychiatry*, *13*, 508–515. Retrieved from http://archpsyc.ama-assn.org/cgi/reprint/13/6/508

Daily monitoring of temporal trajectories of suicidal ideation predict self-injury: A novel application of patient progress monitoring

EMMA RESTIFO[1], SHRADDHA KASHYAP[1], GEOFF R. HOOKE[1,2], & ANDREW C. PAGE[1]

[1]*Department of Psychology, University of Western Australia, Perth, WA, Australia &* [2]*Perth Clinic, West Perth, WA, Australia*

Abstract

Objective: The interpersonal theory of suicide argues that suicidal ideation predicts self-injury. We hypothesized that distinct patterns of suicidal ideation could be identified and these ratings could allow early identification of self-injury. **Method:** The sample consisted of 562 psychiatric inpatients who reported suicidal ideation. **Results:** Latent growth class analysis identified five classes of change in suicidal ideation. Patients who displayed prolonged suicidal ideation could be identified with improved sensitivity (89.66%) and negative predictive power (94%), compared to a model based on routine ratings of suicidality at admission (sensitivity = 50%; negative predictive power = 74%). These patients had a fourfold increased risk of self-injury. **Conclusions:** Daily measurement of suicidal ideation may identify inpatients at risk and inform clinical decision-making.

Introduction

Progress monitoring is a quintessential example of practice-based evidence (Castonguay, Barham, Lutz, & McAleavy, 2013; Page & Stritzke, 2015). Data about patients are regularly collected during psychotherapy (Newnham & Page, 2010). Since assessments (Lambert et al., 2003) occur repeatedly during therapy, clinicians are a key component in feedback and can modify treatment in real time (de Jong, van Sluis, Nugter, Heiser, & Spinhoven, 2012; de Jong et al., 2014). Importantly, the routine feedback of the information about progress to staff (Lambert, 2013; Lutz, Bohnke, & Kock, 2011; Lutz, Wittmann, Bohnke, Rubel, & Steffanowski, 2013; Shimokawa, Lambert, & Smart, 2010) and to both staff and patients (Dyer, Hooke, & Page, 2014, in press; Newnham, Hooke, & Page, 2010) improves treatment outcomes. That is, patients who deviate from an expected trajectory of improvement are less likely to deteriorate when their treating clinician is alerted to the potential of a negative outcome (Lutz, Martinovich, & Howard, 1999; Lutz et al., 2014; Stulz, Lutz, Kopta, Minami, & Saunders, 2013). While progress monitoring has made an important contribution to the quality of care, the full potential for monitoring has not been realized. The present paper will address one area where monitoring can be extended to generate further potential benefits, namely the prediction of suicide and self-injury.

The risk of acting on suicidal thoughts is increased as a person acquires the necessary capability. The concept of this acquired capability is a novel contribution of the interpersonal theory of suicide (Joiner, 2005; Van Orden et al., 2010). Joiner and colleagues argue that proximal predictors of suicide risk occur when there is a confluence of three factors. Suicidal desire occurs when (i) a person's need to social belongingness is thwarted and combined with (ii) a perception that they are a burden on others. Critically, the consequent suicidal desire and associated ideation are not sufficient to predict suicidal behaviour. In addition, a person must (iii) acquire the capability to act on the thoughts. The innate desire for life must be beaten down and any obstacles to acting on suicidal thoughts must be removed (Harrison, Stritzke, Fay, Ellison, & Hudaib, 2014). Thus, in their model, non-suicidal self-injury (NSSI; Hamza, Stewart, & Willoughby, 2012) serves to help a person acquire the capability to die by suicide.

NSSI during a period of treatment and psychotherapy has iatrogenic potential because it increases acquired capability. Although not all NSSI has an immediate impact on suicidal risk, according to the interpersonal theory, it is particularly worrying when combined with suicidal ideation. Furthermore, the probability of the confluence of the three factors described by interpersonal theory of suicide is higher during an inpatient psychiatric admission. Inpatients exhibit an increased risk for suicide attempts and acts (Cassells, Paterson, Dowding, & Morrison, 2005; Hunt et al., 2007) arguably because one reason for admission involves safety concerns (Goldacre, Seagroatt, & Hawton, 1993; Hunt et al., 2009; Large, Sharma, Cannon, Ryan, & Nielssen, 2011; Qin & Nordentoft, 2005). Hence, the prediction of self-injury among people who have already expressed suicidal ideation is important because each act could increase the acquired capability for death by suicide.

Thus, our focus was upon the prediction of self-injurious behaviours among people expressing suicidal ideation during an inpatient psychiatric admission. Yet one issue with the measurement of suicidal ideation is its variability. Suicidal ideation fluctuates across time (Beck, Brown, Steer, Dahlsgaard, & Grisham, 1999; Witte, Fitzpatrick, Joiner, & Schmidt, 2005; Witte, Fitzpatrick, Warren, Schatschneider, & Schmidt, 2006) and therefore depending on a single measurement will ignore the different trajectories of suicidal ideation. For example, endorsement of suicidal ideation at a moderate level on 1 day may mean something different if it occurs within a rising trajectory of suicidal desire as opposed to it occurring within a falling trajectory. Also, individuals with greater variability in suicidal thinking are more likely to have multiple suicide attempts (Witte et al., 2006) and so a pattern of rapid cycling could have a different meaning to a stable pattern. A single assessment of suicidal ideation cannot disambiguate these people.

To the extent that there are different trajectories of suicidal ideation, risk management strategies for those with fleeting suicidality may need to differ from those with more enduring suicidality. Those with more intense enduring suicidal ideation may be more likely to engage in self-injury and thus increase their acquired capability. It was hypothesized that distinct subgroups of psychiatric inpatients could be identified with daily monitoring of suicidal ideation. These subgroups may exhibit different risks of engaging in self-injury and hence the second aim was to examine the degree to which various trajectories of suicidal ideation predicted self-injury, with a view to assisting clinical decision-making by developing a flow chart to inform risk management. Third, assuming that clinically meaningful groupings could be identified, the degree to which the available clinical cross-sectional symptom data could predict these groupings will be contrasted with assessment based on longitudinal data.

Method

Patient Sample

The present sample was selected from a pool of 1060 inpatients admitted to a psychiatric hospital (1 January 2009 to 31 August 2010) diagnosed by their treating psychiatrist according to ICD-10-AM criteria (National Centre for Classification in Health Publications, 2002). To be included in the analysis patients needed to have (i) completed a measure of suicidal ideation on at least three occasions during an admission, to permit modelling of trajectories over time and (ii) endorsed thoughts about killing themselves. The resulting subsample of 562 inpatients (Table I) were mostly female (71.2%) and ages ranged from 16 to 87 years (M = 40; SD = 13.95). The mean length of stay was 24 days (SD = 15.97). Fifty-four percent had at least one previous admission at the hospital (M = 6.15; SD = 9.68). The sample consisted of people with primary diagnoses of mood disorders (64.1%), neurotic disorders (19.2%), substance use (7.7%), psychotic disorders (3.6%), and personality disorders (3.7%). The sample was characterized by severe (scores greater than 28 are in the "extremely severe" range) symptomatology on the Depression Anxiety Stress Scales (DASS-21; Lovibond & Lovibond, 1995; Newnham, Doyle, Sng, Hooke, & Page, 2012; Page, Hooke, & Morrison, 2007; Ronk, Korman, Hooke, & Page, 2013). The research protocol had approval from the university's ethics committee.

Table I. Mean symptom severity of an inpatient sample expressing suicidal ideation, taken at the time of admission and discharge from hospital.

Measure	Admission	Discharge
DASS-21 depression	33.20 (9.54)	16.07 (11.43)
DASS-21 anxiety	22.72 (10.90)	12.47 (10.25)
DASS-21 stress	29.09 (10.21)	16.34 (10.28)
HoNOS total	16.76 (4.55)	6.57 (4.26)

Note. Standard deviations in parentheses.

All observed incidents of self-injury that occurred for each patient during hospitalization were recorded. These self-injury events were documented by hospital staff as part of routine monitoring of adverse events and included acts such as overdose, asphyxiation, and intentional burning, cutting, scratching, puncturing, and hitting of one's body. No distinction was made between self-injury with or without intent to die. Of the original cohort of 1060 patients, 64 patients (6.00%) engaged in at least one incident of self-injury.

Measures and Procedure

Suicidal ideation was assessed with the item: "I have had thoughts about killing myself." The patient would select the most appropriate response from *at no time* (score of 0), *some of the time* (score of 1), *less than half of the time* (score of 2), *more than half of the time* (score of 3), *most of the time* (score of 4), and *all of the time* (score of 5). Patients were invited to complete the item daily during their admission as part of a questionnaire battery administered via touch screens (Newnham et al., 2012).

The Health of the Nation Outcome Scale (HoNOS; Wing et al., 1998), is a 12-item clinician-rated measure consisting exploring behavioural, social, and cognitive problems over the 2 weeks prior to admission. It has good construct validity (Wing et al., 1998) and is sensitive to treatment change (Newnham, Harwood, & Page, 2009; Page, Hooke, & Rutherford, 2001). The internal consistency for the inpatient sample was acceptable (Cronbach's α = .70) given it assesses diverse domains (Trauer, 1999).

The shortened form of the DASS-21 (Lovibond & Lovibond, 1995) measured depression, anxiety, and stress over the previous week. The DASS-21 has sound construct validity (Page et al., 2007; Ronk, Hooke, & Page, 2012; Ronk et al., 2013) and demonstrated good reliability in the current sample (Cronbach's α for depression = .92, anxiety = .85, stress = .88).

Statistics

Latent class growth analysis (LCGA). The number of distinct patterns of early change in suicidal ideation was determined using LCGA (using Mplus 6; Muthén & Muthén, 2010). The presence of suicidal ideation was defined as any score above zero on the suicidal thinking item.

To determine the rate at which suicidal thinking changed, scores were plotted against time (in days), with time zero being the initial endorsement of the suicidal ideation item above zero. The Bayesian Information Criterion (BIC; Schwarz, 1978), a model fit index that balances goodness of fit and parsimony was used to determine the optimal number of classes. Entropy and posterior probabilities for each model (Andruff, Carraro, Thompson, Gaudreau, & Louvet, 2009; Jung & Wickrama, 2008) were also used to select the optimal number of classes.

The growth model assumed a log-linear relationship between suicidal ideation and time. This assumption was supported by the log-linear growth model having a superior fit to a linear model (linear model: −3166.93; log-linear model: −3029.18).

Logistic regression and model comparison. After using LCGA to identify subpopulations, logistic regression analysis in SPSS identified the predictors that distinguished patients who demonstrated a reduction in their suicidal ideation from those whose suicidality remained high. The selection of predictor and outcome variables was based both on the classes identified in the LCGA as well as patient information available at admission. Predictive models were used diagnostic performance criteria outlined by Kessel and Zimmerman (1993).

Missing Values Analysis

A missing values analysis revealed that missing cases were missing completely at random [Little's MCAR test: χ^2 (3415) = 3435.86; p = .397]. Therefore, Full Information Maximum Likelihood was used to impute missing data for LCGA analyses (Enders, 2010). Since data were missing completely at random, listwise deletion was used for the logistic regression.

Results

Identifying Subgroups of Suicidal Inpatients

Considering the fit criteria as a whole, five classes represented the optimal number. Starting with a single latent class model, additional latent classes were added into the LCGA until the optimal number of latent classes was found. The Vuong–Lo–Mendell–Rubin Likelihood Ratio Test (Lo, Mendell, & Rubin, 2001) favoured a five-class solution as adding an extra group significantly improved model fit until the sixth class (one class vs. two classes: p = .000; two classes vs. three classes: p = .000; three classes vs. four classes: p = .007; four classes vs. five classes: p = .008; five classes vs. six classes: p = .144). Likewise, the BIC decreased from one to five class solutions (8130.56, 6859.26, 6469.71, 6298.17, and 6197.66) but showed minimal change with the addition of a sixth class (BIC = 6143.14). Entropy—a summary measure of the classification quality of cases into latent classes (Ramaswamy, DeSarbo, Reibstein, & Robinson, 1993)—was less clear, but five classes were one of the best models (two classes: .92; three classes: .89; four classes: .91; five classes: .90; six classes: .90). Taking these fit indices as a group, on balance, it was decided that five classes provided the best solution.

Average posterior probabilities of group assignment ranged from 0.87 to 0.97, indicating that the trajectories discriminated well between individuals with similar and dissimilar patterns of change (Andruff et al., 2009). To check that solutions were not local the analysis was repeated using the seed values from the two highest-ranked log likelihood values and comparing the model parameter estimates. The replication of the estimates confirmed that this was not a local solution.

As shown in Figure 1, one patient group (i.e., Pattern 1, comprising 10.2% of the sample) was characterized by a high degree of suicidality with no early improvement. Patients repeatedly indicated they thought about suicide "most of the time." Of the 57 patients in this class, 17 (29.8%) engaged in self-injury during their admission.

Three patient groups were characterized by improvements in suicidal ideation but differed in initial severity and rates of change. One group exhibited minimal initial suicidal ideation, with patients reporting thinking of suicide "some of the time" during the initial 24-hr period (i.e., Pattern 5, comprising 57.5% of the sample). Patients in this class experienced a reduction in suicidal ideation over the 7-day period. Of the 323 patients identified as belonging to this class, only 12 (3.7%) engaged in self-injury during admission.

A second group was characterized by moderate suicidality with some improvement over the 7-day period (i.e., Pattern 3, comprising 9.6% of the sample), with patients reporting thinking of suicide "more than half of the time." Of the 54 patients classified into this class, 14 (25.9%) engaged in self-injury during their admission.

A third group was characterized by a high degree of initial suicidal ideation, with a large and rapid improvement (i.e., Pattern 2, comprising 14.2% of the sample). Patients within this subgroup reported suicidal ideation "more than half the time," which then reduced to minimal levels over the following few days. Of the 80 patients in this class, only 8 (10%) engaged in self-injury during their admission.

Finally, there was a subgroup characterized by low suicidality with minor increases in severity (i.e., Pattern 4, comprising 8.5% of the sample). On average, patients in this subgroup reported suicidal ideation "some of the time," which then increased to "less than half the time" after 7 days. Of the 48 patients belonging to this class, only 1 (2.1%) engaged in self-injury during their admission.

Clinical Utility

The rate of self-injury in the total inpatient sample (n = 1060) was 6.0%. Breaking this down further, 1.6% of those who did not report thoughts of suicide engaged in self-injury. Of the 562 inpatients who endorsed suicidal ideation at least once during an admission, 9.96% engaged in self-injury. Since 12 of these 56 incidents of self-injury occurred before endorsement on the questionnaire they could not be predicted by scale and are analyzed separately. The rates of self-injury are displayed in Figure 2

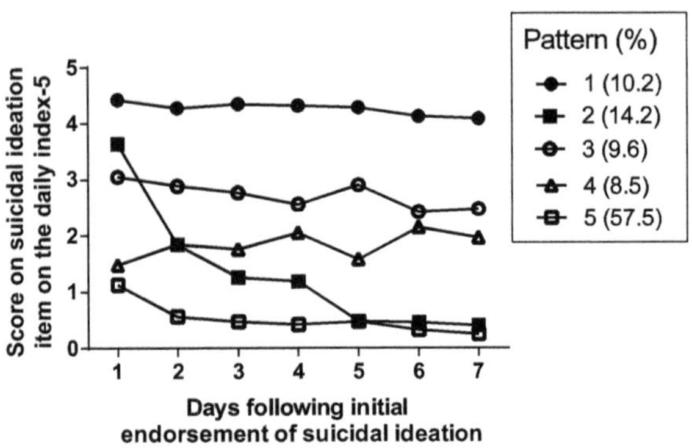

Figure 1. Observed patterns of early change in the days following initial suicidal ideation. Pattern 1: high degree of suicidality with no improvement; Pattern 2: high degree of suicidality with large and rapid improvement; Pattern 3: moderate degree of suicidality with some early improvement; Pattern 4: low suicidality with an increase in severity; Pattern 5: low suicidality with some improvement.

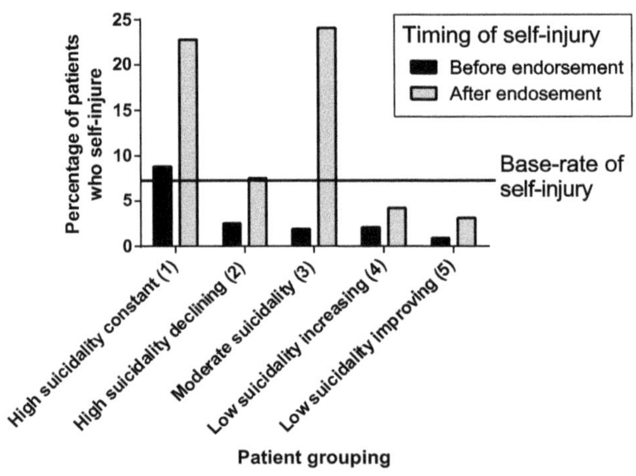

Figure 2. Histogram showing percentage of patients who self-injure before or after endorsing the suicide question broken down by groupings of temporal trajectories of suicidal thoughts (numbers in parentheses refer to patterns identified by the LCGA).

broken down into those which occurred before endorsement of the suicide question and after endorsement. What is evident is that overall the frequency of self-injury increases from 2.1% in the period before this subset of patients have endorsed the suicide question to 7.8% after they have endorsed it. That is, consistent with the interpersonal theory of suicide, the occurrence of suicidal ideation appears to drive acquiring the capability via self-injury. More importantly, there are differences between the groups. Notably, patients who consistently endorse the suicide question highly exhibit high probability of subsequent self-injury (22.8%) as well as high rates (average number of incidents per patient is 2.2), whereas patients who endorse the item highly transiently have subsequent probability of self-injury (7.5%) comparable to the hospital base rate (and the average number of incidents per patient is 1.5). This latter group contrasts with the patients who endorse the suicide question at a moderate level who have high probability of self-injury (24.1%) and higher rates (average number of incidents per patient is 1.8). Together, these data point to the value of understanding the dynamic nature of thoughts about suicide and classifying people accordingly. A flow chart can then be developed that may assist clinical decision-making, by identifying the estimated risk associate with different response profiles (Figure 3).

Predicting Class Membership

Given the importance of distinguishing patients who endorse suicidal thoughts at a moderate to high level continuously, from those who endorse them transiently, subsequent analyses focused on the two groups presenting with more severe suicidal ideation at first endorsement (i.e., Patterns 1 and 2). These two groups will be referred to as those presenting with *remitting suicidality* and *non-remitting suicidality*.

These two groups were selected because both groups presented with frequent suicidal ideation and hence they would be a target for risk assessment. Additionally, these groups diverged rapidly in their trajectories of suicidal thinking in the days following and differed substantially in their proportion of self-injuring patients. Thus, understanding what factors may identify a patient with non-remitting suicidal thinking may assist in risk management, clinical decision-making, and allocation of staff resources.

A backward stepwise binary logistic regression model determined the most parsimonious set of predictors to discriminate between patients with unremitting (n = 22) and remitting suicidal ideation (n = 38). As a baseline against which to evaluate the current model, severity of depression at admission, and staff ratings of current suicidal thinking and behaviour were tested as significant indicators of more severe, longstanding suicidal ideation. Therefore, predictor variables included admission DASS-21 subscale scores and each patient's admission score on the staff-rated non-accidental self-injury item of the HoNOS.

A test of the model against a constant only model was statistically significant, indicating that the model reliably distinguished between remitting and non-remitting suicidal ideation groups [χ^2 (2) = 16.14;

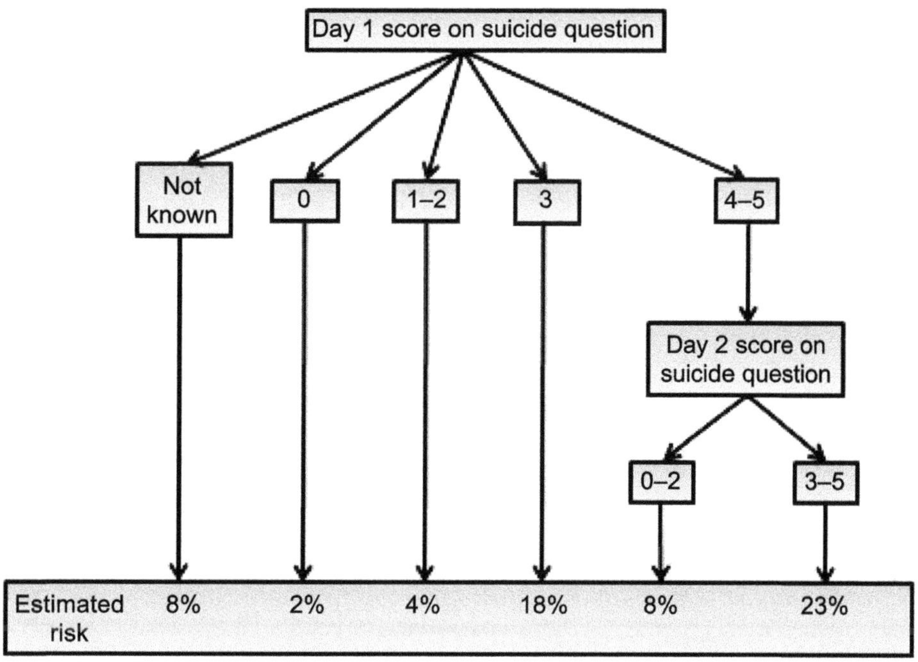

Figure 3. Flow chart reflecting the estimated risk of self-injury based on responses to a question "I have had thoughts of killing myself."

Table II. Observed and predicted frequencies for classification of 60 inpatients into remitting and non-remitting suicidal ideation groups.

	Predicted patient outcome		
Patient outcome	Remitting	Non-remitting	Percent correct
Remitting	31	7	81.60
Non-remitting	11	11	50.00
Overall percent correct			70.00

Note. Sensitivity = 11/(11 + 11)% = 50.00%; specificity = 31/(31 + 7)% = 81.58%; false positive = 7/(7 + 31)% = 18.42%; false negative = 11/(11 + 11)% = 50.00%; positive predictive power = 11/(11 + 7) = 61.11%; negative predictive power = 31/(31 + 11) = 73.81%.

p = .000]. Model fit was acceptable [Hosmer and Lemeshow test; χ^2 (8) = 4.91; p = .767], although only 32.2% of the variation in the dependent variable was explained. As shown in Table II, 70% of patients were correctly classified (81.6% with remitting suicidal ideation and 50% with non-remitting suicidal ideation). The Wald criterion demonstrated that, of the predictors included, only admission scores of the non-accidental self-injury item of the HoNOS significantly contributed to prediction (β = .67; Wald = 8.42; p = .004). The Exp(B) value indicated that for every one unit increase on the non-accidental self-injury item of the HoNOS, a patient is 1.95 times more likely to remain suicidal in the week following initially reporting frequent suicidal thoughts.

To investigate whether the inclusion of the suicidal ideation item improved discrimination between groups, suicidal ideation 24 hrs after initial endorsement was chosen as the variable of interest. Ideation at this time would provide minimum time between initial flagging of potentially at risk patients and classification.

A comparison of the diagnostic performance of these models identified that a score above three on the suicidal ideation item was an optimal threshold for classification of patients into remitting or non-remitting groups (Table III). In the context of the measure, this would mean that identifying patients endorsing suicidal ideation *most of the time* to *all of the time* in a 24-hr period is an accurate and valuable clinical cut-off to begin separating this sample into remitting and non-remitting groups. This model had the highest overall classification rating of all models generated (91.25%), had an excellent agreement (κ = .81), and was the cut-off optimizing the trade-off between sensitivity and specificity (Youden's index = 0.82).

A cut-off score of greater than four on the ideation item, although highly specific, failed to identify almost 25% of patients with non-remitting suicidal ideation. According to Pinto, Whisman, and McCoy (1997), any model discriminating between suicidal individuals should favour superior sensitivity and negative predictive power at the expense of specificity, due to the potential costs of missing individuals at risk. With a high sensitivity rate of 89.66% and a negative predictive power of 94%, a model which used a threshold of four and above to separate patient groups was judged to best balance these considerations with overall predictive power.

In comparing this threshold model to the logistic regression model, it can be seen that the classification accuracy is improved by over 20%. In addition, the model had a far superior sensitivity rate (90% vs. 50%) and negative predictive power (94% vs. 74%). This means that by taking into account suicidality 24 hrs after initially flagging patients as suicidal, fewer patients who go on to express prolonged suicidality and engage in self-injury in the days following are missed.

Discussion

Inpatients who expressed suicidal ideation during their hospital admission could be separated into five separate groups, based on how the intensity of their suicidal thinking changed over the following week. Thus, inpatients who express suicidal thinking are best represented as diverse groups that differ in their

Table III. Number of patients predicted to express prolonged suicidal ideation according to frequency of suicidal ideation 24 hrs after initial endorsement, using a range of cut-off values, and comparing diagnostic performance.

Cut-off score	Remitted	Non-remitted	Sensitivity (%)	Specificity (%)	False positive rate (%)	False negative rate (%)	Classification rate (%)	PPP (%)	NPP (%)	Youden's index	κ
≥0	10	70	100.00	19.61	58.57	0.00	48.75	41.43	100.00	0.36	.150
≥1	21	59	96.55	39.22	52.54	4.76	60.00	47.46	95.24	0.36	.292
≥2	35	45	96.55	66.67	37.78	2.86	77.50	62.22	97.14	0.63	.565
≥3	50	30	89.66	92.16	13.33	6.00	91.25	86.67	94.00	0.82	.812
≥4	66	14	44.83	98.04	7.14	24.24	78.75	92.86	75.76	0.43	.482

Note. PPP = positive predictive power; NPP = negative predictive power.

time course of suicidal ideation. These findings are consistent with previous conclusions that suicidal thinking is not temporally stable (Witte et al., 2006).

The present study also found that inquiring about suicidal thinking in the period can provide important information for the prediction of self-injury. A predictive model based on this information more accurately identified those who continue to express severe suicidality, as opposed to a model based on patient information available at admission alone. These data can then be used to assist clinical decision-making since they allow clinicians to predict self-injury events and to identify with greater precision which groups of patients are at an elevated risk. The data support development of a decision-tree (Figure 2) in which hospital staff could move from knowing that if a person endorses an item concerning thoughts about killing themselves, the risk of self-injury during that admission is doubled. In addition, if the person has a high score (i.e., above 3) and remains elevated for 2 days, then the risk of a self-injury is four times as great as the expected base rate. Such information could be used to manage the risk of self-injury more efficiently.

The occurrence of NSSI is a potentially dangerous event, not only because of the attendant risks that arise from the act itself, but also because of it can be a further step in acquiring the capability to die by suicide. Consistent with predictions from the interpersonal theory of suicide (Van Orden et al., 2010), people with suicidal ideation were more likely to engage in behaviours that would acquire the capability for death by suicide.

It would be of interest to broaden the model to include predictors of group assignment. Taking into account differences in symptom severity, or the presence of key psychological factors, could identify patient characteristics that make someone more vulnerable to elevated suicidal ideation. Alternatively, future research could identify what patient factors may "immunize" a patient against poorer outcomes (Kleiman, Miller, & Riskind, 2012).

The current study used a single-item measure to track suicidal thinking, which was a consequence of monitoring suicidality on a daily basis. Whilst there are a number of well-validated measures that examine suicidal thinking, they are unsuitable for measuring suicidal ideation daily, as they are too lengthy or refer to long-time periods. Thus, while there is evidence to support the use of a single-item measure in effectively tracking patient progress over time (Forman et al., 2012), the information gleaned from a single-item measure is limited and future research may develop this approach by investigating additional predictors.

In drawing conclusions from the present findings it is important to interpret the results cautiously. As such, the classification statistics of the models reported should only be interpreted in relation to each other and cannot be generalized to suicidal attempts or completions. Nonetheless, establishing that intensity in the period after first endorsement is a good predictor of intensity of suicidal thinking 7 days later (Table III) in admission is potentially important in guiding treatment decisions within appropriate time frames.

In conclusion, patient progress monitoring has traditionally been used to identify and respond to patients based on their (lack of) progress towards a good therapy outcome. The present study took this programme of practice-based evidence one step further and showed that the routine monitoring of outcomes could assist in the prediction of adverse events during a period of treatment. Future research will need to evaluate the degree to which the ability to more accurately predict which patients are at a greater risk of self-injury can enhance outcomes. However, the potential clinical benefit appears to lie in the ability of staff to reduce the number of self-injury events. Self-injury is a problem in its own right, but its occurrence increases the risk of death by suicide. By serving to increase the person's acquired capability, incidents of self-injury lower the threshold for suicidal behaviour to occur when suicidal desire is present. More broadly, the present study has shown that patient progress monitoring can be considered not only as a tool for identifying and responding to poor outcomes, but also the identification of adverse events.

Funding

This article is funded by Department of Industry, Innovation, Science, Research and Tertiary Education, Australian Government—Australian Research Council [grant number LP100200749].

References

Andruff, H., Carraro, N., Thompson, A., Gaudreau, P., & Louvet, B. (2009). Latent class growth modelling: A tutorial. *Tutorials in Quantitative Methods for Psychology*, *5*(1), 11–24.

Beck, A. T., Brown, G. K., Steer, R. A., Dahlsgaard, K. K., & Grisham, J. R. (1999). Suicide ideation at its worst point: A predictor of eventual suicide in psychiatric outpatients. *Suicide and Life-threatening Behavior*, *29*(1), 1–9.

Cassells, C., Paterson, B., Dowding, D., & Morrison, R. (2005). Long- and short-term risk factors in the prediction of inpatient suicide. *Crisis: The Journal of Crisis Intervention and Suicide Prevention*, *26*(2), 53–63. doi:10.1027/0227-5910.26.2.53

Castonguay, L., Barham, M., Lutz, W., & McAleavy, A. (2013). Practice-oriented research. In M. J. Lambert (Ed.), *Bergin and Garfield's handbook of psychotherapy and behavior change* (6th ed., pp. 85–133). Hoboken, NJ: Wiley.

de Jong, K., Timman, R., Hakkaart-Van Roijen, L., Vermeulen, P., Kooiman, K., Passchier, J., & Busschbach, J. V. (2014). The effect of outcome monitoring feedback to clinicians and patients in short and long-term psychotherapy: A randomized controlled trial. *Psychotherapy Research, 24*, 629–639. doi:10.1080/10503307.2013.871079

de Jong, K., van Sluis, P., Nugter, M., Heiser, W. J., & Spinhoven, P. (2012). Understanding the differential impact of outcome monitoring: Therapist variables that moderate feedback effects in a randomized clinical trial. *Psychotherapy Research, 22*, 464–474. doi:10.1080/10503307.2012.673023

Dyer, K., Hooke, G., & Page, A. C. (2014). Development and psychometrics of the five item daily index in a psychiatric sample. *Journal of Affective Disorders, 152–154*, 409–415. doi:10.1016/j.jad.2013.10.003

Dyer, K., Hooke, G. R., & Page, A. C. (in press). Effects of providing domain specific progress monitoring and feedback to therapists and patients on outcome. *Psychotherapy Research.* doi:10.1080/10503307.2014.983207

Enders, C. K. (2010). *Applied missing data analysis.* New York, NY: Guilford Press.

Forman, E. M., Chapman, J. E., Herbert, J. D., Goetter, E. M., Yuen, E. K., & Moitra, E. (2012). Using session-by-session measurement to compare mechanisms of action for acceptance and commitment therapy and cognitive therapy. *Behavior Therapy, 43*, 341–354. doi:10.1016/j.beth.2011.07.004

Goldacre, M., Seagroatt, V., & Hawton, K. (1993). Suicide after discharge from psychiatric inpatient care. *The Lancet, 342*, 283–286. doi:10.1016/0140-6736(93)91822-4

Hamza, C. A., Stewart, S. L., & Willoughby, T. (2012). Examining the link between nonsuicidal self-injury and suicidal behavior: A review of the literature and an integrated model. *Clinical Psychology Review, 32*, 482–495. doi:10.1016/j.cpr.2012.05.003

Harrison, D. P., Stritzke, W. G., Fay, N., Ellison, T., & Hudaib, A.-R. (2014). Probing the implicit suicidal mind: Does the death/suicide implicit association test reveal a desire to die, or a diminished desire to live? *Psychological Assessment, 26*, 831–840. doi:10.1037/pas0000001

Hunt, I. M., Kapur, N., Webb, R., Robinson, J. O., Burns, J., Shaw, J., & Appleby, L. (2009). Suicide in recently discharged psychiatric patients: A case-control study. *Psychological Medicine, 39*, 443–449. doi:10.1017/S0033291708003644

Hunt, I. M., Kapur, N., Webb, R., Robinson, J. O., Burns, J., Turnbull, P., … Appleby, L. (2007). Suicide in current psychiatric in-patients: A case-control study. The national confidential inquiry into suicide and homicide. *Psychological Medicine, 37*, 831–837. doi:10.1017/S0033291707000104

Joiner, T. E., Jr. (2005). *Why people die by suicide.* Cambridge, MA: Harvard University Press.

Jung, T., & Wickrama, K. (2008). An introduction to latent class growth analysis and growth mixture modeling. *Social and Personality Psychology Compass, 2*, 302–317. doi:10.1111/j.1751-9004.2007.00054.x

Kessel, J. B., & Zimmerman, M. (1993). Reporting errors in studies of the diagnostic performance of self-administered questionnaires: Extent of the problem, recommendations for standardized presentation of results, and implications for the peer review process. *Psychological Assessment, 5*, 395–399. doi:10.1037/1040-3590.5.4.395

Kleiman, E. M., Miller, A. B., & Riskind, J. H. (2012). Enhancing attributional style as a protective factor in suicide. *Journal of Affective Disorders, 143*, 236–240. doi:10.1016/j.jad.2012.05.014

Lambert, M. J. (2013). *Bergin and Garfield's handbook of psychotherapy and behavior change.* New York, NY: John Wiley & Sons.

Lambert, M. J., Whipple, J. L., Hawkins, E. J., Vermeersch, D. A., Nielsen, S. L., & Smart, D. W. (2003). Is it time for clinicians to routinely track patient outcome? A meta-analysis. *Clinical Psychology: Science and Practice, 10*, 288–301. doi:10.1093/clipsy.bpg025

Large, M. M., Sharma, S., Cannon, E., Ryan, C., & Nielssen, O. B. (2011). Risk factors for suicide within a year of discharge from psychiatric hospital: A systematic meta-analysis. *Australian and New Zealand Journal of Psychiatry, 45*, 619–628. doi:10.3109/00048674.2011.590465

Lo, Y., Mendell, N. R., & Rubin, D. B. (2001). Testing the number of components in a normal mixture. *Biometrika, 88*, 767–778. doi:10.1093/biomet/88.3.767

Lovibond, P. F., & Lovibond, S. H. (1995). The structure of negative emotional states: Comparison of the Depression Anxiety Stress Scales (DASS) with the beck depression and anxiety inventories. *Behaviour Research and Therapy, 33*, 335–343. doi:10.1016/0005-7967(94)00075-U

Lovibond, S. H., & Lovibond, P. F. (1995). *Manual for the Depression Anxiety Stress Scales.* Sydney: Psychology Foundation.

Lutz, W., Bohnke, J. R., & Kock, K. (2011). Lending an ear to feedback systems: Evaluation of recovery and non-response in psychotherapy in a German outpatient setting. *Community Mental Health Journal, 47*, 311–317. doi:10.1007/s10597-010-9307-3

Lutz, W., Hofmann, S. G., Rubel, J., Boswell, J. F., Shear, M., Gorman, J. M., … Barlow, D. H. (2014). Patterns of early change and their relationship to outcome and early treatment termination in patients with panic disorder. *Journal of Consulting and Clinical Psychology, 82*, 287–297. doi:10.1037/a0035535

Lutz, W., Martinovich, Z., & Howard, K. I. (1999). Patient profiling: An application of random coefficient regression models to depicting the response of a patient to outpatient psychotherapy. *Journal of Consulting and Clinical Psychology, 67*, 571–577. doi:10.1037/0022-006X.67.4.571

Lutz, W., Wittmann, W. W., Bohnke, J. R., Rubel, J., & Steffanowski, A. (2013). The TK-project quality monitoring in outpatient psychotherapy from the perspective of the evaluation team – A plea for more psychotherapy research in Germany. *PPmP: Psychotherapie Psychosomatik Medizinische Psychologie, 63*, 225–228.

Muthén, L. K., & Muthén, B. O. (2010). *Mplus (version 6).* Los Angeles, CA: Author.

National Centre for Classification in Health Publications. (2002). *The international statistical classification of diseases and related health problems, tenth revision, Australian modification (ICD-10-AM)* (3rd ed.). Geneva: Author.

Newnham, E. A., Doyle, E. L., Sng, A. A., Hooke, G. R., & Page, A. C. (2012). Improving clinical outcomes in psychiatric care with touch-screen technology. *Psychological Services, 9*, 221–223. doi:10.1037/a0026143

Newnham, E. A., Harwood, K. E., & Page, A. C. (2009). The subscale structure and clinical utility of the Heath of the Nation Outcome Scale. *Journal of Mental Health, 18*, 426–428. doi:10.1080/09638230802522486

Newnham, E. A., Hooke, G. R., & Page, A. C. (2010). Progress monitoring and feedback in psychiatric care reduces depressive symptoms. *Journal of Affective Disorders, 127*(1–3), 139–146. doi:10.1016/j.jad.2010.05.003

Newnham, E. A., & Page, A. C. (2010). Bridging the gap between best evidence and best practice in mental health. *Clinical Psychology Review, 30*(1), 127–142. doi:10.1016/j.cpr.2009.10.004

Page, A. C., Hooke, G. R., & Morrison, D. L. (2007). Psychometric properties of the Depression Anxiety Stress Scales (DASS) in depressed clinical samples. *British Journal of Clinical Psychology, 46*, 283–297. doi:10.1348/014466506X158996

Page, A. C., Hooke, G. R., & Rutherford, E. M. (2001). Measuring mental health outcomes in a private psychiatric clinic: Health of the Nation Outcome Scales and Medical Outcomes Short Form SF-36. *Australian and New Zealand Journal of Psychiatry*, *35*, 377–381. doi:10.1046/j.1440-1614.2001.00908.x

Page, A. C., & Stritzke, W. G. K. (2015). *Clinical psychology for trainees: Foundations of science-informed practice* (2nd ed.). Cambridge: Cambridge University Press.

Pinto, A., Whisman, M. A., & McCoy, K. J. (1997). Suicidal ideation in adolescents: Psychometric properties of the suicidal ideation questionnaire in a clinical sample. *Psychological Assessment*, *9*(1), 63–66. doi:10.1037/1040-3590.9.1.63

Qin, P., & Nordentoft, M. (2005). Suicide risk in relation to psychiatric hospitalization: Evidence based on longitudinal registers. *Archives of General Psychiatry*, *62*, 427–432. doi:10.1001/archpsyc.62.4.427

Ramaswamy, V., DeSarbo, W. S., Reibstein, D. J., & Robinson, W. T. (1993). An empirical pooling approach for estimating marketing mix elasticities with PIMS data. *Marketing Science*, *12*(1), 103–124. doi:10.1287/mksc.12.1.103

Ronk, F. R., Hooke, G. R., & Page, A. C. (2012). How consistent are clinical significance classifications when calculation methods and outcome measures differ? *Clinical Psychology: Science and Practice*, *19*, 167–179. doi:10.1111/j.1468-2850.2012.01281.x

Ronk, F. R., Korman, J. R., Hooke, G. R., & Page, A. C. (2013). Assessing clinical significance of treatment outcomes using the DASS-21. *Psychological Assessment*, *25*(4), 1103–1110. doi:10.1037/a0033100

Schwarz, G. (1978). Estimating the dimension of a model. *The Annals of Statistics*, *6*, 461–464. doi:10.1214/aos/1176344136

Shimokawa, K., Lambert, M. J., & Smart, D. W. (2010). Enhancing treatment outcome of patients at risk of treatment failure: Meta-analytic and mega-analytic review of a psychotherapy quality assurance system. *Journal of Consulting and Clinical Psychology*, *78*, 298–311. doi:10.1037/a0019247

Stulz, N., Lutz, W., Kopta, S. M., Minami, T., & Saunders, S. M. (2013). Dose-effect relationship in routine outpatient psychotherapy: Does treatment duration matter? *Journal of Counseling Psychology*, *60*, 593–600. doi:10.1037/a0033589

Trauer, T. (1999). The subscale structure of the Health of the Nation Outcome Scales (HoNOS). *Journal of Mental Health*, *8*, 499–509. doi:10.1080/09638239917193

Van Orden, K. A., Witte, T. K., Cukrowicz, K. C., Braithwaite, S. R., Selby, E. A., & Joiner, T. E., Jr. (2010). The interpersonal theory of suicide. *Psychological Review*, *117*, 575–600. doi:10.1037/a0018697

Wing, J. K., Beevor, A. S., Curtis, R. H., Park, S. B., Hadden, S., & Burns, A. (1998). Health of the Nation Outcome Scales (HoNOS). Research and development. *British Journal of Psychiatry*, *172*, 11–18. doi:10.1192/bjp.172.1.11

Witte, T. K., Fitzpatrick, K. K., Joiner, T. E., Jr., & Schmidt, N. B. (2005). Variability in suicidal ideation: A better predictor of suicide attempts than intensity or duration of ideation? *Journal of Affective Disorders*, *88*(2), 131–136. doi:10.1016/j.jad.2005.05.019

Witte, T. K., Fitzpatrick, K. K., Warren, K. L., Schatschneider, C., & Schmidt, N. B. (2006). Naturalistic evaluation of suicidal ideation: Variability and relation to attempt status. *Behaviour Research and Therapy*, *44*, 1029–1040. doi:10.1016/j.brat.2005.08.004

Extreme deviations from expected recovery curves and their associations with therapeutic alliance, social support, motivation, and life events in psychosomatic in-patient therapy

THOMAS PROBST[1], MICHAEL J. LAMBERT[2], THOMAS H. LOEW[3], REINER W. DAHLBENDER[4], & KARIN TRITT[3]

[1]*Deparment of Psychology, University of Regensburg, Regensburg, Germany;* [2]*Department of Psychology, Brigham Young University, Provo, UT, USA;* [3]*Department of Psychosomatics, University Clinic of Regensburg, Regensburg, Germany &* [4]*Clinic for Psychosomatic Medicine and Psychotherapy, University Clinic of Ulm, Ulm, Germany*

Abstract

Objectives: Within the clinical support tools (CST) of the OQ-Analyst, the "Assessment for Signal Cases" (ASC) evaluates the therapeutic alliance, social support, motivation, and life events. We investigated whether the ASC covers domains of importance in treatment weeks with extreme deviations from expected recovery curves (ERCs). **Methods:** Psychosomatic in-patients were monitored weekly with the ASC and the "Outcome Questionnaire" (OQ-45). The ERCs of the OQ-45 empirical algorithm were used to define treatment weeks with extreme positive deviations (EPD), extreme negative deviations (END), or without extreme deviations (NO). Associations between the ASC scales and EPD as well as END were analyzed by multilevel models. **Results:** While each ASC scale was positively associated with EPD, only the social support and life events scales were negatively related to END. **Conclusions:** CSTs prioritizing social support and life events might be more effective in preventing treatment failure.

Introduction

In patient-focused research (Howard, Moras, Brill, Martinovich, & Lutz, 1996), the individual patient's progress is continuously monitored with patient reported outcome measures (Greenhalgh, 2009) throughout treatment. By tracking patient progress during psychotherapies, time intervals with considerable positive or negative change can be identified for individual patients.

Different methods have been applied in psychotherapy research to operationalize considerable change with no agreed-upon standard procedure. For example, the "Reliable Change Index" (RCI; Jacobson & Truax, 1991) can be applied to define reliable positive and negative change. The method of percent improvement (Hiller, Schindler, & Lambert, 2013) was suggested to evaluate response and remission. A definition proposed by Tang and DeRubeis (1999) should operationalize sudden dramatic change in the positive (sudden gains: e.g., Tang & DeRubeis, 1999) or negative (sudden losses: e.g., Lutz et al., 2013) direction. In another method to identify considerable positive or negative change, the progress of a given patient is compared with his or her expected recovery curve (ERC) derived from a norm group consisting of patients with characteristics comparable to the patient in question (e.g., comparable levels of distress at intake; Finch, Lambert, & Schaalje, 2001; Newnham, Hooke, & Page, 2010). Extreme positive or negative deviations of the individual patient's progress from his or her ERC can be considered as either considerable positive or considerable negative change depending on the direction of change. It has been shown that extreme positive/negative deviations from ERCs as well as sudden gains/sudden losses during treatment are predictive of treatment success/treatment failure (Aderka, Nickerson, Bøe, & Hofmann, 2012; Haas, Hill, Lambert, & Morrell, 2002; Lambert, Whipple et al., 2002; Lutz et al., 2013; Spielmans, Masters, & Lambert, 2006).

A variety of mechanisms associated with considerable change have been critically discussed especially for sudden gains in cognitive-behavior therapy (CBT) of depression. Some authors advocate the possible causal role of specific treatment mechanisms (Andrusyna, Luborsky, Pham, & Tang, 2006; Tang & DeRubeis, 1999; Tang, DeRubeis, Beberman, & Pham, 2005). Others have speculated that common factors—i.e., factors viewed as active in all types of psychotherapy—or client variables are crucial, particularly for considerable positive change in the early phases of treatment (Ilardi & Craighead, 1994; Lambert, 2005).

A central question to be addressed is which factors should be considered as relevant with regard to considerable change. Taking quantitative findings into account, Asay and Lambert (1999) estimated that each of the following four general factors are more or less relevant for psychotherapy outcome: The contribution to treatment response was considered to amount to 40% for client and extratherapeutic factors, 30% for therapeutic relationship factors, 15% for hope and expectancy factors, and 15% for models and technique factors. A recent meta-analysis provided empirical evidence for these estimations regarding the psychotherapy outcome of depressive disorders (Cuijpers et al., 2012). Building on these findings, the self-report questionnaire "Assessment for Signal Cases" (ASC; Lambert et al., 2007) was developed. Within the ASC, the extratherapeutic factors are operationalized with two scales (social support scale and life events scale), the therapeutic relationship factors are evaluated with a therapeutic alliance scale, and the hope and expectancy factors are covered by a motivation scale. The models and technique factors are not included in the ASC, but other questionnaires are available to assess these factors, e.g., the "Multitheoretical List of Therapeutic Interventions" (MULTI; McCarthy & Barber, 2009).

Providing therapists with feedback on the ASC results constitutes the first part of the clinical support tools (CSTs) of the monitoring and feedback software OQ-Analyst (Lambert, 2012): When a patient deviates significantly negatively from his or her ERC (such a patient is considered at-risk of treatment failure; Lambert, Whipple et al., 2002; Spielmans et al., 2006), the therapist should administer the ASC to this patient and examine the ASC scores (pertaining to the last week) to identify possible problem areas that could account for the at-risk classification. The second part is recommended when patients show problematic scores on ASC scales. This part consists of a decision tree supporting therapists in organizing problem-solving strategies as well as in selecting interventions to improve problematic ASC domains (Lambert et al., 2007).

When therapists receive CSTs in addition to patient progress feedback, the outcome of patients at risk of treatment failure has been shown to improve in counseling (Harmon et al., 2007; Slade, Lambert, Harmon, Smart, & Bailey, 2008; Whipple et al., 2003), outpatient psychotherapy (Simon, Lambert, Harris, Busath, & Vazquez, 2012), outpatient substance abuse treatment (Crits-Christoph et al., 2012), and psychosomatic in-patient therapy (Probst et al., 2013).

Although the ASC comprises domains shown to be relevant for the prevention of treatment failure as well as for psychotherapy outcome/progress (therapeutic alliance: e.g., Horvath, Del Re, Flückiger, & Symonds, 2011; social support: e.g., Bankoff & Howard, 1992; motivation: e.g., Pelletier, Tuson, & Haddad, 1997; and life events: e.g., Sexton, 1996), the influence of those domains on considerable change during psychotherapy remains unclear. Previous studies examining associations between those domains and considerable change either on a patient-level or an assessment-level showed inconsistent results:

The patient-level studies compared patients who experienced considerable change at least at one assessment point during the entire course of psychotherapy against patients without any considerable change: It has been shown that neither the therapeutic alliance of the first psychotherapy session (Hardy et al., 2005), nor social support at the time of pretreatment (Hopko, Robertson, & Carvalho, 2009; Keller, Feeny, & Zoellner, 2014), nor life events during the course of psychotherapy (Hardy et al., 2005) differed between patients with and without at least one sudden gain. Furthermore, the therapeutic alliance during the entire course of psychotherapy did not differ between patients with at least one sudden gain assessment and patients with at least one sudden loss assessment (Lutz et al., 2013).

As the presence or absence of considerable change can be investigated at each available assessment point (this does not hold for the intake assessment, since at least two assessments are necessary to obtain a change score), a patient reaching considerable change at least at one assessment can also provide assessments not coded as considerable change during the course of treatment. The instability of considerable change has for instance been shown for sudden gains (Lutz, Bachmann, Tschitsaz, Smart, & Lambert, 2007).

Therefore, the assessment-level studies investigated how variables of interest (here the ASC domains) are related to individual assessments coded as considerable change. Those studies revealed that patients with depressive disorders rate the therapeutic alliance higher not before but after sudden gain assessments (Tang & DeRubeis, 1999) and that higher motivation preceded assessments coded as sudden gains in patients with eating disorders (Cavallini & Spangler, 2013). Moreover, independent observers considered therapists as more distanced and impatient in sudden loss sessions but more empathetic in sessions without considerable change in outpatient psychotherapies (Tschitsaz-Stucki & Lutz, 2009). Furthermore, the patients' motivation as well as their amount of life events were rated higher in sessions without considerable change, but their expectations were considered to be more realistic in sessions coded as sudden gains (Tschitsaz-Stucki & Lutz, 2009).

The cited studies did not investigate associations between considerable change and the ASC domains in psychosomatic in-patient therapy. Therefore, the present study examined with psychosomatic in-patients whether the ASC scales are of importance during treatment weeks with considerable change. We hypothesized that the weekly ASC scale scores are (1) positively related to treatment weeks with considerable positive change and (2) negatively associated with treatment weeks coded as considerable negative change.

Methods

Questionnaires

In this study, two questionnaires were administered to the patients simultaneously on a weekly basis:

Assessment for Signal Cases (ASC): The self-report questionnaire ASC (Lambert et al., 2007) contains 40 items which are rated on a five-point Likert scale. The ratings pertain to the previous week. The ASC covers four domains: Therapeutic alliance (11 items, range: 11–55), social support (11 items, range: 11–55), motivation (9 items, range: 9–45), and life events (9 items, range: 9–45). The higher the ASC scores, the better the therapeutic alliance, social support, motivation, and life events. For this study, the ASC was translated into German using the back-translation method as well as cognitive debriefings with 10 in-patients (Wild et al., 2005). The internal consistency coefficients (Cronbach's Alpha) of the scales of the German ASC were calculated with the ASC assessments at intake resulting in the following Cronbach's Alphas: Therapeutic alliance scale: 0.89; social support scale: 0.76; motivation scale: 0.78; life events scale: 0.71.

Outcome Questionnaire (OQ-45): The OQ-45 (Lambert, Hannöver, Nisslmüller, Richard, & Kordy, 2002; Lambert, Kahler, Harmon, Burlingame, & Shimokawa, 2011) is a self-report questionnaire which comprises 45 items rated on a five-point Likert scale. All ratings refer to the last week. In this paper, only the total scale of the OQ-45 (min: 0, max: 180) was used to measure the general distress level due to psychological problems and to define considerable change (see below). For the total scale of the German version of the OQ-45, the internal consistency reached 0.93 and the retest reliability amounted to 0.88 (Lambert, Hannöver et al., 2002). The higher the OQ-45 score, the worse was the impairment.

Study Design

Patients of two psychosomatic in-patient clinics were monitored over the course of their treatment. They were asked to fill out the German paper and pencil versions of the OQ-45 and the ASC once a week (between Friday and Sunday) during their stay. While all patients of the Psychosomatics Department of the Hospital in Donaustauf, Germany—treated from 10/01/2010 to 07/06/2012—were asked to participate in the study, only patients with private health care of the Psychosomatic Hospital "Am Schönen Moos" in Bad Saulgau, Germany—treated from 01/16/2012 to 04/06/2012—were encouraged to take part in the study. In both clinics, a multi-professional team (consisting mainly of psychologists, physicians, and nurses) provides a multimodal treatment with more than 24 treatment hours a week. This includes at least two individual psychotherapy sessions per week, group psychotherapy, relaxation and mindfulness training as well as art, music, and dance therapy and—if required—crisis intervention, visitations by nurses, and medical consultations.

In our overall project, patients were randomly assigned either to the control group or to the experimental group. For patients belonging to the experimental group, the therapists responsible for individual therapy received continuous patient progress (OQ-45) feedback as well as feedback on the ASC results. This paper analyses the scores of both control group and experimental group patients. The feedback effects were reported in other publications (Probst et al., 2013; Probst, Lambert, Dahlbender, Loew, & Tritt, 2014). The study was approved by the Ethics Committee of the University Clinic of Regensburg.

Definition of Considerable Change

Using the monitoring and feedback software OQ-Analyst (Lambert, 2012), the "empirical algorithm" of the OQ-45 was applied to define the presence or absence of considerable change on a weekly basis.

The "empirical algorithm" provides an ERC for each patient as a function of the patient's intake OQ-45 score. The ERC of a given patient is based on a norm group of at least 220 patients with OQ-45 intake scores comparable to the patient in question (Finch et al., 2001). Since the intake score and the change from session 1 to 3 has been shown to account for 40% of the outcome variance and adding other variables (e.g., diagnosis, therapy schools) did not prove itself useful in explaining more variance in the final outcome (Lambert, 2013), only the intake score functions as the baseline for the ERC.

For each treatment week following the intake assessment, the OQ-45 score of a given patient was compared with his or her ERC. When the OQ-45 score of a patient deviated positively from the patient's ERC and this score ranged within the top 10% of the norm group used to generate the ERC ("blue signal patients"; Lambert, 2012), the week was coded as treatment week with an extreme positive deviation (EPD). When an OQ-45 score deviated negatively by at least one standard deviation from the patient-specific ERCs (bottom 16% of the norm group), the week was coded as treatment week with an extreme negative deviation (END). This criterion has also been used to define patients at risk of treatment failure ("not-on-track" patients) in previous studies (Lambert, Whipple et al., 2002; Spielmans et al., 2006). Weeks with OQ-45 scores not deviating as described from the ERCs were classified as treatment weeks without extreme deviations (NO).

Statistical Analysis

The statistical analysis was done with SPSS 21. Means (*M*), standard deviations (*SD*), and percentages (%) were calculated as descriptive statistics.

For investigating associations between the ASC scales and considerable change, the following analyses were done with the weekly assessments (it should be kept in mind that the assessments taken during the intake week were only used to determine the patient's ERC and are hence not included in any further calculations).

For examining treatment weeks with EPD, the variable EPD was created for each treatment week: If an OQ-45 assessment was classified as EPD, this new variable was coded as 1 and if an OQ-45 assessment was classified as END or NO, this variable was coded as 0.

To analyze treatment weeks with END, the variable END was also created for each treatment week: If an OQ-45 assessment was classified as END, this variable was coded as 1 and if an OQ-45 assessment was classified as EPD or NO, this variable was coded as 0.

Two multilevel models for dichotomous outcomes (Heck, Thomas, & Tabata, 2012) were performed to study associations between the ASC scales and EPD or END. Both models were binary logistic models within the "Generalized Estimating Equations" (GEE) in SPSS. Multilevel models were chosen due to the nested structure of the data: Assessment points as level 1 nested within patients as level 2. In GEE, patients were therefore designated as subject variable and assessment points as within-subject variable. The therapists and clinics were not added as levels to the multilevel models due to the confidentiality agreement with the therapists and clinics.

Model 1 investigated associations between the ASC scales and EPD. EPD was the binary outcome: 1 (treatment week coded as EPD) was set as the answer and 0 (treatment week coded as either END or NO) as the reference.

Model 2 analyzed associations between the ASC scales and END. In this model, END was the binary outcome: Again, 1 (treatment week coded as END) was defined as the answer and 0 (treatment week coded as either EPD or NO) as the reference.

In both models, the four ASC scales (therapeutic alliance, social support, motivation, life events) were added as covariates (time-dependent: the ASC scale scores always pertained to the same treatment week as the EPD, END, or NO classifications). The four covariates were grand-mean centered, since the ASC scales do not have a meaningful 0 value. In GEE, the main-effects setting was selected to obtain a main-effects term for each of the four covariates. Moreover, the following settings were chosen for both models: Covariance matrix = robust estimator, analysis type = type 3, confidence interval = 95%, chi-square statistics = Wald, log quasi likelihood function = full.

Regarding the working correlation matrix structure, we tried three structures: Unstructured, exchangeable (compound symmetry structure), and autoregressive. Of those three structures, the one was chosen as the final structure of model 1/model 2 with which the model produced convergence and the smallest QIC (quasi likelihood under independence model criterion).

All tests were performed two-tailed with a *p*-value of ≤ 0.05. No corrections for multiple testing (e.g., Bonferroni) were applied due to the explorative nature of our study (Abt, 1987).

Participants

The patients included in this paper had to fulfill two criteria. First, they had to provide an intake OQ-45 score and at least one more OQ-45 score. We excluded all other patients, since the intake OQ-45 scores are necessary to plot the ERCs of the empirical OQ-45 algorithm and only assessments following the intake assessments can be classified as either EPD, END, or NO. Second, patients were only included if they completed the OQ-45 and the ASC simultaneously at least at one assessment point following intake, since at least one simultaneous OQ-45 and ASC assessment is necessary to study associations between considerable change (here: EPD, END) and the ASC scales.

Of all 436 registered patients, 271 patients (62%) fulfilled these inclusion criteria. The excluded 165 patients either did not provide an OQ-45 score for the intake week, since they were too distressed or not motivated to take part in the study (65% of 165) or they did not complete the OQ-45 and ASC simultaneously at least at one assessment point after the intake assessment (35% of 165).

The characteristics of the 271 patients included in this study are presented in Table I. The diagnoses were made by the clinical teams according to chapter V of the ICD-10 (World Health Organization [WHO], 1992). Taking psychological comorbidity into account, all diagnoses of the included patients (not only the main diagnosis) are reported in Table I.

Results

Treatment weeks with EPD, END, or NO. Altogether the included patients provided 791 weekly OQ-45 assessments following the intake assessment that were classified as either EPD, END, or NO: Of all these assessments, 178 (22.5%) were classified as EPD, 75 (9.5%) as END, and the rest (538, 68.0%) as NO. The 178 weeks with EPD belonged to 94 patients (34.7% of 271), the 75 weeks with END to 38 patients[1] (14.0% of 271), and the 538 weeks with NO to 231 patients (85.2% of 271).

Importance of the ASC scales during treatment weeks with EPD. The multilevel model used to study associations between the ASC scales and EPD did not converge with the unstructured working correlation matrix structure. However, the model converged with the autoregressive structure and the exchangeable structure. The autoregressive structure showed a slightly smaller QIC (688.92) than the exchangeable structure (689.60). Therefore, the results of the model with the autoregressive structure are reported in Table II.

As can be seen in Table II, each ASC scale was significantly positively ($\beta > 0$, $\text{Exp}(\beta) > 1$, $p < 0.05$) associated with EPD when the other ASC scales were held constant at their grand-means.

Relevance of the ASC scales during treatment weeks with END. The multilevel model performed to analyze associations between the ASC scales and END converged with the unstructured, the autoregressive, as well as with the exchangeable working correlation matrix structure. The autoregressive structure produced a smaller QIC (436.70) than the exchangeable structure (443.92) and the unstructured structure (444.61). Table III thus presents the results of the model with the autoregressive structure.

Table III illustrates that only the ASC social support scale and the ASC life events scale were significantly negatively ($\beta < 0$, $\text{Exp}(\beta) < 1$, $p < 0.05$) related to END when the other ASC scales were held constant at their grand-means.

Table I. Sample characteristics

Gender *n* (%)	Female	161 (59.4)
	Male	110 (40.6)
Education *n* (%)	Higher seconday school	53 (19.6)
	Intermediate secondary school	76 (28.0)
	Lower secondary school	118 (43.5)
	Other type of graduation	24 (8.9)
Amount of patients with specific diagnoses *n* (%)	Depressive disorders (F32/F33)	178 (65.7)
	Anxiety disorders (F40/F41)	69 (25.5)
	Obsessive compulsive disorders (F42)	8 (3.0)
	Reaction to severe stress, and adjustment disorders (F43)	42 (15.5)
	Somatoform disorders (F45)	158 (58.3)
	Eating disorders (F50)	35 (12.9)
	Disorders of adult personality and behavior (F6)	20 (7.4)
	Other disorders (all F diagnoses except the already mentioned)	57 (21.0)
Number of diagnoses according to chapter V of the ICD-10 *M* (*SD*)		2.26 (1.06)
Age *M* (SD)		48.36 (13.08)
OQ total score of the intake week *M* (*SD*)		81.52 (25.70)
Treatment weeks from intake to discharge *M* (*SD*)		4.65 (2.13)

Table II. Results of the multilevel model with the extreme positive deviation classification (EPD) as binary outcome (treatment week with EPD = 1; treatment week without EPD = 0) and the scales of the "Assessment of Signal Cases" (ASC) as time-dependent covariates

Parameter	Regression coefficient β	Standard error	95% Wald confidence interval: Lower bound	95% Wald confidence interval: Upper bound	Wald-chi-square	Degrees of freedom	p-value	Exp(β)
Intercept	−1.640	0.151	−1.936	−1.344	117.863	1	<0.01	0.194
ASC therapeutic alliance scale	0.052	0.022	0.009	0.094	5.732	1	0.017	1.053
ASC social support scale	0.066	0.014	0.039	0.094	22.482	1	<0.01	1.069
ASC motivation scale	0.093	0.032	0.031	0.155	8.595	1	<0.01	1.097
ASC life events scale	0.081	0.020	0.043	0.120	17.053	1	<0.01	1.085

Discussion

This study investigated in two psychosomatic in-patient clinics whether the domains of the questionnaire "Assessment for Signal Cases" (ASC)—therapeutic alliance, social support, motivation, and life events—are of importance when patients deviate extremely from their expected recovery curves (ERCs). The ERCs of the OQ-45 empirical algorithm (Finch et al., 2001) were applied to define treatment weeks with extreme positive deviations (EPD), with extreme negative deviations (END) or without extreme deviations (NO). The ASC and the OQ-45 were administered to patients simultaneously on a weekly basis during their in-patient stay so that the ASC scale scores pertained to the weeks coded as either EPD, END, or NO.

The percentage of patients with at least one END (14.0%) during the entire course of treatment was within the range found in previous studies that also used the OQ-45 algorithms to operationalize considerable negative change (Amble, Gude, Stubdal, Andersen, & Wampold, 2014; Crits-Christoph et al., 2012; Shimokawa, Lambert, & Smart, 2010; Simon et al., 2012: 11%–56%). Although the method used to operationalize considerable positive change in this study (OQ-45 algorithm) differs from previous research (which mostly used the sudden gain definition proposed by Tang & DeRubeis, 1999), our result of 34.7% patients with at least one EPD also lies within the 11%–50% interval of sudden gain patients found in other investigations (Lutz et al., 2013).

Of all assessments taken during the weeks following intake, 23% were classified as EPD and 10% were coded as END. To investigate the relevance of the ASC scales during treatment weeks with considerable change (EPD, END), multilevel models for dichotomous outcomes were applied. When the other ASC scales were held constant, each ASC scale was significantly positively related to EPD. However, significant negative associations with END were found (again when holding the other ASC scales constant) only for the ASC social support scale and the ASC life events scale, but neither for the ASC motivation scale nor for the ASC therapeutic alliance scale.

Table III. Results of the multilevel model with the extreme negative deviation classification (END) as binary outcome (treatment week with END = 1; treatment week without END = 0) and the scales of the "Assessment of Signal Cases" (ASC) as time-dependent covariates

Parameter	Regression coefficient β	Standard error	95% Wald confidence interval: Lower bound	95% Wald confidence interval: Upper bound	Wald-chi-square	Degrees of freedom	p-value	Exp(s)
Intercept	−2.865	0.265	−3.385	−2.345	116.513	1	<0.01	0.057
ASC therapeutic alliance scale	−0.009	0.026	−0.060	0.041	0.136	1	0.713	0.991
ASC social support scale	−0.077	0.022	−0.121	−0.034	12.127	1	<0.01	0.926
ASC motivation scale	−0.044	0.033	−0.109	0.021	1.727	1	0.189	0.957
ASC life events scale	−0.087	0.025	−0.135	−0.039	12.441	1	<0.01	0.917

Taking the sheltered in-patient setting of our sample into account, the importance of extratherapeutic factors for EPD and END was somewhat surprising for us. The usefulness of the extratherapeutic scales of the ASC—especially of the social support scale—has been questioned for the psychosomatic in-patient setting (Probst et al., 2013). However, this study highlights the relevance of extratherapeutic factors (especially for END) even in psychosomatic in-patient therapy. Social support could for instance be important for considerable change in in-patient settings, since in-patients might experience more or less social support from other in-patients. Social support could therefore be at least partially related to cohesiveness, a curative factor proven to influence patient progress in psychosomatic in-patient therapy (Dinger & Schauenburg, 2010). Due to the possible overlap of social support and cohesiveness in in-patient settings, social support might be both an extratherapeutic factor and a factor within therapy in in-patient settings. Life events could be associated with considerable change as some in-patients undergo stress tests (trials of momentary coping abilities) on the weekends during their in-patient stay. Moreover, as in-patients live some weeks of their lives in the clinics, they may experience life events (e.g., receiving bad news from relatives or work) also during their in-patient stay.

Our significant associations between considerable positive change and social support as well as life events seem to contradict previous studies which applied the sudden gain definition to operationalize considerable positive change: The relationship between social support and sudden gains did not attain statistical significance in the studies of Hopko et al. (2009) and Keller et al. (2014). However, these studies assessed social support only at pretreatment and did not analyze the association between individual assessments and social support over the course of treatment. Furthermore, although Hardy et al. (2005) assessed life events on a session-by-session basis, they failed to show a significant relationship between sudden gains and life events. Besides the different methods used to operationalize considerable positive change, two more differences between our investigation and the study of Hardy et al. (2005) should be considered and could also explain the ambiguous results: First, Hardy et al. (2005) compared life events over the course of treatment between patients with at least one sudden gain against patients without any sudden gain. In contrast, we analyzed life events pertaining to weeks with and without considerable change. Second, Hardy et al. (2005) dichotomized the life events score (good vs. bad life events); we in turn used a life events scale score.

The impact of motivation as well as of the therapeutic alliance could have turned out being stronger for EPD than for END in our study because we applied a more rigorous criterion for defining EPD than for defining END. The top 10% of the norm group were the reference for our EPD classification, and the bottom 16% of the norm group for our END classification. The different criteria applied to operationalize EPD and END could be viewed as a limitation of this study. Wanting to enhance the comparability to other studies, we decided to use the bottom 16% to define END since patients scoring in this range were considered "not-on-track" patients, signal cases, or patients at risk of treatment failure in previous research (Lambert, Whipple et al., 2002; Spielmans et al., 2006). The top 10% were used to define EPD since the OQ-Analyst labels patients scoring in this range as "blue signal patients" (Lambert, 2012).

Another limitation refers to our examination of only four domains (therapeutic alliance, social support, motivation, life events) in weeks with and without considerable change. Other domains shown to influence patient progress in psychosomatic in-patient therapy (e.g., Dinger & Schauenburg, 2010; Mander et al., 2013, 2014) were not assessed in this study. In addition, we did not assess specific therapeutic factors, which have been shown to interact with common factors (Boswell, Castonguay, & Wasserman, 2010). Furthermore, some of the therapeutic factors might be associated with considerable negative change (Lilienfeld, 2007) and some of them have been shown to foster considerable positive change: e.g., cognitive changes have been shown to precede sudden gains in CBT (Tang & DeRubeis, 1999; Tang et al., 2005) and therapist interpretation accuracy to predict sudden gains in supportive-expressive therapy (Andrusyna et al., 2006).

One should keep in mind that our associations between the ASC scales and EPD / END do not allow drawing causal inferences. On the one hand, better/worse ASC scale scores could lead to EPD/END. On the other hand, EPD/END could lead to better/worse therapeutic alliance, social support, motivation, and life events.

Despite these limitations, our findings provide validity for the ASC social support scale and the ASC life events scale as scales assessing possible problem areas that may account for deterioration in psychotherapy. In clinical practice, when the OQ-Analyst warns therapists that a patient's progress predicts a negative treatment outcome (i.e., when an END occurs) therapists are encouraged to use CSTs, i.e., administer the ASC to patients, attend to items and scale scores that are problematic, use a decision tree to organize problem-solving, and then consider the relevant interventions that are recommended through this approach (Lambert et al., 2007). The results of this study indicate that lower scores on the ASC social support scale and the ASC life events scale are associated with unusually large negative treatment response.

In contrast to other comparable approaches and methods of outcome informed care that include problem-solving tools (e.g., Bickman, 2005; Duncan & Miller, 2008; Kopta & Lowry, 2002), the OQ-Analyst includes measures of social support, motivation and life events rather than relying solely on therapeutic alliance ratings. The results of the present study provide evidence that the additional variables social support and life events may affect considerable negative change even more than the therapeutic alliance (and motivation).

Finally, if these results are replicated in other settings, they could suggest a modification of the CSTs of the OQ-Analyst. The current CSTs include a decision-tree with a stepwise procedure when an END occurs: Therapists are encouraged to examine the therapeutic alliance in a first step, to check motivation in a second step, to inspect social support in a third step, and to investigate life events in a fourth step (Lambert et al., 2007). This procedure gives priority to the therapeutic alliance and motivation. Our results indicate that CSTs prioritizing social support and life events could be more effective in preventing treatment failure.

Conclusions

The quality of life events as well as the quality of social support were associated with considerable positive and negative change, whereas the quality of the therapeutic alliance and the quality of motivation were related only to considerable positive change.

Clinical Implications

The results of this study indirectly suggest that encouraging therapists to help poorly responding patients deal with life events as well as build a social network can be of importance when trying to improve treatment outcome.

Note

[1] The number of patients with END amounted to 38 in this paper. This sample differs from the 43 patients with END analyzed by Probst et al. (2013) since 5 of those 43 patients did not complete the ASC in their treatment weeks classified as END.

References

Abt, K. (1987). Descriptive data analysis: A concept between confirmatory and exploratory data analysis. *Methods of Information in Medicine, 26*, 77–88.

Aderka, I. M., Nickerson, A., Bøe, H. J., & Hofmann, S. G. (2012). Sudden gains during psychological treatments of anxiety and depression: A meta-analysis. *Journal of Consulting & Clinical Psychology, 80*(1), 93–101. doi:10.1037/a0026455

Amble, I., Gude, T., Stubdal, S., Andersen, B. J., & Wampold, B. E. (2014). The effect of implementing the outcome questionnaire-45.2 feedback system in Norway: A multisite randomized clinical trial in a naturalistic setting. *Psychotherapy Research*, epub ahead of print.

Andrusyna, T. P., Luborsky, L., Pham, T., & Tang, T. Z. (2006). The mechanisms of sudden gains in supportive-expressive therapy for depression. *Psychotherapy Research, 16*, 526–536. doi:10.1080/10503300600591379

Asay, T. P., & Lambert, M. J. (1999). The empirical case for the common factors in therapy: Quantitative findings. In M. A. Hubble, B. L. Duncan, & S. D. Miller (Eds.), *The heart and soul of change: What works in therapy* (pp. 23–55). Washington, DC: American Psychological Association.

Bankoff, E. A., & Howard, K. I. (1992). The social network of the psychotherapy client and effective psychotherapeutic process. *Journal of Psychotherapy Integration, 2*, 273–294.

Bickman, L. (2005). A common factors approach to improving mental health services. *Mental Health Services Research, 7*(1), 1–4. doi:10.1007/s11020-005-1961-7

Boswell, J. F., Castonguay, L. G., & Wasserman, R. H. (2010). Effects of psychotherapy training and intervention use on session outcome. *Journal of Consulting & Clinical Psychology, 78*, 717–723. doi:10.1037/a0020088

Cavallini, A. Q., & Spangler, D. L. (2013). Sudden gains in cognitive-behavioral therapy for eating disorders. *International Journal of Cognitive Therapy, 6*, 292–310. doi:10.1521/ijct.2013.6.3.292

Crits-Christoph, P., Ring-Kurtz, S., Hamilton, J. L., Lambert, M. J., Gallop, R., McClure, B., ... Rotrosen, J. (2012). A preliminary study of the effects of individual patient-level feedback in outpatient substance abuse treatment programs. *Journal of Substance Abuse Treatment, 42*, 301–309. doi:10.1016/j.jsat.2011.09.003

Cuijpers, P., Driessen, E., Hollon, S. D., van Oppen, P., Barth, J., & Andersson, G. (2012). The efficacy of non-directive supportive psychotherapy for adult depression: A meta-analysis. *Clinical Psychology Review, 32*, 280–291. doi:10.1016/j.cpr.2012.01.003

Dinger, U., & Schauenburg, H. (2010). Effects of individual cohesion and patient interpersonal style on outcome in psychodynamically oriented inpatient group psychotherapy. *Psychotherapy Research, 20*(1), 22–29. doi:10.1080/10503300902855514

Duncan, B. L., & Miller, S. D. (2008). *The outcome and session rating scales: The revised administration and scoring manual, including the child outcome rating scale*. Chicago, IL: Institute for the Study of Therapeutic Change.

Finch, A. E., Lambert, M. J., & Schaalje, B. G. (2001). Psychotherapy quality control: The statistical generation of expected recovery curves for integration into an early warning system. *Clinical Psychology & Psychotherapy, 8*, 231–242. doi:10.1002/cpp.286

Greenhalgh, J. (2009). The applications of PROs in clinical practice: What are they, do they work, and why? *Quality of Life Research, 18*, 115–123. doi:10.1007/s11136-008-9430-6

Haas, E., Hill, R. D., Lambert, M. J., & Morrell, B. (2002). Do early responders to psychotherapy maintain treatment gains? *Journal of Clinical Psychology, 58*, 1157–1172. doi:10.1002/jclp.10044

Hardy, G. E., Cahill, J., Stiles, W. B., Ispan, C., Macaskill, N., & Barkham, M. (2005). Sudden gains in cognitive therapy for depression: A replication and extension. *Journal of Consulting & Clinical Psychology, 73*(1), 59–67. doi:10.1037/0022-006X.73.1.59

Harmon, S. C., Lambert, M. J., Smart, D. M., Hawkins, E., Nielsen, S. L., Slade, K., & Lutz, W. (2007). Enhancing outcome for potential treatment failures: Therapist client feedback and clinical support tools. *Psychotherapy Research, 17*, 379–392. doi:10.1080/10503300600702331

Heck, R. H., Thomas, S. L., & Tabata, L. N. (2012). *Multilevel modeling of categorical outcomes using IBM SPSS*. New York, NY: Routledge.

Hiller, W., Schindler, A., & Lambert, M. J. (2013). Defining response and remission in psychotherapy research: A comparison of the RCI and the method of percent improvement. *Psychotherapy Research, 22*(1), 1–11. doi:10.1080/10503307.2011.616237

Hopko, D. R., Robertson, S. M. C., & Carvalho, J. P. (2009). Sudden gains in depressed cancer patients treated with behavioral activation therapy. *Behavior Therapy, 40*, 346–356. doi:10.1016/j.beth.2008.09.001

Horvath, A. O., Del Re, A. C., Flückiger, C., & Symonds, D. (2011). Alliance in individual psychotherapy. *Psychotherapy: Theory, Research, Practice, Training, 48*, 9–16.

Howard, K. I., Moras, K., Brill, P. L., Martinovich, Z., & Lutz, W. (1996). Evaluation of psychotherapy: Efficacy, effectiveness, and patient progress. *American Psychologist, 51*, 1059–1064. doi:10.1037/0003-066X.51.10.1059

Ilardi, S. S., & Craighead, W. E. (1994). The role of nonspecific factors in cognitive-behavior therapy of depression. *Clinical Psychology-Science & Practice, 1*, 138–155. doi:10.1111/j.1468-2850.1994.tb00016.x

Jacobson, N. S., & Truax, P. (1991). Clinical significance: A statistical approach to defining meaningful change in psychotherapy research. *Journal of Consulting & Clinical Psychology, 59*, 12–19.

Keller, S. M., Feeny, N. C., & Zoellner, L. A. (2014). Depression sudden gains and transient depression spikes during treatment for PTSD. *Journal of Consulting & Clinical Psychology, 82*(1), 102–111. doi:10.1037/a0035286

Kopta, S. M., & Lowry, J. L. (2002). Psychometric evaluation of the behavioral health questionnaire-20: A brief instrument for assessing global mental health and the three phases of psychotherapy outcome. *Psychotherapy Research, 12*, 413–426. doi:10.1093/ptr/12.4.413

Lambert, M. J. (2005). Early response in psychotherapy: Further evidence for the importance of common factors rather than "placebo effects". *Journal of Clinical Psychology, 61*, 855–869. doi:10.1002/jclp.20130

Lambert, M. J. (2012). Helping clinicians to use and learn from research-based systems: The OQ-analyst. *Psychotherapy, 49*(2), 109–114. doi:10.1037/a0027110

Lambert, M. J. (2013). Outcome in psychotherapy: The past and important advances. *Psychotherapy, 50*(1), 42–51. doi:10.1037/a0030682

Lambert, M. J., Bailey, R., Kimball, K., Shimokawa, K., Harmon, S. C., & Slade, K. (2007). *Clinical support tools manual-brief version-40*. Salt Lake City, UT: OQMeasures.

Lambert, M. J., Hannöver, W., Nisslmüller, K., Richard, M., & Kordy, H. (2002). Questionnaire on the results of psychotherapy: Reliability and validity of the German translation of the outcome questionnaire 45.2 (OQ-45.2). *Zeitschrift für Klinische Psychologie und Psychotherapie, 31*, 40–47.

Lambert, M. J., Kahler, M., Harmon, S. C., Burlingame, G. M., & Shimokawa, K. (2011). *Administration and scoring manual for the outcome questionnaire-45.2*. Salt Lake City, UT: OQMeasures.

Lambert, M. J., Whipple, J. L., Bishop, M. J., Vermeersch, D. A., Gray, G. V., & Finch, A. E. (2002). Comparison of empirically derived and rationally derived methods for identifying clients at risk for treatment failure. *Clinical Psychology & Psychotherapy, 9*(3), 149–164. doi:10.1002/cpp.333

Lilienfeld, S. O. (2007). Psychological treatments that cause harm. *Perspectives on Psychological Science, 2*(1), 53–70. doi:10.1111/j.1745-6916.2007.00029.x

Lutz, W., Bachmann, F., Tschitsaz, A., Smart, D. W., & Lambert, M. J. (2007). Temporal and sequential patterns of nonlinear change psychotherapy. The phenomenon of sudden gains and sudden losses in its context. *Zeitschrift für Klinische Psychologie und Psychotherapie, 36*, 261–269.

Lutz, W., Ehrlich, T., Rubel, J., Hallwachs, N., Röttger, M.-A., Jorasz, C., … Tschitsaz-Stucki, A. (2013). The ups and downs of psychotherapy: Sudden gains and sudden losses identified with session reports. *Psychotherapy Research, 23*(1), 14–24. doi:10.1080/10503307.2012.693837

Mander, J., Schlarb, A., Teufel, M., Keller, F., Hautzinger, M., Zipfel, S., Sammet, I. (2014). The individual therapy process questionnaire: Development and validation of a revised measure to evaluate general change mechanisms in psychotherapy. *Clinical Psychology & Psychotherapy*, published online.

Mander, J. V., Wittorf, A., Schlarb, A., Hautzinger, M., Zipfel, S., & Sammet, I. (2013). Change mechanisms in psychotherapy: Multiperspective assessment and relation to outcome. *Psychotherapy Research, 23*(1), 105–116. doi:10.1080/10503307.2012.744111

McCarthy, K. S., & Barber, J. P. (2009). The multitheoretical list of therapeutic interventions (MULTI): Initial report. *Psychotherapy Research, 19*(1), 96–113. doi:10.1080/10503300802524343

Newnham, E. A., Hooke, G. R., & Page, A. C. (2010). Progress monitoring and feedback in psychiatric care reduces depressive symptoms. *Journal of Affective Disorders, 127*(1–3), 139–146. doi:10.1016/j.jad.2010.05.003

Pelletier, L. G., Tuson, K. M., & Haddad, N. K. (1997). Client motivation for therapy scale: A measure of intrinsic motivation, extrinsic motivation, and amotivation for therapy. *Journal of Personality Assessment, 68*, 414–435. doi:10.1207/s15327752jpa6802_11

Probst, T., Lambert, M. J., Loew, T. H., Dahlbender, R. W., Göllner, R., & Tritt, K. (2013). Feedback on patient progress and clinical support tools for therapists: Improved outcome for patients at risk of treatment failure in psychosomatic in-patient therapy under the conditions of routine practice. *Journal of Psychosomatic Research, 75*, 255–261. doi:10.1016/j.jpsychores.2013.07.003

Probst, T., Lambert, M. J., Dahlbender, R. W., Loew, T. H., & Tritt, K. (2014). Providing feedback on patient progress and clinical support tools for therapists: Is the therapeutic process of patients on-track to recovery improved in psychosomatic in-patient therapy under the conditions of routine practice? *Journal of Psychosomatic Research, 76*, 477–484. doi:10.1016/j.jpsychores.2014.03.010

Sexton, H. (1996). Process, life events, and symptomatic change in brief eclectic psychotherapy. *Journal of Consulting & Clinical Psychology, 64*, 1358–1365. doi:10.1037/0022-006X.64.6.1358

Simon, W., Lambert, M. J., Harris, M. W., Busath, G., & Vazquez, A. (2012). Providing patient progress information and clinical support tools to therapists: Effects on patients at risk of treatment failure. *Psychotherapy Research, 22*, 638–647. doi:10.1080/10503307.2012.698918

Shimokawa, K., Lambert, M. J., & Smart, D. W. (2010). Enhancing treatment outcome of patients at risk of treatment failure: Meta-analytic and mega-analytic review of a psychotherapy quality assurance system. *Journal of Consulting & Clinical Psychology, 78*, 298–311. doi:10.1037/a0019247

Slade, K., Lambert, M. J., Harmon, S. C., Smart, D. W., & Bailey, R. (2008). Improving psychotherapy outcome: The use of immediate electronic feedback and revised clinical support tools. *Clinical Psychology & Psychotherapy, 15*, 287–303. doi:10.1002/cpp.594

Spielmans, G. I., Masters, K. S., & Lambert, M. J. (2006). A comparison of rational versus empirical methods in prediction of negative psychotherapy outcome. *Clinical Psychology & Psychotherapy, 13*, 202–214. doi:10.1002/cpp.491

Tang, T. Z., & DeRubeis, R. J. (1999). Sudden gains and critical sessions in cognitive-behavioral therapy for depression. *Journal of Consulting & Clinical Psychology, 67*, 894–904. doi:10.1037/0022-006X.67.6.894

Tang, T. Z., DeRubeis, R. J., Beberman, R., & Pham, T. (2005). Cognitive changes, critical sessions, and sudden gains in cognitive-behavioral therapy for depression. *Journal of Consulting & Clinical Psychology, 73*, 168–172. doi:10.1037/0022-006X.73.1.168

Tschitsaz-Stucki, A., & Lutz, W. (2009). Identification and clarification of sudden gains and sudden losses in individual psychotherapy courses. *Zeitschrift für Klinische Psychologie und Psychotherapie, 38*, 13–23.

Whipple, J. L., Lambert, M. J., Vermeersch, D. A., Smart, D. W., Nielsen, S. L., & Hawkins, E. J. (2003). Improving the effects of psychotherapy: The use of early identification of treatment and problem-solving strategies in routine practice. *Journal of Counseling Psychology, 50*(1), 59–68. doi:10.1037/0022-0167.50.1.59

Wild, D., Grove, A., Martin, M., Eremenco, S., McElroy, S., Verjee-Lorenz, A., & Erikson, P. (2005). Principles of good practice for the translation and cultural adaptation process for patient-reported outcomes (PRO) measures: Report of the ISPOR task force for translation and cultural adaptation. Value Health, *8*, 94–104. doi:10.1111/j.1524-4733.2005.04054.x.

World Health Organization (WHO). (1992). *ICD-10: The ICD-10 classification of mental and behavioural disorders*. Geneva: Author.

Using the Assessment for Signal Clients as a feedback tool for reducing treatment failure

MELISSA M. WHITE[1], MICHAEL J. LAMBERT[1], BENJAMIN M. OGLES[1], STEVIE B. MCLAUGHLIN[1], RUSSELL J. BAILEY[2], & K. MORGAN TINGEY[1]

[1]*Department of Psychology, Brigham Young University, Provo, UT, USA & [2]Department of Counseling and Psychological Services, Brigham Young University, Provo, UT, USA*

Abstract

Objective: The Clinical Support Tools (CSTs) were developed to help therapists organize and target potential problems that might account for negative outcomes in psychotherapy. The core of CST feedback is the Assessment for Signal Clients. The purpose of this study was to describe and identify patterns of problems that typically characterize off-track cases. **Method:** The responses and scores from 107 off-track clients from a hospital-based outpatient clinic were analyzed. **Results:** A cluster analysis of the 107 off-track clients revealed three client types: those whose problems were characterized by alliance and motivational difficulties; those characterized by social support and life event difficulties; and those whose problems had an indistinguishable pattern. Log-linear modeling showed that if patients had less therapeutic alliance problems they were also less likely to have motivational problems. Findings were also consistent with the cluster analysis, which showed that a relatively higher percentage of not-on-track participants received signal alerts for the social support items and scale. **Conclusions:** Individuals whose progress goes off-track while in psychotherapy appear to have their greatest difficulty with social support, followed closely by motivation for therapy and therapeutic alliance.

Keywords: treatment failure; progress feedback; psychotherapy outcome; therapeutic alliance; Assessment for Signal Clients

Lambert and colleagues at Brigham Young University (BYU) have developed methods of predicting and preventing deterioration in psychotherapy by alerting clinicians that a client is predicted to leave treatment in a deteriorated state. As part of this effort they developed Clinical Support Tools (CSTs; Lambert et al., 2007) to help therapists organize and target potential problems that might account for negative outcomes. Shimokawa, Lambert, and Smart (2010) performed a meta-analysis of clinical trials carried out by the BYU group and found a large effect size between no feedback clients (treatment-as-usual) and progress feedback clients plus CSTs (d = .70) treated by the same therapists. The core of CST feedback is a 40-item self-report questionnaire (Assessment for Signal Clients—ASC) that is given to those clients who are predicted to deteriorate. The ASC attempts to identify problems with the therapeutic alliance, motivation, social support, and problematic life events. ASC feedback provides clinicians with information regarding which areas and which specific items are significantly below normative values. The ASC feedback thereby alerts therapists to possible target areas for problem-solving in therapy. The ASC results are provided to therapists by the OQ-Analyst software that also provides recommendations for interventions that therapists can consider using.

The ASC targets general areas considered important across types of psychotherapy and a wide range of disorders common in adult treatment, outpatient practice. The CSTs also provide a decision tree to organize therapist problem-solving, directing therapists to first consider the strength of the therapeutic relationship, then motivation, then social supports external to psychotherapy, followed by negative life events, all of which are measured by the ASC. The decision tree then directs therapists to reconsider the patient's diagnosis and the possible need for medication referral and reconsideration of the treatment method. While the CST feedback cannot provide prescriptive information for getting the patient back on-track for a positive outcome, clinicians have found the CST feedback useful in their work with clients, with experimental data demonstrating reduced deterioration rates in predicted treatment failures from a baseline of 20% to 5.5% and the rate of positive outcomes from 22% to 50.5% (Shimokawa et al., 2010). We cannot attribute the success of the CST intervention to the use of the ASC but hypothesize it is essential because of its focus on specific areas of client functioning.

In creating the ASC we considered its primary function to be quantification of the quality of the psychotherapy relationship given the strength of the empirical relationship between *client's perception* of therapist attitudes and behavior and the outcome of psychotherapy (Horvath, Del Re, Flückiger, & Symonds, 2011). The relationship may be of special importance in negative treatment as alliance ruptures occur over the course of therapy and can be repaired by the therapist (Safran & Muran, 2000). Given that the therapist's perception of their relationship with the client does not have as strong a relationship with the client perception of the relationship, there is a specific need to provide therapists with client-reported perceptions, including specific indicators of alliance problems. This is facilitated through the use of cut scores that delineate a "problem" or "no problem" with particular aspects of the relationship. In the case of the ASC, the therapeutic alliance was operationalized with the possibility that the alliance, in general, was not only problematic but also assumed that any of the alliance could be problematic or not. Since the alliance is made up of the strength of the affective bond, agreement on therapeutic tasks and agreement of goals, cut-off scores can be provided for each. In addition, while a specific aspect (bond, task, or goal) may not be problematic, individual items within each area could be. If a risk of a negative outcome is detected during therapy, evaluating specific items within the alliance that are below normative values could speed problem-solving and lead to corrective actions.

Another important variable that is included in the ASC and that has been shown to affect outcome is client motivation (Bohart & Wade, 2013). Specifically, clients who worsen during treatment may lose or lack motivation for psychotherapy because they fail to have their expectations met or become discouraged with their progress. The extent to which a client is motivated to change while in therapy varies among clients. According to the stages of change model, clients move through motivational stages throughout treatment (Prochaska & Norcross, 2003). This model of change shows that people who are in the process of changing a behavior will cycle through low levels of motivation to high levels of motivation to change. This means that a lack of success in therapy could be associated with a client's motivation and the degree to which therapists' attitudes and behaviors are responsive to motivational stages. Given this information, when creating the ASC it was hypothesized that it would be important for the therapist to become aware of motivational problems and respond to them if the client went off-track.

Two "outside of therapy" variables that were also included in the ASC are social support and life events. Social support is the degree to which clients feel their family and friends support them, i.e., that the client can rely on a support system. Social support can be defined through the amount of interpersonal connection an individual has with others and the quality of those relationships (Chronister, Johnson, & Berven, 2006). Research suggests that strong interpersonal relationships reduce psychological disturbance and augment the effectiveness of therapy (Thoits, 1983; Zimet, Dahlem, Zimet, & Farley, 1988). In addition, having adequate social support seems to help with long-term benefits of psychotherapy. For example, Lindfors, Ojanen, Jääskeläinen, and Knekt (2014) found at a 3-year follow-up that patients with a low level of social support before treatment did not benefit as much from psychotherapy as those with high levels of support. Furthermore, when a client is predicted to deteriorate in therapy, they have lower amounts of social support compared to those who are progressing in therapy (Probst, Lambert, Loew, Dahlbender, & Tritt, 2014). Likewise, situations outside of therapists control may contribute to deterioration, such as negative life events (Lambert & Cattani-Thompson, 1996). Life events characterized by loss as well as physical pain appear to be of particular importance and may need to be addressed in therapy (Lambert et al., 2007). Additionally, a more recent study has found that negative life events contribute to client deterioration while in psychotherapy (Probst, Lambert, Loew, et al., 2014).

Although there is evidence showing that the use of OQ alarm signals plus CST feedback reduces deterioration in off-track clients and substantially bolsters positive outcomes, little is known about the frequency with which off-track clients subscribe to specific items and scales within the ASC. Details about the factors associated with flagging progress in therapy, particularly from the client's perspective, may provide rich clinical material to psychotherapists and possibly answer specific questions about deteriorating clients. The information gathered may shed light on which items and scales (alliance, motivation, social support, life events) are most often problematic in off-track cases. In addition, identifying patterns of problems across off-track clients (i.e., clustering patients into typical types) and understanding relationships between the ASC four problems may be determined. Such research has yet to be undertaken and more empirical data could help clinicians use the ASC to enhance their problem-solving in therapy for those clients predicted to leave treatment in a deteriorated state.

Methods

Participants

Participant data were drawn from a previously published study carried out in a hospital-based outpatient clinic in the Western USA (Simon, Lambert, Harris, Busath, & Vazquez, 2012). Of the 464 patients who consented to participate in that study and were randomly assigned to either a feedback condition or a treatment-as-usual condition, 107 completed the ASC after they were identified as not-on-track (NOT) to have a positive treatment outcome. Completion of the ASC took place immediately after they first signaled as being off-track. The session at which the patient signaled varied from patient to patient.

Prior to completion of the Simon et al. (2012) study, the participants' data were de-identified. The de-identified data as well as the descriptive information for the overall sample were available to the researchers of this study. For the whole sample the mean age was 36.10 years (*SD* = 13.32). Sixty-four percent of the sample was female with 93% being Caucasian. The primary diagnosis for the participants was mood disorders (64%), followed by anxiety disorders (30%) and substance abuse (5%) with 46% meeting criteria for two or more disorders. Fifty-nine percent of participants were married and 59% were currently employed. Fourteen percent of participants had received individual psychotherapy in the past and 74% were taking psychoactive medication when they entered individual psychotherapy at the beginning of treatment.

Instruments

Outcome Questionnaire-45 (OQ-45). Client level of disturbance and identification as an off-track case was based on the Outcome Questionnaire (OQ-45; Lambert et al., 2013), and algorithms for identifying off-track cases were embedded in the OQ-Analyst software. The OQ-45 was designed to measure client progress in therapy and to be repeatedly administered during the course of treatment and at termination. It assesses three aspects of the client's life: subjective discomfort/symptoms; problems in interpersonal relationships; and problems in social role performance. The items also measure personally and socially relevant characteristics that affect the individual's quality of life, attempting to quantify both positive and negative functioning. Each item is scored on a 5-point scale and the total score yields a range of possible scores of 0–180, where higher values indicate higher levels of client distress and pathology.

Completion of the OQ-45 takes approximately 5–7 min and is typically administered prior to each treatment session. When clients complete the measure they are instructed to reflect back over the last week. The OQ-45 has adequate internal consistency (r = .93) and 3-week test–retest reliability (r = .84). Concurrent validity is moderate to high (r = .50–.85) when correlated with measures most often used to assess psychotherapy outcome in clinical trials such as the Symptom Checklist-90 and Beck Depression Inventory. Most importantly, the OQ-45 has been shown to be sensitive to change in clients over short-time periods while remaining stable in untreated individuals (Vermeersch, Lambert, & Burlingame, 2000; Vermeersch et al., 2004).

Further details about the OQ-45 can be found in the Administration and Scoring Manual (Lambert et al., 2013). Most relevant to the current study is the accuracy identifying treatment failures. Finch, Lambert, and Schaalje (2001) developed algorithms to identify cases at risk for deterioration based on a sample of more than 11,000 patients receiving treatment from across the USA. The actuarial method developed for the OQ-45 has been tested in four studies (Ellsworth, Lambert, & Johnson, 2006; Hannan et al., 2005; Lambert et al., 2002; Spielmans, Masters, & Lambert, 2006) and they appear to be successful at predicting which patients will have negative treatment outcomes, accurately identifying from 80% to 100% of clients who are deteriorated at the end of therapy.

Assessment for Signal Clients (ASC). The ASC is a 40-item self-report scale that enquires into patient experiences over the prior week using a 5-point Likert scale with anchors ranging from strongly agree to strongly disagree. It has four scales: Therapeutic Alliance (TA; 11 items), Motivation (M) for Therapy (9 items), Social Support (SS; 11 items), and Life Events (LE; 9 items) but a total score of the four scales is not calculated.

TA items inquire about the therapeutic bond, shared goals, and agreement on therapeutic tasks, as well as alliance rupture. M items focus on low or inadequate motivation for treatment, including negative reactions to the treatment process and negative expectations. Social support items inquire into the degree to which individuals feel that their family and close friends can be counted on. Life event items focus on recent negative life events related to loss and illness and are intended to alert therapists to life crises that might need to be addressed in therapy.

The ASC feedback report is given to the therapist and consists of the ASC items endorsed as problematic, along with a cut-off score signaling if there is an overall problem in any of the four scales. Identification of a problematic scale or item score was based on normative data. The normative data included 400 individuals participating in psychotherapy. One hundred and sixty-nine of these individuals were served in a community mental health setting that included lower socioeconomic status and severe psychopathology with the rest coming from a university counseling center setting. For an item (or scale) to be potentially problematic it had to be subscribed to by 20% or fewer of the normative sample. The rationale for providing individual item feedback is that it enhances clinician problem-solving by making feedback more specific. From the specific answers to these questions, a report is given indicating to the therapist which scale questions may be a possible concern. Of note, according to the present state of the literature, there is no evidence supporting the use of specific cut-off scores for specific items or scales of the ASC for feedback. Rather the existing evidence suggests that delivering the ASC feedback along with the decision tree effects outcome.

According to Kimball (2010), the Cronbach's α coefficient for each scale is: TA (.87); M for Therapy (.81); SS (.88); and LE (.81). Similarly, Probst, Lambert, Dahlbender, et al. (2014) found similar values in Germany with Cronbach's αs ranging from .89 to .71. These coefficients were based on all clients in treatment (both on-track and off-track clients). Generally, items in the scales contributed to their respective internal consistency. Confirmatory factor analysis suggested the factor structure was consistent with the content of the designed scales (Al-Alim, 2012). More detailed presentation of the theoretical background of the ASC scales can be found in the administration and scoring manual (Lambert et al., 2007).

Procedure

The ASC results for NOT clients from the Simon et al. (2012) study ($N = 107$) were analyzed through frequency counts of signal items (items identified as meeting the below 20% cut-off) to identify the frequency of problematic items and their respective scales. Of note, analyses focused on patterns of signal alerts for both the ASC items and the overall alliance scale, motivation scale, social support scale, and life event scale for two reasons. First, the inclusion of item signal alerts seemed appropriate, given that the OQ-Analyst provides feedback to therapists for both individual items, as well as the alliance, motivation, social support, and life event scales. Due to the manner in which the ASC is scored, a client may receive a signal alert on an item but not signal on the scale associated with that item. Thus, important information may have been ignored if the focus of analysis was solely on scales. Second, 45 out of the 107 NOT clients (41.4%) did not obtain signal alerts for any of the four scales (see Table I for patterns of scale signal alerts), thus leaving a narrow range of power and complexity with which to detect patterns in the data.

In addition to frequency counts, a cluster analysis was performed in order to identify similar and distinct problematic participant types. A cluster

Table I. Frequency of patterns of signal alerts for scales of the ASC.

ASC scale(s) with signal alert	Total number (percentage) of participants with signal alerts for scale(s) (n = 107)
No signal alerts for ASC scales	45 (41.4%)
SS (only)	20 (18.69%)
LE (only)	9 (8.4%)
M (only)	6 (5.6%)
TA (only)	5 (4.6%)
SS and M	4 (3.7%)
TA, SS, and M	4 (3.7%)
TA and M	4 (3.7%)
TA and LE	3 (2.8%)
TA and SS	2 (1.8%)
TA, SS, M, and LE	1 (0.9%)

Table II. Descriptive statistics for item signal alerts.

	All 40 ASC items	TA scale items	SS scale items	M scale items	LE scale items
Total number of signal alerts (across participants)	1074	296	330	221	227
Mean number of signal alerts (per participant) and SD	10.03 ± 6.29	2.77 ± 2.99	3.08 ± 2.54	2.06 ± 2.07	2.12 ± 1.95
Median number of signal alerts (per participant)	10	2	3	1	2
Mode number of signal alerts (per participant) and percentage of participants with that value	10 (9.3%)	0 (28.9%)	0 (18.7%)	0 (28.0%)	0 (27.1%)

analysis is a multivariate procedure for separating cases into their naturally occurring homogeneous groupings. The aim of cluster analysis research "is to uncover structure in data without making prior assumptions" (Chignell & Stacey, 1981, p. 133). Although there are numerous ways to perform a cluster analysis, there are generally four steps: First, data are collected on a large sample of subjects. Second, profile similarities among subjects are computed using a coefficient such as correlation or Euclidian distance. Third, a computer algorithm is used to search for homogeneous subgroups based on objective criteria. Specifically, subjects in one cluster are deemed to be more similar to each other on objective criteria than they are to subjects classified into another cluster. Fourth, the clusters are typically replicated with new samples and validated against several outcome measures. As a final step in these analyses, the relationship among constructs on the ASC was examined using log-linear analysis to identify potential co-occurring patterns of endorsement among ASC items and scales. Log-linear modeling is a technique that can be used to identify patterns in frequency counts across levels of categorical variables and provides information for both main effects and interactions between variables (Agresti, 2007, p. 204).

Results

Analyses were carried out using IBM SPSS Statistics Version 21. When referring to ASC items and scales, Therapeutic Alliance will be abbreviated "TA," Motivation "M," Social Support "SS," and Life Events "LE."

Descriptive Information

As shown in Table I, 41.4% of the NOT clients received signal alerts for none of the ASC *scales*. Clinicians using the ASC feedback can expect a large minority of clients not to have enough signaling items within a particular scale to identify a significant overall alarm based on therapeutic alliance, motivation, social support, or life event alerts. Forty individuals (37.5%), another large minority of clients, alerted on a single scale. Importantly, the most common scale to achieve alert status was SS (31 alerts, 28.9% of clients identified as having significant problems in this area), followed by TA and the M scale (each scale with 19 alerts, 17.7% of clients), followed by the LE scale (13 alerts, 12.1% of clients). Overall these data suggest the need for clinicians (and designers of the OQ-Analyst) to be prepared with as many suggestions as possible for interventions related specifically to social support.

Table II provides descriptive information regarding signal alert patterns at the item level, and Table III provides frequency information for the total number of signal alerts per item across the 107 participants. Measures of central tendency reveal that it was common for each patient to have two to four signal alert items within each scale and around 10 item signal alerts total. Table III provides the rank ordering for the frequency with which the cut-offs were identifying item endorsement problems that may need to be addressed in psychotherapy with NOT cases. Interestingly, therapists received alerts on about 50% of NOT participants on two of the items within the social support scale, the highest percentage for any ASC items. As can be seen in Table III, the top two SS items were quite similar in nature with both suggesting the absence of a person in the client's network of close friends or family who could be trusted with emotionally challenging feelings.

Cluster Analysis

In order to determine the natural groupings among NOT patients, a cluster analysis was performed using the 40 ASC items. The two-step cluster method (with log-likelihood as the distance measure) was chosen to conduct the analysis because of its utility for categorical data. The number of clusters was chosen automatically as part of the SPSS algorithm using Schwarz's Bayesian criterion and resulted in a three cluster solution. Table IV provides frequency data for the 40 ASC items grouped by cluster.

Table III. Frequency and item signal alerts of across NOT clients.

Total number and percentage of signal alerts for NOT clients	ASC items
107-60 alerts (100 to 56%)	None
59-50 alerts (55 to 47%)	#16 There was a special person who was around when I was in need. #17 There was a special person with whom I could share my joys and sorrows.
49-40 alerts (46 to 37%)	#4 I felt like I could trust my therapist completely.
39-30 alerts (36 to 28%)	#1 I felt cared for and respected as a person. #3 I found the suggestions my therapist made were useful. #9 My therapist seemed to be glad to see me. #10 My therapist and I seemed to work well together to accomplish what I want. #12 I could count on my friendships when things went wrong. #15 I got the emotional help and support I needed from someone in my family. #22 Some subjects were so sensitive I could not talk with anyone about them. #28 I have no desire to work out my problems. #32 I had an interaction with another person that I found upsetting. #33 I felt rejected or betrayed by someone. #38 I had health problems (such as physical pain).
29-20 alerts (27 to 19%)	#6 I felt there was a breakdown in the relationship with my therapist. #7 I felt like my therapist disapproved of me. #8 At times, the tone of my therapist's voice seemed critical or impatient. #13 I could talk about problems with my friends. #14 I could talk about problems with my family. #20 I felt accepted by someone other than my therapist. #21 I felt connected to a higher power. #24 Honestly, I really do not understand what I can get from therapy. #25 I am not really sure what to work on in therapy. #26 I had thoughts about quitting therapy; it's just not for me. #27 I do not think therapy will help me feel any better. #29 Although I am currently unhappy with life, there is nothing I can do about it now. #31 I am in therapy because someone is requiring it of me. #34 I made a mistake that I cannot undo. #35 I received bad news that was difficult for me. #37 There was trouble at home, work, or school. #40 I had difficulty adjusting to an occurrence in my life.

As can be seen in Table IV, the 21 NOT clients in Cluster 1 had high rates of signal endorsement of items in the therapeutic alliance and motivation scales. As a result, we labeled this the "Internal" cluster to represent their focus on in-therapy or internal issues that may influence their flagging progress in therapy. In addition, clients in Cluster 1 endorsed the largest number of all items in the signal range with an average of 17.9 (SD = 4.27). The 31 clients in Cluster 2 had higher signal endorsement rates of items in the life events and social support scales. As a result, we labeled them the "External" cluster to represent their focus on outside of therapy issues as influencing their flagging progress in therapy. Individuals in Cluster 2 endorsed an average of 12.5 items (SD = 3.59) in the signal range on the ASC. The 55 NOT clients in Cluster 3 endorsed an average of 5.3 items (SD = 3.16) in the signal range and had no particular pattern of item endorsement. No individual item had more than 40% signal endorsement. The two items endorsed by individuals in Cluster 3 at greater than 30% were a social support item #16 "There was a special person who was around when I was in need" and a motivation item #31 "I am in therapy because someone is requiring it of me".

A one-way analysis of variance comparing the mean number of items endorsed within each cluster was significant, F (2, 104) = 109.80, $p < 0.001$, and post hoc tests (Scheffe) indicated that all three averages were significantly different from each other.

Log-linear Modeling: Examination of Associations between Variables

In order to transform the data into categorical form, for the log-linear portion of the analysis, NOT participants were categorized based on the number of item signal alerts a participant received on items within each separate scale. Four dummy variables were created (i.e., Therapeutic Alliance [TAd], Social Support [SSd], Motivation [Md], Life Events [LEd]) and a participant was assigned a "0" value for a scale if he or she was identified as having 0 or 1 item alert(s) within a scale and a "1" value if he or she was identified as having 2 or more item alerts within a scale. For example, if a NOT participant had 3 item alerts (out of the 11 possible items) within the TA scale, he or she was coded as a "1" for TAd and would be considered a "high scorer" for that scale. If he or she had 0 item alerts within the SS scale (out of the 11 possible items), he or she was coded as a "0" for SSd and would be considered a "low scorer" for that scale. Our cut-off criteria for categorization as a "high" or "low scorer" were to choose the cut-off that resulted in the most evenly distributed cell frequency counts within each dummy variable (e.g., 50% of participants were valued "0" for SSd), which is commonly recommended as a means to meet the minimum

Table IV. Cluster item frequency.

	Cluster 1		Cluster 2		Cluster 3	
Item type	Number of clients	Percent of clients	Number of clients	Percent of clients	Number of clients	Percent of clients
#1 (TA)	18	**85.7**	7	22.6	7	12.7
#2 (TA)	11	**52.4**	1	3.2	0	0
#3 (TA)	20	**95.2**	6	19.4	5	9.1
#4 (TA)	17	**81.0**	14	45.2	12	21.8
#5 (TA)	10	47.6	6	19.4	2	3.6
#6 (TA)	10	47.6	9	29.0	4	7.3
#7 (TA)	12	**57.1**	7	22.8	10	18.2
#8 (TA)	9	42.9	4	12.9	7	12.7
#9 (TA)	15	**71.4**	10	32.3	10	18.2
#10 (TA)	20	**95.2**	10	32.3	9	16.4
#11 (TA)	11	**52.4**	3	9.7	0	0
#12 (SS)	9	42.9	21	**67.7**	5	9.1
#13 (SS)	6	28.6	12	38.7	3	5.5
#14 (SS)	2	9.5	18	**58.1**	2	3.6
#15 (SS)	9	42.9	20	**64.5**	4	7.3
#16 (SS)	13	**61.9**	20	**64.5**	21	38.2
#17 (SS)	12	**57.1**	23	**74.2**	16	29.1
#18 (SS)	2	9.5	7	22.6	4	7.3
#19 (SS)	5	23.8	10	32.3	3	5.5
#20 (SS)	6	28.6	15	48.4	2	3.6
#21 (SS)	8	38.1	11	35.5	7	12.7
#22 (SS)	8	38.1	14	45.2	12	21.8
#23 (M)	15	**71.4**	3	9.7	1	1.8
#24 (M)	17	**81.0**	1	3.2	5	9.1
#25 (M)	13	**61.9**	8	25.8	7	12.7
#26 (M)	14	**66.7**	1	3.2	11	20.0
#27 (M)	13	**61.9**	4	12.9	5	9.1
#28 (M)	9	42.9	9	29.0	14	25.5
#29 (M)	6	28.6	10	32.3	8	14.5
#30 (M)	6	28.6	2	6.5	10	18.2
#31 (M)	8	38.1	4	12.9	17	30.9
#32 (LE)	5	23.8	18	**58.1**	14	25.5
#33 (LE)	6	28.6	18	**58.1**	8	14.5
#34 (LE)	6	28.6	18	**58.1**	8	14.5
#35 (LE)	7	33.3	7	22.6	9	16.4
#36 (LE)	2	9.5	6	19.4	3	5.5
#37 (LE)	5	23.8	12	38.7	12	21.8
#38 (LE)	2	9.5	17	**54.8**	12	21.8
#39 (LE)	6	28.6	8	25.8	2	3.6
#40 (LE)	9	42.9	10	32.3	7	12.7

Note. *N* (Cluster 1) = 21; *N* (Cluster 2) = 31; *N* (Cluster 3) = 55. Client percentages were greater than 50% signal endorsement bolded.

expected cell frequencies for goodness-of-fit tests (Warner, 2008, p. 156).

As shown in Table V (contingency table for the four dummy variables), for the current analysis, 43% of the expected cell frequencies were below five, which is less than recommended for cell frequency analyses (Wickens, 1989). This could be considered a limitation of the analysis, though none of the frequencies were less than 1 (the lowest frequency was 2.5), and there have been arguments that this condition is likely acceptable (Everitt, 1977). Thus, though the results might be interpreted with this limitation in mind, this issue was deemed minor enough that analysis could proceed. A correction for continuity was applied for goodness-of-fit tests, such that 0.5 was added to every negative observed and expected cell frequency and subtracted from every positive cell frequency (Wickens, 1989).

A backward elimination approach was taken for the current study, which means that a model was first developed so as to include all main effects and higher order associations (i.e., terms) and then, starting with the highest order interaction (i.e., TAd × SSd × Md × LEd), a term was removed one by one, and a statistical test was performed to determine whether dropping the term lead to a significant change in the model. For a more in-depth explanation of log-linear analysis, see Agresti (2007) and Wickens (1989). Removal of four- and three-way associations did not result in significant changes

Table V. Contingency table for dummy variables.

		SSd = 0		SSd = 1	
		LEd = 0	LEd = 1	LEd = 0	LEd = 1
TAd = 0	Md = 0	13 (low all scales)	6 (LEd high)	8 (SSd high)	14 (LEd and SSd high)
	Md = 1	3 (Md high)	2 (LEd and Md high)	7 (SSd and Md high)	4 (Md, SSd, and LEd high)
TAd = 1	Md = 0	3 (TAd high)	2 (TAd and LEd high)	3 (TAd and SSd high)	6 (TAd, SSd, and LEd high)
	Md = 1	2 (TAd and Md high)	5 (TAd, Md, and LEd high)	7 (TAd, Md, and SSd high)	22 (TAd, Md, SSd, and LEd high)

High, high scorer.

in the model. The following two-way interactions were found significant at $p < 0.05$: SSd × Md ($p = 0.042$), SSd × LEd ($p = 0.04$), and TAd × Md ($p = 0.00$). Both Pearson ($\chi^2 = 4.224$; $df = 7$; $p = 0.754$) and likelihood ratio ($\chi^2 = 4.446$; $df = 7$; $p = 0.727$) goodness-of-fit tests were not significant, indicating a good fit to the model. In further support for model fit, none of the standardized residuals for the final model were greater than ±1.96.

Table VI includes parameter estimates, z scores, significance levels, and confidence intervals for each main effect and interaction estimates of parameters are calculated as odds expressed in logarithmic terms. Significant effects occurred solely for the TAd × Md interaction (estimate = 0.38; $z = 3.314$; $p = 0.001$; 95% confidence interval: 0.155 to 0.602) and SSd main effect (estimate = −0.32; $z = -2.182$; $p = 0.005$; 95% confidence interval: −0.546 to −0.098). These results suggest that if a participant was a low scorer for TA, they were also likely (above chance) to be a low scorer on Md, and that was generally less likely (below chance) for participants to be low scorers on SSd. This is consistent with the preceding descriptive tables and cluster analysis, which showed that a relatively higher percentage of NOT participants received signal alerts for the SS items and scale, and there seems to be a grouping of clients who align on "internal" to therapy issues. The lack of significant effects for the other two interactions indicated for the model (SSd × Md and SSd × LEd) suggest less confidence can be held for their association, but this potential relationship might be a consideration for future studies.

Discussion

Lambert and colleagues found that alerting therapists to probable treatment failure improved psychotherapy outcomes for NOT clients but still a portion went on to deteriorate or were not improved at termination. In an attempt to further prevent treatment failure they developed a problem-solving tool based on a 40-item self-report scale (the ASC) administered if and when a client became NOT for a positive outcome. Use of this intervention in controlled trials further reduced deterioration and bolstered positive treatment response (Shimokawa et al., 2010). Southwick and Lambert (2014) found in a qualitative study that therapists tend to use the CSTs in a manner consistent with their design.

The current study explored ASC data from 107 predicted treatment failures from a hospital-based

Table VI. Parameter estimates for main effects and interactions of dummy variables.

Effect	Parameter estimate	z Score	Significance	Confidence interval (95%)
TAd × SSd × Md × LEd	0.05	0.43	0.66	−0.17 to 0.27
TAd × SSd × Md	−0.03	−0.29	0.77	−0.26 to 0.19
TAd × SSd × LEd	−0.01	−0.09	0.92	−0.23 to 0.21
TAd × Md × LEd	−0.14	−1.23	0.22	−0.36 to 0.08
SSd × Md × LEd	0.13	1.14	0.25	−0.09 to 0.35
TAd × SSd	0.11	0.97	0.33	−0.11 to 0.33
TAd × Md	0.38	3.31	0.001*	0.15 to 0.60
SSd × Md	0.16	1.40	0.16	−0.06 to 0.38
TAd × LEd	0.20	1.76	0.08	−0.02 to 0.42
SSd × LEd	0.15	1.28	0.19	−0.08 to 0.37
Md × LEd	0.06	0.52	0.60	−0.16 to 0.28
TAd	0.12	1.06	0.29	−0.10 to 0.34
SSd	−0.32	−2.82	0.005*	−0.55 to −0.098
Md	0.07	0.63	0.53	−0.15 to 0.29
LEd	−0.07	−0.62	0.54	−0.29 to 0.15

*$p < 0.01$.

outpatient clinic (Simon et al., 2012) in order to describe the frequency and nature of problems clients noted on the ASC that met criterion (Lambert et al., 2007) for being problematic. Both scale feedback and specific item feedback were examined in the current study. Within the current sample of outpatients who were predicted to deteriorate about 58% of patients had enough problems within a unique scale to trigger a scale alarm signal. Surprisingly, the SS scale (instead of the TA scale) was triggered most often, with 29% of all NOT clients meeting criterion for an overall problem in this area. About 40% of clients did not have enough items within any of the four scales to bring the overall scale score to the critical threshold for an alarm. At the item level clients had an average of 10 items (SD = 6.29) that passed the threshold for an alert, giving therapists numerous specific issues that they could explore with the NOT client while also limiting the list of likely problems.

As would be expected from the *scale* results, the most frequently identified problematic *items* were from the SS scale ("There was a special person who was around when I was in need." "There was a special person with whom I could share my joys and sorrows." "I could count on my friendships when things went wrong."). Cumulatively, these items suggest that many NOT clients are missing a close person in their social network with whom they can confide at the time they go off-track for a positive outcome. This suggests the need for therapists to consider interventions that could strengthen the social network of such clients, help them with social skills, including a significant other in the psychotherapy process, or make referrals to group psychotherapy or support groups as an adjunct to individual psychotherapy. These results are consistent with the findings of Probst, Lambert, Loew, et al. (2014) who suggested that the social support scales were so commonly endorsed that the decision tree that guides problem-solving for therapists should be reorganized so that social support precedes rather than follows alliance. Such a change in emphasis may come as a relief to therapists as it implies that predicted deterioration is most likely caused by a weak social support network rather than themselves. Of course replication of these results will be necessary before modifying the decision tree.

The ASC also identified alliance problems in NOT cases with items like: "I felt like I could trust my therapist completely" and "My therapist seemed glad to see me." There also seemed to be evidence of collaboration difficulties leading the way (e.g., "My therapist and I seemed to work well together to accomplish what I want."). Certainly alliance problems would seem to be more easily solved than social support difficulties since the therapist can rather readily become more responsive to patient needs than engineer their social environment. Therapists may also find some relief in knowing that bond problems (e.g., empathy, respect) do not fully explain the off-track client's negative change. It may be a problem of renegotiating the therapeutic contract by (re)presenting the therapeutic rationale and its connection to in-session therapeutic procedures. This consideration also applies to motivational problems. NOT clients require help in overcoming hindering motivational states. Recall the association between the alliance and motivational items as shown in the results of log-linear modeling and the identification of an "internal" cluster in the cluster analysis. Hansen, Lambert, and Vlass (2014) in their study of off-track clients compared to early dramatic treatment responders found little difference in the bond aspects of the alliance, but evidence of task aspects of the alliance and motivational problems.

When considering clusters or groups of NOT clients with similar profiles, three clusters emerged. Cluster 1 included about 20% of the NOT clients who endorsed a larger number of items in the signal range (an average of 17), with a pattern of high endorsement in the therapeutic alliance and motivation scales. If this pattern holds in future studies, clinicians might expect about 20% of clients who are NOT to report a variety of problems "internal" to therapy (i.e., alliance and motivation to change). In contrast, Cluster 2 included about 29% of the NOT clients who had an average number of items endorsed (12) but a different pattern in that they endorsed more social support and life event items (i.e., external to therapy issues) as contributing to their lack of progress in treatment.

These two clusters may represent contrasting explanations for treatment deterioration. The internal cluster may relate to a breakdown in the process of therapy itself. A therapist interpreting the results of an ASC administration may focus Cluster 1 clients on factors that relate directly to the process of therapy and may also choose to adjust interventions accordingly. However, Cluster 2 explains deterioration in terms of problems external to therapy and suggests a client having a context or experiences in that context that exceed her/his resources for coping. There may be merit for future discussion on an internal versus external split in explaining treatment deterioration.

The remaining 51% of clients, in Cluster 3, had no specific pattern of item endorsement on the ASC, although two facts stand out. First, 30% of the clients in Cluster 3 report participating in treatment as a result of pressure from a third party and 38%

reported problems with social support. Second, NOT clients in Cluster 3 had an overall lower rate of endorsement of ASC items in general. This may suggest that something other than alliance, motivation, social support, or life events was contributing to their poor progress in therapy.

Alliance and motivation problems appear to be related as "internal to therapy" problems and indicate to a therapist working with such problems to use interventions within the context of therapy that focus on improving the relationship and enhancing motivation. External to therapy issues (i.e., social support and life events) may present more of a challenge, since therapists have a less direct influence on such issues. Therapists working with such clients may need to more seriously consider a client's context outside of therapy and how relationships with others may contribute to distress. It is noted, however, that interventions from a broad spectrum of theoretical orientations may be used to enhance social support. Behavioral activation may include taking action to enhance social support while cognitive restructuring may help a client reframe their perspective on available sources of support. Humanistic and psychodynamic approaches may focus on a client's relational framework and on enhancing relationships to maximize a client's benefit from these relationships.

More research may be needed to address how therapists can enact social support interventions. Policy-makers may take note how this study's findings emphasize that possible explanations for treatment deterioration for mental health clients tend to be complex and idiosyncratic. NOT clients may require the commitment of more clinical resources to determine how best to provide effective intervention.

The cluster analysis provides an interesting starting point for further examination of NOT clients. In this sample, three distinct profile types emerged that provide provocative clinical information that may be useful to the therapist. Of particular help is the finding that 50% of the NOT clients may have either alliance and motivation issues—internal cluster—or social support and disruptive life events—external cluster. The remaining 50% it is a bit more difficult to identify a prototypical pattern. Given the lack of data examining cluster stability and reliability, these initial findings must remain tentative. More cluster analyses may be conducted with similar, as well as different populations (e.g., NOT clients in different settings) to determine whether these findings can be replicated. Future studies may further clarify the types and groups of clients who are NOT in treatment. In particular, future studies may address how these clusters relate to eventual outcome, including recovery or deterioration. While these results appear to be valid for a general mental health population (mood and anxiety disorders), these clusters may also be studied relative to diagnosis or other presenting problems. Should these results be replicated and found to generalize across other treatment populations, typing patients and providing this information to therapists could speed problem-solving with at least a portion of NOT patients.

References

Agresti, A. (2007). Loglinear models for contingency tables. In *An introduction to categorical data analysis* (p. 204). Hoboken, NJ: Wiley-Interscience.

Al-Alim, O. (2012). *Psychometric evaluation of a Dutch translation of the Assessment for Signal Clients Questionnaire* (Doctoral dissertation). Department of Psychology, Leiden University, The Netherlands.

Bohart, A. C., & Wade, A. G. (2013). The client in psychotherapy. In M. J. Lambert (Ed.), *Bergin & Garfield's handbook of psychotherapy & behavior change* (6th ed., 219–257). New York, NY: Wiley.

Chignell, M. H., & Stacey, B. G. (1981). The classification of patients into diagnostic groups using cluster analysis. *Journal of Clinical Psychology*, *37*, 151–153. doi:10.1002/1097-4679(198101)37:1<151::AID-JCLP2270370129>3.0.CO;2-4

Chronister, J. A., Johnson, E. K., & Berven, N. L. (2006). Measuring social support in rehabilitation. *Disability & Rehabilitation*, *28*(2), 75–84. doi:10.1080/09638280500163695

Ellsworth, J. R., Lambert, M. J., & Johnson, J. (2006). A comparison of the Outcome Questionnaire-45 and Outcome Questionnaire-30 in classification and prediction of treatment outcome. *Clinical Psychology & Psychotherapy*, *13*, 380–391. doi:10.1002/cpp.503

Everitt, B. (1977). Log-linear models for contingency tables. In *The analysis of contingency tables* (p. 70). London: Chapman and Hall; Wiley (Distributed in the USA by Halsted Press).

Finch, A. E., Lambert, M. J., & Schaalje, B. G. (2001). Psychotherapy quality control: The statistical generation of expected recovery curves for integration into an early warning system. *Clinical Psychology & Psychotherapy*, *8*, 231–242. doi:10.1002/cpp.28

Hannan, C., Lambert, M. J., Harmon, C., Nielsen, S. L., Smart, D. W., Shimokawa, K., & Sutton, S. W. W. (2005). A lab test and algorithms for identifying clients at risk for treatment failure. *Journal of Clinical Psychology*, *61*, 155–163. doi:10.1002/jclp.20108

Hansen, B., Lambert, M. J., & Vlass, E. N. (2014). *Sudden gains: A pluralistic approach to the patient and therapist experience* (Unpublished doctoral dissertation). Brigham Young University, Provo, UT.

Horvath, A. O., Del Re, A. C., Flückiger, C., & Symonds, D. (2011). Alliance in individual psychotherapy. *Psychotherapy*, *48*(1), 9–16. doi:10.1037/a0022186

Kimball, K. L. (2010). *Toward determining best items for identifying therapeutic problem areas* (Unpublished doctoral dissertation). Brigham Young University, Provo, UT.

Lambert, M. J., Bailey, R. J., Kimball, K., Shimokawa, K., Harmon, S. C., & Slade, K. (2007). *Clinical Support Tools Manual: Brief Version-40*. Salt Lake City, UT: OQ Measures, LLC.

Lambert, M. J., & Cattani-Thompson, K. (1996). Current findings regarding the effectiveness of counseling: Implications for practice. *Journal of Counseling & Development*, *74*, 601–608. doi:10.1002/j.1556-6676.1996.tb02299.x

Lambert, M. J., Kahler, M., Harmon, C., Burlingame, G. M., Shimokawa, K., & White, M. (2013). *Outcome Questionnaire OQ-45.2* (4th ed.). Salt Lake City, UT: OQ Measures, LLC.

Lambert, M. J., Whipple, J. L., Bishop, M. J., Vermeersch, D. A., Gray, G. V., & Finch, A. E. (2002). Comparison of empirically-derived and rationally-derived methods for identifying patients at risk for treatment failure. *Clinical Psychology & Psychotherapy, 9*, 149–164. doi:10.1002/cpp.333

Lindfors, O., Ojanen, S., Jääskeläinen, T., & Knekt, P. (2014). Social support as a predictor of the outcome of depressive and anxiety disorder in short-term and long-term psychotherapy. *Psychiatry Research, 216*(1), 44–51. doi:10.1016/j.psychres.2013.12.050

Probst, T., Lambert, M. J., Dahlbender, R. W., Loew, T. H., Thomas, H., & Tritt, K. (2014). Providing patient progress feedback and clinical support tools to therapists: Is the therapeutic process of patients on-track to recovery enhanced in psychosomatic in-patient therapy under the conditions of routine practice? *Journal of Psychosomatic Research, 76*, 477–484. doi:10.1016/j.jpsychores.2014.03.010

Probst, T., Lambert, M. J., Loew, T. H., Dahlbender, R. W., & Tritt, K. (2014). Extreme deviations from expected recovery curves and their associations with therapeutic alliance, social support, motivation, and life events in psychosomatic in-patient therapy. *Psychotherapy Research*. Advance online publication. doi:10.1080/10503307.2014.981682

Prochaska, J. O., & Norcross, J. C. (2003). *Systems of psychotherapy: A transtheoretical analysis* (5th ed.). Pacific Grove, CA: Brooks/Cole.

Safran, J. D., & Muran, J. C. (2000). Resolving therapeutic alliance ruptures: Diversity and integration. *Journal of Clinical Psychology, 56*, 233–243. doi:10.1002/(SICI)1097-4679(200002)56:2<233::AID-JCLP9>3.0.CO;2-3

Shimokawa, K., Lambert, M. J., & Smart, D. W. (2010). Enhancing treatment outcome of patients at risk of treatment failure: Meta-analytic and mega-analytic review of a psychotherapy quality assurance system. *Journal of Consulting and Clinical Psychology, 78*, 298–311. doi:10.1037/a0019247

Simon, W., Lambert, M. J., Harris, M. W., Busath, G., & Vazquez, A. (2012). Providing patient progress information and clinical support tools to therapists: Effects on patients at risk of treatment failure. *Psychotherapy Research, 22*, 638–647. doi:10.1080/10503307.2012.698918

Southwick, J., & Lambert, M. J. (2014). *Therapists' experience with structured feedback procedures: Review and discussion of research literature*. Unpublished manuscript, Department of Psychology, Brigham Young University, Provo, UT.

Spielmans, G. I., Masters, K. S., & Lambert, M. J. (2006). A comparison of rational versus empirical methods in the prediction of psychotherapy outcome. *Clinical Psychology & Psychotherapy, 13*, 202–214. doi:10.1002/cpp.491

Thoits, P. A. (1983). Direct, indirect, and moderating effects of social support on psychological distress and associated conditions. In *Psychosocial stress: Trends in theory and research* (pp. 105–155). New York, NY: Academic Press.

Vermeersch, D. A., Lambert, M. J., & Burlingame, G. M. (2000). Outcome Questionnaire: Item sensitivity to change. *Journal of Personality Assessment, 74*, 242–261. doi:10.1207/S15327752JPA7402_6

Vermeersch, D. A., Whipple, J. L., Lambert, M. J., Hawkins, E. J., Burchfield, C. M., & Okiishi, J. C. (2004). Outcome Questionnaire: Is it sensitive to changes in counseling center clients? *Journal of Counseling Psychology, 51*(1), 38–49. doi:10.1037/0022-0167.51.1.38

Warner, R. M. (2008). *Applied statistics*. Los Angeles, CA, London, New Delhi, and Singapore: Sage.

Wickens, T. D. (1989). *Multiway contingency tables analysis for the social sciences*. Hillsdale, NJ: Lawrence Erlbaum.

Zimet, G. D., Dahlem, N. W., Zimet, S. G., & Farley, G. K. (1988). The multidimensional scale of perceived social support. *Journal of Personality Assessment, 52*(1), 30–41. doi:10.1207/s15327752jpa5201_2

Index

Note: Page numbers in **bold** type refer to figures
Page numbers in *italic* type refer to tables

For Product Safety Concerns and Information please contact our EU
representative GPSR@taylorandfrancis.com
Taylor & Francis Verlag GmbH, Kaufingerstraße 24, 80331 München, Germany

www.ingramcontent.com/pod-product-compliance
Ingram Content Group UK Ltd.
Pitfield, Milton Keynes, MK11 3LW, UK
UKHW050059200926
475702UK00019B/2922

9780367029012